ONE WEEK L

I

HISTORICAL GUIDES
TO AMERICAN AUTHORS

The Historical Guides to American Authors is an interdisciplinary, historically sensitive series that combines close attention to the United States' most widely read and studied authors with a strong sense of time, place, and history. Placing each writer in the context of the vibrant relationship between literature and society, volumes in this series contain historical essays written on subjects of contemporary social, political, and cultural relevance. Each volume also includes a capsule biography and illustrated chronology detailing important cultural events as they coincided with the author's life and works, while photographs and illustrations dating from the period capture the flavor of the author's time and social milieu. Equally accessible to students of literature and of life, the volumes offer a complete and rounded picture of each author in his or her America.

RECENT TITLES

A Historical Guide to Walt Whitman
Edited by David S. Reynolds

A Historical Guide to Ralph Waldo Emerson
Edited by Joel Myerson

A Historical Guide to Henry David Thoreau
Edited by William E. Cain

A Historical Guide to Edgar Allan Poe
Edited by J. Gerald Kennedy

A Historical Guide to Nathaniel Hawthorne
Edited by Larry Reynolds

A Historical Guide to Mark Twain
Edited by Shelley Fisher Fishkin

A Historical Guide to Edith Wharton
Edited by Carol J. Singley

A Historical Guide to Langston Hughes
Edited by Steven C. Tracy

A Historical Guide to Emily Dickinson
Edited by Vivian R. Pollak

A
Historical Guide
to Emily Dickinson

EDITED BY
VIVIAN R. POLLAK

OXFORD
UNIVERSITY PRESS
2004

OXFORD
UNIVERSITY PRESS

Oxford   New York

Auckland   Bangkok   Buenos Aires   Cape Town   Chennai
Dar es Salaam   Delhi   Hong Kong   Istanbul   Karachi   Kolkata
Kuala Lumpur   Madrid   Melbourne   Mexico City   Mumbai   Nairobi
São Paulo   Shanghai   Taipei   Tokyo   Toronto

Copyright © 2004 by Oxford University Press, Inc.

Published by Oxford University Press, Inc.
198 Madison Avenue, New York, New York 10016

www.oup.com

Library of Congress Cataloging-in-Publication Data
A historical guide to Emily Dickinson / edited by Vivian R. Pollak.
p. cm.— (Historical guides to American authors)
Includes bibliographical references and index.
ISBN 0-19-515134-8; 0-19-515135-6 (pbk.)
1. Dickinson, Emily, 1830–1886—Criticism and interpretation.
2. Literature and history—Massachusetts—History—19th century.
3. Women and literature—Massachusetts—History—19th century.
I. Pollak, Vivian R.   II. Series.
PS1541.Z5 H57 2003
811'.4—dc21   2003002308

1 3 5 7 9 8 6 4 2
Printed in the United States of America
on acid-free paper

Contents

Introduction   3
Vivian R. Pollak

Emily Dickinson, 1830–1886:
A Brief Biography   13
Vivian R. Pollak and Marianne Noble

DICKINSON IN HER TIME

"Is Immorality True?":
Salvaging Faith in an Age of Upheavals   67
Jane Donahue Eberwein

Public and Private in Dickinson's War Poetry   103
Shira Wolosky

Dickinson and the Art of Politics   133
Betsy Erkkila

Dickinson in Context:
Nineteenth-Century American Women Poets   175
Cheryl Walker

The Sound of Shifting Paradigms,
or Hearing Dickinson in the Twenty-First Century   201
Cristanne Miller

Illustrated Chronology   235

Bibliographical Essay   255
Jonathan Morse

Contributors   285

Credits   289

Index   291

A HISTORICAL GUIDE TO
Emily Dickinson

Introduction

Vivian R. Pollak

Emily Dickinson's language leads in many different directions. Virtually unpublished during her lifetime and seemingly ambivalent about publication in the future, she emerged dramatically in the twentieth century as one of America's most distinguished and distinctive poets. But if Dickinson's originality is universally credited, her generative affiliations—the emotional and intellectual loyalties that made her who she was—are more difficult to discern, and many of the essays in this volume address the question, "For and to whom does Dickinson speak?"

There is an emerging consensus that Dickinson wrote most powerfully during the Civil War, and that she participated in a larger national debate about the meaning of life itself when pressured by death. As a poet of the inner civil war, she used images of death and dying to clarify her own experience, and she frequently psychologized military tropes. The essays in this volume, all previously unpublished, either seek to identify the various personal and cultural traumas to which Dickinson was responding or to recuperate nineteenth-century literary and social contexts that our collective cultural memory has seemingly erased. The contributors themselves present some of the most exciting new approaches to Dickinson—approaches that not only situate her in history but that also appreciate the particular and unique angle of her vision and of the historically specific contexts in which she has been and is currently being read.

Although in one of her meditations on death Dickinson uses the phrase "None may teach it" to suggest that highly individuated feelings may not be communicable, ever since the first posthumous publication of poems in 1890, she has proved herself to be a great teacher. Dickinson inspires dialogue, and a recently published volume called *Visiting Emily: Poems Inspired by the Life and Work of Emily Dickinson* is only one sign of her continuing presence among us. Women poets in particular are often compared to Dickinson, while visual artists, musicians, fiction writers, even the U.S. government with its notable "stamp," have testified to Dickinson's importance as a cultural commodity. For many readers, however, Dickinson represents the rebellious, antinomian strain in American culture and the courage to be oneself. As a great experimental realist, she troubles our certainties. As an extravagant dreamer, she invites us to dwell "in Possibility - / A fairer House than Prose." Her emotional range is wide, and both her poetry and her letters are full of surprises.

Like other richly representative mid-nineteenth-century American authors, Dickinson was deeply influenced by an ideology of self-reliance; Ralph Waldo Emerson, with whom this philosophy is often identified, was one of the writers she most admired. Unlike Emerson, however, Dickinson is not obviously a theorist of national identity, and when Emerson came to Amherst in December 1857, she did not attend his lecture. She could easily have met him face to face, since he was the houseguest of her brother and sister-in-law. She chose not to. Notwithstanding her apparent indifference to the role of poet-citizen, Dickinson's language leaps across social and historical barriers to create remarkable communities of knowledge. Like Whitman, Dickinson asks us to confront some of the most enduring issues of American life and of life anywhere: for example, the problem of death, the problem of God, and the problem, too, of love. Anticipating some of the "elite" aesthetic strategies of twentieth-century modernism, Dickinson has much to say to readers who resist popular measures of success. "How dreary - to be - somebody," she wrote, "How public - like a Frog."

Known during her youth for her humor, Dickinson emerged in the poetry of her maturity as a supreme ironist. She was witty and tart, but there was a deeper purpose. Irony defended her against single-mindedness and against emotional pain. "Mirth," she wrote, is "the mail of Anguish." Armored in mirth, she resisted the pressures to conform to codes of gentility that she had already begun to describe in her first extant letter to her beloved brother Austin. In her teens, she was remarkably self-aware, and in her twenties, she was developing those habits of observation that made her such a remarkable witness to the (il)logics and conditions that robbed life of its fullest meaning.

Despite the eventual vulnerability of her social being, Emily Dickinson was a largehearted and generous woman, and both the vulnerability and the generosity come through in her writing. Dickinson's poems are difficult and accessible, intellectually challenging and emotionally intense. Short and far-reaching, they are memorable and mnemonic, as are her letters, although the early letters are longer. After she became socially reclusive in her midtwenties, her correspondence sustained her, as did family relationships. (She continued to interact with children and servants after she had "lost the run of the roads" [L 410].)[1] While most of the letters she received were destroyed when she died— this was the custom of the time—three volumes of her letters have been published. This one-sided correspondence forms the basis for much of what we know about her life, and her letters are important guides to her reading. For example, in 1865, when she was suffering from her mysterious and threatening eye ailment, she wrote that the physician was finally permitting her to read again. She turned to Shakespeare and asked, "Why is any other book needed." But on the whole there were many books that Dickinson needed, including books by women writers such as Charlotte and Emily Brontë, George Eliot, and Elizabeth Barrett Browning, one of the poets who most demonstrably influenced her. Her early letters, too, are filled with descriptions of the vibrant religious culture that defined public life in Amherst, and in both poems and letters, the Bible is her most frequently quoted source.

The sermonesque quality of public rhetoric in Amherst is the butt of Dickinson's satire in several early poems and informs her early correspondence as well. For example, at the age of eleven she begins her first extant letter, written to her brother Austin while he was away at boarding school, "As Father was going to Northampton and thought of coming over to see you I thought I would improve the opportunity and write you a few lines." The phrase "improve the opportunity" captures the moral earnestness of Dickinson's youth, as does her first extant poem, an 1850 comic valentine satirizing romantic and religious convention. The two were intimately linked. Over time, however, the letters become more elliptical and take on the coded, gnomic quality that caused her to sign herself to one of her 1863 correspondents, "Your Gnome." Gradually, the social and intellectual context out of which the letters emerge becomes more difficult to discern. One has the sense of an omitted center—of a single traumatic narrative or of many traumatic narratives pressing against the language and needing to be recovered.

Directly and indirectly, all the essays in this volume ask questions about Dickinson's development as an artist. In the opening biographical essay, Marianne Noble and I discuss the major familial, religious, and erotic crises of her life as recounted by her poems and letters and as supplemented by the observations of others, including Thomas Wentworth Higginson, the 1863 correspondent to whom she signed herself "Your Gnome." What was the effect of Dickinson's social isolation on her career? There is a sense in which this question is unanswerable, but Noble and I extend other biographical accounts that foreground Dickinson's incremental knowledge of the house of pain, knowledge that Emerson faulted himself for not having. Despite her intense self-absorption, however, Dickinson was not intellectually isolated, and Jane Donahue Eberwein's essay locates the poet firmly in a religious community that changed over time, becoming more liberal over the course of the nineteenth century. Eberwein describes the Congregational religion that Dickinson inherited, the intellectual traditions to which it responded, and Dickinson's tenacity in probing and dismantling conventional beliefs. As described by Eberwein, Dickinson looks longingly both backward and forward—back toward greater epistemological security and forward to greater emotional freedom. Shira Wolosky is also concerned with Dickinson's religious aesthetic, yet her version of Dickinson is more agonistic. Wolosky's Dickinson is a poet of many wars who finds reality unacceptable. She interrogates God, takes him to task, and finds no solution other than truthtelling. Authenticity turns out to be Dickinson's personal salvation, although the fate of her nation is more vexed. Betsy Erkkila provides a thick-textured description of Dickinson's immediate political environment, which in certain respects was resolutely antidemocratic. Arguing against the view that Dickinson is adequately understood as a personal or private poet, she sees Dickinson as engaged in an ongoing debate with the political culture of antebellum, wartime, and Gilded Age society. Erkkila also explores Dickinson's racial views, and the news is not as encouraging as some might like, since Dickinson was not untouched by the prejudices of her class position. Within this context, Dickinson emerges as both a trenchant critic of political corruption during the Gilded Age and as a precursor of modernist elitism.

Cheryl Walker looks at Dickinson from quite a different angle, suggesting that there is much to be learned from reading Dickinson in the context of other nineteenth-century American women poets. She demonstrates linguistic links between Dickinson and less frequently read writers such as Rose Terry (Cooke) and Maria (White) Lowell. Without denying that Dickinson was a thoroughgoing original, Walker argues for a balanced appreciation of Dickinson's relationship to her contemporaries. Cristanne Miller also reads Dickinson in relation to her contemporaries, but Miller focuses on Longfellow, whom she characterizes as the century's most popular and esteemed poet. In recent years, textual critics such as Susan Howe, Jerome McGann, Martha Nell Smith, Ellen Louise Hart, and Marta Werner have argued for the importance of *visual* elements in Dickinson's manuscripts. Miller, however, believes that Dickinson in her time was a more *aural* poet and that indeed she was steeped in a poetic culture in which *sound* rather than sight was the key element.

Finally, Jonathan Morse offers an overview of the editing of Dickinson's poems and letters, concluding that in the twenty-first century, electronic media will contribute greatly to our understanding of a poet who refused to see her works into print. Morse believes that twenty-first century critical theories and technologies are at last ready to present us with more authentic texts. His essay considers the extraordinary history of her manuscripts and of attempts to locate the "real" Emily Dickinson among a wealth of competing critical and biographical approaches.

The poetry of Dickinson's maturity is conventionally dated from 1858. She left most of her manuscripts untitled and undated, and statements about the dates in which particular poems were written are based on elaborate guesswork. Only ten poems are known to have been published during her lifetime, seven of them in the Massachusetts newspaper, the *Springfield Republican*, and none of them at her own instigation. Friends tried to coax her into print, but she demurred. Dickinson nevertheless sent about a third of her poems to family and friends in letters, and some of these letters can be accurately dated. In the 1950s, the textual scholars Thomas Johnson and Theodora Ward used changes in Dickinson's handwriting in letters to suggest approximate dates for the poetry. This process has been further refined by Ralph Franklin, who has recently edited a new variorum of the poems. When this variorum appeared in 1998, it inspired much debate about the true text of Dickinson's poems. No one doubts that Dickinson's manuscripts contain features that are not reproduced in standard editions of her work and that careful consideration of the visual features of her manuscripts, including capitalization, punctuation, and line breaks can lead to fresh new readings of her poems. Dickinson's intentions, however, are more difficult to recover. What forms would she have sanctioned, had she chosen to print? Are some features of her manuscripts accidental? Do twentieth and twenty-first century eyes historicize or dehistoricize her texts? Cristanne Miller argues that many features of Dickinson's manuscripts are indeed accidental, in that she would not have imagined them as forming part of her printed text. This debate is ongoing in Dickinson studies, and readers are encouraged to turn to the Notes and concluding bibliography for other points of view.

When Emily Dickinson died in May 1886, her sister Lavinia was astonished by what she found. She had always believed that Emily was a genius, and now there was proof. Lavinia succeeded in interesting Mabel Loomis Todd and Thomas Wentworth Higginson in editing a small volume for the Boston firm of Roberts Brothers. It appeared late in 1890, in time for the Christmas trade, contained forty-two poems, and was widely reviewed both in England and in the United States. Some reviewers found the poet wayward, or worse, but many were inclined to look for the rationale behind her off-rhymes and other subversions of conventional literary forms. In the book's "Preface," Higginson insisted that the poet was only "seemingly wayward," and the debate over intentionality continues to this day. Are there any accidentals to her style? Is it useful to encounter the word "upon" spelled "opon"? How much attention should be paid to her capitalization? What do her dashes mean?

These "small picture" issues are related to larger ones. From 1858 to 1865, Dickinson copied or recopied some eight hundred poems into larger groupings, or "fascicles," which a later editor, possibly Mabel Loomis Todd, disassembled. In 1981, Ralph Franklin published *The Manuscript Books of Emily Dickinson*, which reestablished the original order (to the extent possible). These forty manuscript books contain between eleven and twenty-nine poems each, and their purpose has been hotly debated. What, then, were her literary ambitions and which writers, if any, did she see as her peer group? Did she have any "natural" companions?

Although Dickinson once described herself facetiously as a "Nobody," she lived in a New England college town that, while provincial in its own ways, was a center of intellectual exchange. And she came from a well-established family in this town, a family that valued education even for women. Both Emily and her sister Lavinia went to good schools, as did her brother Austin, who attended Amherst College as an undergraduate and then went on to Harvard Law School before returning home to go into law practice with Emily's father, who was himself a Yale College graduate, class of 1821. And for the men, formal education went further back in Emily Dickinson's paternal line. But the nineteenth century was a time when a high school dropout such as Walt Whitman could, in Emerson's terms, author one of "the greatest piece[s] of wit and wisdom that America has yet produced." Whitman came from a financially hard-pressed farming and laboring family. He learned to write as a printer's apprentice and then as a newspaperman, and before long, while still in his early twenties, he was editing a newspaper and publishing melodramatic fictions. Before he was out of his teens, Whitman expressed the desire to produce a book, in fact, a ponderous book. Bookmaking, it seems, was in his blood. Dickinson, on the other hand, had friends who wanted her to publish books, and she declined to do so. In fact, she declined piecemeal publication of her poems as well and commercial publication, in general. She seems to have turned her back on everything we might associate with a literary career in the nineteenth century, except her love of reading and writing. That kept her going.

The essays in this volume situate Dickinson primarily as she has been read in modern times: in editions that take apart her small, handsewn booklets and in the interest of a more fluid but also more solidly historical presentation. Fascinating as they are, Dickinson's forty poem sequences raise questions of authorial authority that are better discussed elsewhere, and the essays in this volume reflect the hybrid editorial practices by which most readers, including other poets, have come to know her. These essays therefore situate Dickinson in both the public and private spheres, teasing out their interconnections. They focus on her personal relationships, her religious beliefs, her politics, her public and private wars, her relations with other American women poets, and her language. They demonstrate that Dickinson is indeed a representative American, both in her need for a legitimate community of readers and in her commitment to self: to having it out at last, as the contemporary poet Adrienne Rich has said, "on [her] own premises." Although for complex reasons Dickinson resisted the demands of a public career, she would have been pleased, I think, by many (though not all) elements of her posthumous reception. All her life, she sought "the rare Ear /

Not too dull" and I am pleased to introduce these rare twenty-first century readers in this volume.

NOTE

1. Citation from Letters (L) refers to *The Letters of Emily Dickinson*, ed. Thomas H. Johnson and Theodora Ward, 3 vols. (Cambridge, Mass.: Harvard University Press, 1958).

EMILY DICKINSON
1830–1886

A Brief Biography

Vivian R. Pollak and Marianne Noble

In the spring of 1862, Emily Dickinson read an essay in the *Atlantic Monthly* that was destined to make a distinct mark on American literary history. "Letter to a Young Contributor" was by the former Unitarian minister Thomas Wentworth Higginson, and this compendium of practical and moral advice caught her eye. A few days later, on April 15, Dickinson sent him four poems and a letter of her own. It began:

> Mr Higginson,
>   Are you too deeply occupied to say if my Verse is alive?
>   The Mind is so near itself—it cannot see, distinctly—and I have none to ask—
>   Should you think it breathed—and had you the leisure to tell me, I should feel quick gratitude—(L 260)[1]

She did not sign her name but included it on a calling card and intimated that she'd like him to keep it a secret.

Higginson responded quickly and generously. He expressed interest in who she was, how long she had been writing verse, and how she understood her relationship to conventional literary forms. He asked questions about her reading and education, as well as her "Companions." Responding ten days later "from [her] pillow" (she had been ill), Dickinson adopted a deferential stance toward her potential mentor, who was a graduate of Harvard College and Harvard Divinity School and a renowned advocate for radical political causes. She explained, "I went to school—but in your manner of the phrase—had no education." Although she had been writing poetry for many years, the thirty-one-year-old Dickinson chose to represent herself as a neophyte: "You asked how old I was? I made no verse—but one or two—until this winter—Sir." And then, she added dramatically, "I had a terror— since September—I could tell to none—and so I sing, as the Boy does by the Burying Ground—because I am afraid" (L 261). The likelihood is that her terror of September 1861 was real, that something happened which endangered both her peace of mind and her writing life. The two were intertwined.

In any event, this mysterious terror captured Higginson's attention, and as Dickinson sent him further poems, her cover letters continued to stimulate his interest. For example, in early June she explained her terror as follows: "My dying Tutor told me that he would like to live till I had been a poet, but Death was much of Mob as I could master—then—And when far afterward—a sudden light on Orchards, or a new fashion in the wind troubled my attention—I felt a palsy, here—the Verses just relieve" (L 265). In the next month, however, the Dickinson who had initially emphasized the autotherapeutic value of her project was cautioning Higginson against biographical literalism: "When I state myself as the Representative of the Verse—it does not mean—me—but a supposed person" (L 268). The poems, she suggested, were not necessarily about herself as most people understood her to be.

By the end of the year, Higginson was in South Carolina, distinguishing himself as the colonel of a black regiment.[2] He had less time to consider remote and possibly fantastic terrors. Dickinson continued the correspondence, telling him less about her life but alluding to previous losses that heightened her nervousness about his safety. "Perhaps Death—gave me awe for friends," she wrote, "striking sharp and early, for I held them since—in a brittle love—of more alarm, than peace" (L 280). When the war ended, she continued to express interest in meeting Higginson. He pressed her to come to Boston, where he could introduce her to his literary friends. Dickinson declined, making up face-saving excuses (L 316, L 319) and eventually stating categorically, "I do not cross my Father's ground to any House or town" (L 330). She pressed him to come to Amherst, as she had done previously, and while revealing nothing particular about her terror, she indicated both that he had saved her life and that "My life has been too simple and stern to embarrass any" (L 330). Puzzled, Higginson continued to hope that a face-to-face interview would explain the "strange power" of Dickinson's letters and verses and prove that the reclusive and mysterious correspondent who "enshroud[ed]" herself in a "fiery mist" was "real" (L 330a). These epistolary friends met for the first time in August 1870 in Amherst, in a "parlor dark & cool & stiffish"(L 342a), and when Higginson wrote to his wife the next day, he remarked, "I never was with any one who drained my nerve power so much. Without touching her, she drew from me. I am glad not to live near her. She often thought me *tired* & seemed very thoughtful of others" (L 342b). Recalling the interview after the poet's death, Higginson concluded, in the *Atlantic Monthly*, "The impression undoubtedly made on me was that of an excess of tension, and of an abnormal life" (L 342b).

Nothing specific had been said about her terror, but Higginson was well aware that in 1864 and 1865 Dickinson feared that she was losing her eyesight. During their interview, she said to him, "'When I lost the use of my Eyes it was a comfort to think there were so few real *books* that I could easily find some one to read me all of them'" (L 342a). Although she was nervous, it appears that her sense of humor was much in evidence. There is no reason to believe that her terror of September 1861 was related to eye problems. Rather, it is more likely that in September 1861, an event transpired that Dickinson experienced as a death, conditioned to such traumas as she had been by a history of "brittle love" (L 280).

The relationship between the historical Emily Dickinson and her Supposed Person(s) can never be fully demystified. But when she described her life as "too simple and stern to embarrass any," she was hinting at desires which, if revealed in their riotous complexity, would discomfort many. Dickinson refused to be confined by the normalizing realities of her time and place and struggled against the narrowing demands of her immediate environment. Yet in some measure she had internalized an ideology that confined women to the domestic sphere, and she deflected opportunities to publish during her lifetime: only ten of her poems were published before her death in 1886. Idealistically, as she explained in her poem "I dwell in Possibility," Dickinson committed herself to the power of poetic vision, which was "More numerous of Windows - / Superior - for Doors." In its limitless amplitude, this alternative world of possibility was also "Impregnable of eye" (Fr 466).[3] It allowed her to think independently beyond the withering scrutiny of a judgmental society. Ideally, then, the poet's imagination could liberate her from public history and personal fate. Ideally, poetry had the power to transform the self.

Yet if "spreading wide my narrow Hands / To gather Paradise" was Dickinson's goal (Fr 466), her mission was often thwarted, and biographies of her imagination have been more successful in defining Dickinson's frustrations than in explaining how she kept her faith in "Paradise"—whatever that meant to her, and however much her imagination of "Paradise" changed during the course of her writing life. Dickinson's personal paradise could not be represented in traditional terms, and in a poem perhaps written in 1861, she asked jocosely

> What is - "Paradise" -
> Who live there -
> Are they "Farmers" -
> Do they "hoe" -
> Do they know that this is "Amherst" -
> And that I - am coming - too -
>
> Do they wear "new shoes" - in "Eden" -
> Is it always pleasant - there -
> Wont they scold us - when we're hungry -
> Or tell God - how cross we are -
>
> You are sure there's such a person
> As "a Father" - in the sky -

So if I get lost - there - ever -
Or do what the Nurse calls "die" -

I shant walk the "Jasper" - barefoot -
Ransomed folks - wont laugh at me -
Maybe - "Eden" a'nt so lonesome
As New England used to be! (Fr 241)

Dickinson's imagination of paradise was structured by competing and even inconsistent grammars, as exemplified in the lines
just quoted by her startling use or nonuse of apostrophes. The
traditional Eden, the "Eden" in quotation marks, could not contain her. Dwelling in possibility and thinking independently,
Dickinson, who was schooled in New England traditions of *self*-
definition, resisted social and literary pressures to conform.

This is not to deny that as a person Dickinson puzzled many
people, including herself; her writings are at once self-revealing
and biographically elusive. Perhaps her deepest authorial consistency was her desire to connect with "the rare Ear / Not too
dull" (Fr 945), and she was a generous and inspiring letter writer,
if somewhat opaque. People who received letters from Emily
Dickinson tended to save them: her friends appreciated the bril-
liance of her language, even if they felt partially shut out by the
ellipses of her style. Despite, then, the difficulty of identifying
the real Emily Dickinson through her letters, in one of her signature poems, she famously referred to her project as a "letter to
the World" (Fr 519). For much of her adult life, she was reclusive
and homebound and letters provided her with a social context
that was otherwise lacking. Her poems include poignant descriptions of herself as sending and receiving letters in particular
ways. Consider the following example, which is conventionally
dated 1863, a year in which Dickinson drafted, revised, or transcribed close to three hundred poems:

The Way I read a Letter's - this -
Tis first - I lock the Door -
And push it with my fingers - next -
For transport it be sure -

And then I go the furthest off
To counteract a knock -
Then draw my little Letter forth
And slowly pick the lock -

Then - glancing narrow, at the Wall -
And narrow at the floor
For firm Conviction of a Mouse
Not exorcised before -

Peruse how infinite I am
To no one that You - know -
And sigh for lack of Heaven - but not
The Heaven God bestow - (Fr 700)

Reading such a poem, we wonder about its occasion: What inspired it? And is Dickinson describing an actual or imagined event? If, as seems likely, she is combining fact and fiction, history and prophecy, what are the facts? Assuming that someone wrote to her, who was it? And was the poem *written* in 1863 or transcribed in that year? Was she writing or rewriting her history? While Dickinson's letters facilitate biographical inquiry—three volumes have been published—there are demonstrable exaggerations and ellipses in some of her most widely quoted correspondences, including her correspondence with Higginson. Thus, the relationship between Dickinson's poems and letters is controversial, and for some readers the idea of dwelling in possibility, or, as she also phrased it, "invent[ing] a Life" (Fr 747), gets at her refusal to respect the lines that traditionally separated fact from fiction, history from prophecy, poetry from prose.

In varying degrees, Dickinson's letters, so essential for her biography, are marked by humor and anger and eagerness and traumatized self-representations. Beginning in 1842 with a long letter to her brother Austin, these remarkable addresses to family and friends and potential friends show the young Emily Dickinson as first engaged with the social world of Amherst and then, as she turned toward poetry in the 1850s, stylistically more withdrawn. That is, the letters of Dickinson's maturity provide further evidence of her quarrel with dominant literary histories, especially those that privileged goals such as publication and marriage and motherhood and formal traditions, including formal religious traditions, that she was unwilling to claim as her own. Perhaps only an inconsistent outsider *could* defiantly dwell in possibility, but in ways that we shall describe, Dickinson was an insider as well. Her education was special, as were her friendships. And despite some lapses, real or imagined, she was a dutiful daughter.[4] So when we refer to social goals that Dickinson was unwilling to claim as her own, we mean that, as expressed in the poetry of her maturity, her claims on ordinary happiness were partial, oblique, discontinuous. She was always looking for something less lonesome, more permanent, and, paradoxically, more intense. Her project, while gloriously selfish, was also capacious. When she spoke of "internal difference, / Where the Meanings, are" (Fr 320), she was extrapolating from her own experience and wanted to create a history more universal than her own. Ironically, then, Dickinson's understanding of community was founded on her awareness of difference and was often linked in her poetry to a seemingly personal experience of exclusion from grace, joy, wild nights, freedom, nation, even from life itself. The vocabulary is wonderfully varied.[5]

As the "Representative of the Verse" (L 268), Dickinson was not only describing her own experience, she was scrutinizing public definitions of failure and success and testing them against her own realities. As a woman poet, she probed the gender conventions that both sustained and traumatized her. She continues to be read as a great poet of the almost, of desire deferred, of ecstatic possibility that is never (or rarely) realized. Why was happiness so difficult to attain? For all her boldness, Emily Dickinson was often conflicted about her own ambitions. In part, she wanted to be empowered in conventional terms: to close the gap between romance and reality. In part, she was cynical about reality and refused to be satisfied with metaphors of fulfillment that sustained others. Oscillating between "heaven" and "earth," she refused perfectionist religious culture, which she associated with the repression of glorious, sensuously gratifying particulars, and with death. "Their Hight in Heaven comforts not - / Their Glory - nought to me," she wrote, "'Twas best imperfect - as it

was - I'm finite - I cant see" (Fr 725). Similarly, she resisted normative definitions of citizenship, writing to Higginson, "To an Emigrant, Country is idle except it be his own" (L 330). Emily Dickinson never emigrated but she often wanted to do so. "Dwelling
alone" on her own hard-won premises, what forms of perfection
and imperfection did she settle for?

For those inclined toward literary pilgrimages, the actual house
in which Emily Elizabeth Dickinson was born on December 10,
1830, remains a popular tourist attraction. It was built by her paternal grandfather, Samuel Fowler Dickinson, in 1813, was supposedly the first brick house in Amherst, and is still one of the
most elegant homes in the town. A victim of his own enthusiasm, Samuel Fowler was a problematic ancestor. The son of
a prosperous Amherst farmer, he entered Dartmouth College
at sixteen and graduated in 1795 as the salutatorian of his class.
He then studied for the ministry with an older brother, but as
Cynthia Griffin Wolff observes, "His restless ambition chafed
under the scholarly contemplative mode of life, and he soon
abandoned it to study law." Samuel Fowler married outspoken
Lucretia Gunn in 1802, set up his law practice, and speculated
successfully in real estate on the side. But as Wolff further notes,
"He did nothing by halves."[6] A founder of Amherst Academy in
1814 and of Amherst College in 1821, Emily Elizabeth Dickinson's
paternal grandfather was a schemer and dreamer whose career
got off to a fast start and then disintegrated, as his enthusiasm
outstripped his prudence. Amherst College survived its difficult
opening years and eventually flourished, but in the end her
grandfather's affairs were in a "sorry mess."[7] In 1833, he was
forced to emigrate to Cincinnati, Ohio, then the raw West, followed by his disgruntled wife Lucretia Gunn (1775–1840) and
their two unmarried daughters. He went because of the promise
of a steady job at a theological seminary, and they went because
they saw no alternative.

Edward Dickinson (1803–1874) was determined not to repeat
his zealous father's mistakes. He too furthered religious and educational causes, but he took fewer risks. Edward's goal was to re-

coup the family name and fortune, to (re)establish himself and his growing family in the community, the region, and the state. In the event, these goals were realized and as early as the spring of 1830, he was able to purchase half of The Homestead, as the brick mansion came to be called, moving in with his wife and one-year-old son, while his father's family continued to occupy the other side in their reduced circumstances as tenants. His wife Emily Norcross Dickinson (1804–1882) also came from a family that valued education and religion, but compared to Squire Dickinson (as Edward's father was called), her prosperous father, who was a shrewd farmer, businessman, and investor, was a model of cautious consistency in his philanthropic ventures. He was not universally beloved, however, and when he died, the principal of Monson Academy, which he had helped to create, remarked that it was "pretty generally conceded that Monson has lost a benefactor in Mr Norcross though many hated him heartily while he lived."[8] For all his virtues, plainspoken Joel Norcross frequently stepped on other people's toes.

Unfortunately, the Norcross children were not robust, and when Emily Norcross Dickinson's mother died in 1829 at the age of fifty-two after a terrible illness, an obituary notice remarked on the "severe afflictions, which she was called repeatedly to endure in the sickness and death of children," four of whom had predeceased her.[9] (Both Emily Norcross and Edward Dickinson came from large families—there were nine children each.) Her mother's illness and death, together with the deaths of four of her siblings, affected Emily Norcross Dickinson deeply and reinforced her tendency toward anxiety and introversion. Her father remarried in 1831 and her younger, more outgoing sister Lavinia, after whom she named her own daughter, was not pleased.[10] Characteristically, Emily Norcross Dickinson kept her own counsel; her response to her father's remarriage is unrecorded.

The poet Emily Elizabeth Dickinson inherited some of her father's energy and some of her mother's shyness. The middle child and close in age to both her older brother Austin and younger sister Lavinia, she took pride in their accomplishments and was fiercely loyal to them throughout her life. Toward the end, she was especially close to Lavinia, who was to all intents and purposes her literary executor. Without Lavinia's efforts, Dickinson's "letter[s] to the world" would not have been published. Moreover, Mabel Loomis Todd, the editor who did so much to publicize Dickinson's poems and letters in the 1890s, was for many years involved in an adulterous liaison with Austin.[11] In both its public and private dimensions, Emily Dickinson's career cannot be separated for very long from the history of her family, which was further inflected by Dickinson's relationship to her sister-in-law, Susan Gilbert Dickinson. We will hear more about the forceful and mercurial Susan and her controversial role in inspiring and disseminating Dickinson's letter(s) to the world later on.

When the future poet was nine, the Dickinsons moved into an undivided home, a spacious wooden one on Pleasant Street. The brick mansion on Main Street continued to haunt Edward, though, and in 1855 he repurchased, refurbished, and added onto the house that his father had built and lost. Although recently defeated in his bid for reelection to Congress, Edward's property romance had been realized.[12] Emily Dickinson was more ambivalent about the move, referring to herself as an emigrant with a *"gone-to-Kansas* feeling." "They say that 'home is where the heart is,'" she wrote to her close friend Elizabeth Holland in January 1856. "I think it is where the *house* is, and the outlying buildings" (L 182). Later that year, Edward consolidated his gains when, on a building lot adjacent to The Homestead, he financed the construction of The Evergreens, a fashionable Italianate villa, which became the residence of Austin and Sue after their marriage that July. Austin had been restless, but the house was a powerful inducement to remain in Amherst and Edward offered to make him a partner in his law practice. Austin acceded and he did.

Real estate romance and family romance diverged, however, for the 1850s played out very differently for the poet's parents. Leaving the Pleasant Street house, where she had raised her family, unsettled Mrs. Dickinson both physically and emotionally. Her daughters were proving to be capable housekeepers, and after Austin's marriage to a highly literate and socially poised daughter-in-law, with whom she had little in common, her listlessness deepened. One biographer (Alfred Habegger) has suggested that she may have been suffering from a blocked grief reaction, that, in her prosperity and comparative leisure, the family deaths she had had to put behind her as a busy young wife and mother had finally caught up with her.[13] This seems as good an explanation of her midlife crisis as any, although it makes the most sense if we factor in her growing estrangement from Edward, or her need for more emotional support from him, which was probably not forthcoming. Whatever the causes of her discontent, after the move, Emily Norcross Dickinson, whose life had been her home and family, was feeling displaced. Her daughter Emily was sensitive to her feelings, writing poignantly in 1858 of depression that seems a combination of her mother's and her own (L 190).

Writing to her uncle Joseph A. Sweetser in the early summer of 1858, Dickinson explained both frankly and evasively:

> Much has occurred, dear Uncle, since my writing you—so much—that I stagger as I write, in its sharp remembrance. Summers of bloom—and months of frost, and days of jingling bells, yet all the while this hand upon our fireside. Today has been so glad without, and yet so grieved within—so jolly, shone the sun—and now the moon comes stealing, and yet it makes none glad. I cannot always see the light—please tell me if it shines. (L 190)

Dickinson was already commenting on her reluctance to leave home in 1854, when she declined an invitation to visit her pious friend Abiah Root, identifying herself as "your quaint, old fashioned friend," and explaining, "I dont go from home, unless emergency leads me by the hand, and then I do it obstinately, and draw back if I can. Should I ever leave home, which is improbable, I will with much delight, accept your invitation; till then, my dear Abiah, my warmest thanks are your's, but dont expect me. I'm so old fashioned, Darling, that all your friends would stare" (L 166). With one exception, Dickinson was true to her word.[14] As far as overnight travels were concerned, she journeyed only when "emergency" took her by the hand, as it did in 1864, when she spent seven months in Cambridge, Massachusetts, returning to Cambridge for another extensive stay the following year. She was receiving medical treatment for her eye problems and after her return to Amherst in the fall of 1865, she never left the town again.[15] Nor did she usually visit *in* the town, not even at The Evergreens. Nor did she freely receive visitors at home.

Before moving on, we should note one happy offshoot of these medically mandated sojourns "in the wilderness," as Dickinson called them, which was that she developed one of the most important relationships of her life, with her cousins, Frances and Louisa Norcross. She lived with them at Mrs. Bangs's Boarding-house in Cambridgeport, one mile from Harvard College, while she was undergoing her eye treatments. Fanny and Loo were the daughters of Dickinson's Aunt Lavinia—her mother's sister, who died in 1860, while their grieving father died in January 1863. The recently orphaned Norcross sisters were seventeen and twenty-two years old at the time of Dickinson's first boardinghouse stay, while Dickinson herself was thirty-three. Over the years, she maintained an extensive correspondence with these "Little Cousins" (L 1046), in which she described her feelings and day-to-day experiences with unusual candor and clarity. The sisters later moved to Concord, where they participated in the Concord Saturday Club, a small group devoted to the study of literature, whose members included Louisa May Alcott, William Ellery Channing, and Ralph Waldo Emerson. As these impressive acquaintances indicate, among the reasons Dickinson may have valued her relationship with her Norcross cousins was their intelligence and their interest in literature.

As previously noted, after 1865 Emily Dickinson was homebound. According to a plausible legend, one evening, probably in September 1868, she went with her brother "as far as a certain tree in the hedge in order to see the new church."[16] (Her father had spoken at the dedication ceremony, and the pastor and his family were her friends.) According to an equally plausible legend, when she visited her dying nephew Gilbert in 1883, she was paying her first call to The Evergreens in fifteen years.[17] Yet this is the poet who could write, "Doom is the House without the Door" (Fr 710), and "Exultation is the going / Of an inland soul to sea" (Fr 143), and "I never hear the word 'Escape' / Without a quicker blood" (Fr 144). Dickinson repeatedly suggested that "Water, is taught by thirst" (Fr 93), and that we "learn the Transport by the Pain - / As Blind Men learn the sun!" (Fr 178). She wanted to believe that there was value in deprivation and that her imagination of freedom was intensified by her physical confinement, in what toward the end of her life she described as a "magic Prison," which by then was earth itself, in its aspect of nonheaven:

> Of God we ask one favor, that we may be forgiven -
> For what, he is presumed to know -
> The Crime, from us, is hidden -
> Immured the whole of Life
> Within a magic Prison
> We reprimand the Happiness
> That too competes with Heaven - (Fr 1675)

Elsewhere, she wrote that "A Prison gets to be a friend" (Fr 456).[18]

Why *did* Emily Dickinson shut herself up in The Homestead and leave the wider social world behind? In various forms, this question has haunted Dickinson's biography. Writing in 1918, for example, the Imagist poet Amy Lowell asked pointedly, "I wonder what made Emily Dickinson as she was. She cannot be accounted for by any trick of ancestry or early influence." Lowell was certain, however, that Dickinson was the victim of some undiagnosed nervous disorder, and that "All her friends were in the conspiracy of silence":

As the years went on, she could scarcely be induced to leave her own threshold; what she saw from her window, what she read in her books, were her only external *stimuli*. Those few people whom she admitted to her friendship were loved with the terrible and morbid exaggeration of the profoundly lonely. In this isolation, all resilience to the blows of illness and death was atrophied. She could not take up her life again because there was no life to take. Her thoughts came to be more and more preoccupied with the grave. Her letters were painful reading indeed to the normal-minded. Here was a woman with a nice wit, a sparkling sense of humour, sinking under the weight of an introverted imagination to a state bordering upon neurasthenia; for her horror of publicity would now certainly be classed as a "phobia." The ignorance and unwisdom of her friends confused illness with genius, and, reversing the usual experience in such cases, they saw in the morbidness of hysteria, the sensitiveness of a peculiarly artistic nature.[19]

Lowell dreamed of breaking through this conspiracy of silence by writing a Dickinson biography, but as she predicted in a letter to Mabel Loomis Todd, it never materialized.[20]

Although Dickinson did not shut herself up "in Prose" (Fr 445), she certainly shut herself up in a particular house and with a particular family for most of her adult life. There is a high probability that she suffered from agoraphobia. At the very least, she suffered from extreme social shyness.[21] Her father, however, was often in the limelight, and he figured prominently in early accounts of her life. She was thought to have a father complex. Her relations with her father were considered "peculiar." She said on one occasion, "I am not very well acquainted with father."[22] Under the pressure of feminist inquiry, in the 1970s and 1980s Dickinson's mother was increasingly written into the picture, as were her brother Austin (1829–1895) and sister-in-law Sue (1830–1913). Mother. Father. Older brother. Younger sister. Mercurial sister-in-law. The sister-in-law who taught her more about people than anyone except Shakespeare. "To say that sincerely is strange praise" (L 757).

The Dickinsons were one of the most important families in Amherst, Massachusetts, population 3,057 in 1850 and 4,298 in 1880. They were part of an economic, political, and philanthropic elite. In 1871, when *The Amherst Record* published "Pen Portraits of the Prominent Men of Amherst," they included the following notice about Emily's father:

HONORABLE EDWARD DICKINSON. If there is a native of Amherst
to whom the name at the head of this article is a stranger,
he must indeed be a curiosity. . . . The name of Dickinson
. . . is so identified with everything that belongs to Amherst,
that any attempt to speak of town history in which that name
should not appear the most prominent would be impossible.

Curiously, *The Record* suggested that under the circumstances,
Edward Dickinson was something of a shrinking violet, certainly
"averse to notoriety, and were the choice left with him [he]
would have avoided all contact with affairs which we class as *political*." The writer further described him as "A gentleman of the
elder school" and suggested that

> he is by no means a fogy . . . we believe we transgress no
> law of propriety in claiming him to be the most prominent of
> the living men of Amherst. . . . Inheriting an integrity that
> was in itself a fortune, he has ever maintained it in its purity,
> hence the wealth he is now possessed of does not contain
> within it the gall of a wrong inflicted or the curse of another's
> sigh. . . . Mr. and Mrs. Dickinson have been blessed with
> three children—one son and two daughters. We hope he will
> pardon our intrusion upon him.[23]

Edward was a lifelong trustee of the Amherst Academy, the
secondary school which Emily attended, and he was treasurer of
Amherst College for thirty-seven years.[24] Deeply involved in
local affairs, Edward frequently served as moderator of the Town
Meeting and was active in the First Church Parish Committee,
the Temperance Society, the Hampshire Colonization Society,
the Agricultural Society, and was on the board of the Northampton Lunatic Asylum. These are only some of the positions he
held. Devoted to sound financial management of public institutions, Edward was also committed to solid Whig politics and was
active at the state level beginning in 1838, when he was a representative to the Massachusetts legislature. After further service
to the state, in 1852 he was elected by a narrow margin to the
United States Congress, where he was a one-term Whig in

the House of Representatives, from 1853 to 1855, at the time of the debates over the Kansas-Nebraska bill, which "finished off the Whig party and gave birth to a new, entirely northern Republican party."[25] A faithful Whig, Edward did not adapt to new times and except for a return to the state legislature during the last year of his life, his political career was effectively over. It is no accident, however, that when he returned to Boston in the spring of 1874, he did so to help bring a larger railroad line to Amherst, since one of his passions had been linking Amherst to other parts of the region and state. Previously, he had been an organizer of and shareholder in the Amherst and Belchertown Railroad, and when this nineteen-mile line opened in June 1853, a crowd came up from New London, Connecticut, to celebrate. As Emily explained to Austin, who was attending Harvard Law School,

> Father was as usual, Chief Marshal of the day, and went marching around the town with New London at his heels like some old Roman General, upon a Triumph Day. . . . Carriages flew like sparks, hither, and thither and yon, and they all said t'was fine. I spose it was—I sat in Prof Tyler's woods and saw the train move off, and then ran home again for fear somebody would see me, or ask me how I did. (L 127)[26]

While on such occasions Edward was in his element, at age twenty-two Emily was already removing herself from crowds and was uncomfortable at the thought of a casual hello.

But this model of civic virtue was less comfortable with his children, who found him stern and regimented. In a December 1851 letter to her brother, who was teaching school in Boston, Emily wrote,

> [these days, w]hen I know of anything funny, I am just as apt to cry, far *more* so than to *laugh*, for I know *who loves jokes* best [Austin], and who is not here to enjoy them. We dont *have* many jokes tho' *now*, it is pretty much all sobriety, and we do not have much poetry, father having made up his mind that its pretty much all *real life*. Fathers real life and *mine* sometimes come into collision, but as yet, escape unhurt! (L 65)

At times, her father's behavior seemed to her little short of tyrannical:

> Tutor Howland was here *as usual*, during the afternoon—after tea I went to see Sue—had a nice little visit with her—then went to see Emily Fowler, and arrived home at 9—found Father in great agitation at my protracted stay—and mother and Vinnie [her sister] in tears, for fear that he would kill me. (L 42)[27]

And it wasn't only his children who found him threatening. The next year, after her friend Martha Gilbert visited, Emily wrote Austin:

> Mat came home from meeting with us last Sunday, was here Saturday afternoon when father came, and at her special request, was secreted by me in the *entry*, until he was fairly in the house, when she escaped, *unharmed*. (L 82)

The Dickinson children did not simply submit to their father's exactions; although they rarely rebelled openly, they found creative forms of resistance and subversion. This was especially true of Austin and Emily, whereas Lavinia was more compliant. And yet, there was a tender and witty side to this stern man too. In an October 1851 letter to her brother, Dickinson wrote:

> There was quite an excitement in the village Monday evening. We were all startled by a violent church bell ringing, and thinking of nothing but fire, rushed out in the street to see. The sky was a beautiful red, bordering on a crimson, and rays of a gold pink color were constantly shooting off from a kind of sun in the centre. People were alarmed at this beautiful Phenomenon, supposing that fires somewhere were *coloring the sky*. The exhibition lasted for nearly 15. minutes, and the streets were full of people wondering and admiring. Father happened to see it among the very first and rang the bell *himself* to call attention to it. (L 53)

It was he who gave Emily a huge dog, Carlo, who was her constant companion, or "Shaggy Ally," for sixteen years (L 280). When his daughter's shyness advanced, he created a nook for Emily among the trees behind their home, where she could sit out-of-doors unobserved. And once, she writes,

> he said he ran out of meeting for fear somebody would ask him what he tho't of the preaching. He says if anyone asks him, he shall put his hand to his mouth, and his mouth in the dust, and cry, Unclean—Unclean!! (L 125)

When she grew older, Dickinson developed compassion for her father's "lonely Life and his lonelier Death" (L 457). Probably in the mid-1860s, she explained to Joseph Lyman, who had been her friend and Vinnie's suitor, "Father says in fugitive moments when he forgets the barrister & lapses into the man, says that his life has been passed in a wilderness or on an island—of late he says on an island." But she also described him as the oldest and oddest sort of a "foreigner."[28] She had dreams about him every night for a year after he died, and in a letter to a friend, she described *his* pleasure in their last moments together, while indicating that she had never been able to figure him out:

> The last Afternoon that my Father lived, though with no premonition—I preferred to be with him, and invented an absence for Mother, Vinnie being asleep. He seemed peculiarly pleased as I oftenest stayed with myself, and remarked as the Afternoon withdrew, he "would like it to not end."
>
> His pleasure almost embarrassed me and my Brother coming—I suggested they walk. Next morning I woke him for the train [to Boston]—and saw him no more.
>
> His Heart was pure and terrible and I think no other like it exists. (L 418)

Inventing an absence for mother was easy; it was harder to know how to respond to father's unique combination of vigilance and reserve.

And what of Emily's mother in her maturity, once she had recovered from the depression that plagued her in the 1850s? In one of her first letters to Higginson, the poet summed up the situation succinctly, if somewhat cruelly, as follows: "My Mother does not care for thought" (L 261). Elaborating on the idea that she and her mother inhabited different worlds, in 1870 she told him, "'I never had a mother. I suppose a mother is one to whom you hurry when you are troubled'" (L 342b). Higginson had to take her word for it, since he never met Mrs. Dickinson either during his 1870 or 1873 visits to The Homestead. Edward, however, put in an appearance, exhibiting what one might think of as normal parental curiosity about his daughter's illustrious caller. With Higginson, Emily Dickinson persisted in this narrative of maternal neglect and abandonment and incomprehension and overall lack of mutual sympathy. In 1874, she wrote him punningly, "I always ran Home to Awe when a child, if anything befell me. He was an awful Mother, but I liked him better than none" (L 405).

Despite Dickinson's statement that "My mother does not care for thought," for a woman in her time and place Emily Norcross Dickinson had a superior education. True, she was never much of a reader, but she did attend a coeducational school in Monson and then studied at a boarding school "for Young Ladies" in New Haven, Connecticut, in 1823, receiving a commendation for "punctual attendance, close application, good acquirements, and discreet behavior."[29] She first met Edward Dickinson, a Yale College graduate who was studying law, in the winter of 1826; they met in Monson, her hometown, where he was serving as a marshal of a military court. Edward was interested in settling down and getting to work on his plan for a life of "rational happiness." He almost immediately identified Emily Norcross as someone he wanted to marry, writing her that he found her "a person, in whom so many of the female virtues are conspicuous."[30]

The young couple corresponded for six months, with Edward writing long and serious letters, to which Emily responded sporadically with short apologetic letters that evince little interest in ideas or in the affection of her beau, but great interest in the daily goings-on of her own domestic circle. Notwithstanding the tepid tone of her letters, Edward was in love, and he extended a sober proposal in a letter written the following June. Based on his "full conviction of [her] merits & [her] virtues," he proposed to make her a "friend" for life.[31] These sententious and less-than-amorous expressions of affection did not set Emily's heart on fire, and she stalled in responding to his proposal—claiming that she needed to consult her father—until later that summer, at which time she did accept. She postponed the marriage for more than a year, though, until May 1828. There was a small ceremony in Amherst, because she wanted "as little noise as possible," did not "wish for company," and wanted to "stand up alone" (without bridesmaids and bridegrooms).[32]

The new bride gave birth to three children within four years: William Austin in April 1829, Emily Elizabeth in December 1830, and Lavinia Norcross in February 1833. A story, perhaps apocryphal, has it that on the eve of the birth of her famous daughter she defied her husband's wishes for the first and only time by inducing a paperhanger to redo their bedroom. She was not active in community affairs and appears to have had no close friends in the town, although she exchanged visits with her own relatives. Emily Norcross Dickinson ran an orderly and immaculate house, loved gardening, and prepared outstanding food. But when Edward was away on business—a not uncommon occurrence—she was anxious about the children, and in 1843 she struck at least one observer as full of her usual "plaintive talk."[33] Whatever the mother's substantial virtues—she was not overly controlling—by the time she was nineteen, the emerging poet Emily Dickinson was writing, "God keep me from what they call *households*" (L 36). Housekeeping as she understood it was a "prickly art," and for an aspiring writer, her "timid" mother was far from inspiring.

Emily Dickinson was an affectionate and verbally gifted child, who was deeply attached to her more self-confident older brother and gregarious younger sister. After attending the local primary school, she enrolled at Amherst Academy, where she created a distinct impression on one of her teachers (Daniel Taggart Fiske), who many years later recalled her as she was in 1842–1843:

a very bright, but rather delicate and frail looking girl; an excellent scholar, of exemplary deportment, faithful in all school duties; but somewhat shy and nervous. Her compositions were strikingly original; and in both thought and style seemed beyond her years, and always attracted much attention in the school, and, I am afraid, excited not a little envy.[34]

Dickinson completed her last term at the Academy in August 1847, and at the end of September she entered Mount Holyoke Female Seminary, in nearby South Hadley. It was only seven miles away and she got over her homesickness quickly, although home continued to be her model of perfection. Shortly after she arrived, she wrote to her friend Abiah Root, "I think I could be no happier at any other school away from home. Things seem much more like home than I anticipated & the teachers are all very kind & affectionate to us. They call on us frequently & urge us to return their calls & when we do, we always receive a cordial welcome from them" (L 18). Mount Holyoke was a serious place of higher learning for young women, with a reputation for fostering practical as well as spiritual traits. There was some economic diversity, which induced a fear of "rough & uncultivated manners" (L 18). But Emily Dickinson does not seem to have minded the light housekeeping chores, whereas her childhood acquaintance and future friend Helen Hunt Jackson refused to go to Mount Holyoke "to learn to make hasty pudding and clean *gridirons!*"[35]

We can get a vivid picture of what life was like at Mount Holyoke from a daily schedule she shared in a letter to her friend Abiah Root:

I will tell you my order of time for the day, as you were so kind as to give me your's. At 6. oclock, we all rise. We breakfast at 7. Our study hours begin at 8. At 9. we all meet in Seminary Hall, for devotions. At 10 1/4. I recite a review of Ancient History, in connection with which we read Goldsmith & Grimshaw. At .11. I recite a lesson in "Pope's Essay on Man" which is merely transposition. At .12. I practice Calisthenics & at 12 1/4 read until dinner, which is at 12 1/2 & after dinner, from

1 $1/2$ until 2 I sing in Seminary Hall. From $23/4$ until $33/4$. I prac-
tise upon the Piano. At $33/4$ I go to Sections, where we give in
all our accounts for the day, including, Absence—Tardiness—
Communications—Breaking Silent Study hours—Receiving
Company in our rooms & ten thousand other things, which I
will not take time or place to mention. At $41/2$. we go into
Seminary Hall, & receive advice from Miss. Lyon in the form
of a lecture. We have Supper at 6. & silent-study hours from
then until the retiring bell, which rings at $83/4$, but the tardy
bell does not ring until $93/4$, so that we dont often obey the
first warning to retire. (L 18)

The schedule was indeed regimented, but despite her anxious
dreams about home (L 16) and her waking fears about the en-
trance exams (L 18), she was in high spirits for much of the time.

Nevertheless, to the Emily Dickinson who preferred to dwell
in possibility, the religious regimentation in which the school
specialized was unsettling. Mary Lyon (1797–1849) had founded
Mount Holyoke with a dual emphasis on intellectual achievement and Christian self-denial, and these values were not always
compatible with each other. Throughout the school year, the
subject of giving oneself up to and for Christ was emphasized;
Miss Lyon held separate meetings for those who had "professed
faith," those who had a "hope," and those who had "no hope."
Emily Dickinson was one of eighty "No-hopers" when she entered; by the end of the term, only twenty-nine remained, including herself. At one point, Miss Lyon asked all those who
wanted to be Christians (and hence to fast on Christmas) to rise.
Emily was one of those who remained seated, a fact remarked
on by her roommate, her cousin Emily Norcross, who commented in one of her letters home to Monson, "Emily Dickinson
appears no different. I hoped I might have good news to write
with regard to her."[36] Emily Dickinson was by no means indifferent to religion, "the all important subject" (L 13), nor was she indifferent to the theme of self-denial. In January 1848, she, along
with sixteen other students who felt an "uncommon anxiety,"
met with Mary Lyon to discuss the state of their souls. Under the
right circumstances, anxiety might be a prelude to hope.

Emily, however, left the three-year course at Mount Holyoke without converting. She completed what was called her "junior" year, and in early May, her father decided that there was no need for her to return to the school as a "senior." Perhaps he was concerned about her health, since health was always an issue in the Dickinson family, and she had been home for a month with a cough that raised the specter of tuberculosis, from which so many suffered. Perhaps, too, he viewed a further Mount Holyoke education as superfluous for a woman who was not expected to become a missionary, support herself, become a professional writer, or enter the learned professions. Emily herself does not seem to have minded. Most Holyoke scholars did not stay the course and the town of Amherst, with its college and reading clubs and literary societies had at least as much, if not more to offer. Nevertheless, Dickinson left Holyoke with a sense of unfinished spiritual business. Although Mary Lyon did not succeed in converting her, she appears to have deepened Dickinson's interest in the relationship between self-discipline and power. Lyon urged women to believe in their own abilities, stating that "We have great powers over ourselves. We may become almost what we will."[37] As a daughter of New England, steeped in the traditions of neo-Puritanism, Dickinson was taught that the projects of perfecting and realizing the self (or soul) were intimately intertwined.

There was a problem, though. While Dickinson felt impelled to confront some of the large questions of life, there were more particular matters that concerned her as well. For example, in February 1848 she complained to her brother that she had not received any valentines, that she had looked in vain for one of "Cupid's messengers." "Your *highly accomplished & gifted elder sister* is entirely overlooked," she explained, and she asked Austin to remind her friend "THOMAS" (otherwise unidentified) to send her one (L 22). Status in a girls' boarding school depended on more than academic accomplishments, and popularity with boys mattered. But how could she ponder the large questions of life and also fulfill conventional gender expectations? Her own father had written a series of essays in the 1820s that had addressed this issue, making it clear that he viewed intellectual women as unsuitable marriage partners. When his essays were published in the local newspaper in 1826–1827, they inspired controversy. He was accused of being a male chauvinist, and in some respects, so he remained.[38] "He buys me many Books," Dickinson later explained, "but begs me not to read them—because he fears they joggle the Mind" (L 261).

Her formal schooling ended, Dickinson returned to Amherst which, in the winter of 1849–1850, was "alive with fun" (L 29) and which, as anticipated, provided her with a "feast in the reading line." What, though, was to be *her* life's work and how was she to express her growing sense of estrangement from the genteel conventions that threatened to entrap her? Would it do to think of herself as a character in a book, someone, say, like Byron's prisoner of Chillon? How powerful *was* her imagination? What would constitute her "almost," the impediments that energized and defined her? Dickinson's letters are full of humor, but there is intermittent loneliness as well and during the revival of 1850, even her stern, unbending father was converted, as was her sister Vinnie. Dickinson, however, took pride in "standing alone in rebellion" (L 35), as it seemed to her she was doing. With deliberate irony, she pictured herself as Satan: a Romantic hero of a Byronic cast, engaged in a heroic course of action. Cultivating this persona helped her through the trying domestic days, in which she stayed home to help a sick mother and denied herself outings with friends. She was a good worker, the queen of the court, if regalia be "dust, and dirt" (L 37).

Yet during the early 1850s, her "*golden* dream[s]," the vague life-ambitions which she discussed with friends, were coming clearer. There were "fancies" she refused to nip in the bud, and there were literary consequences. In 1850, for example, one of her prose valentines appeared in the Amherst College literary magazine (L 34) with a favorable notice. It was a witty send up of classical learning, biblical rhetoric, current political oratory, and discourses of romantic friendship. This rollicking comic valentine was also grandiose. Dickinson compared herself to Judith, the heroine of the Apocrypha, and, together with her friend George Gould, to the United States of America! Intent on distinguishing herself, Dickinson was opting for "metaphor" rather than marriage and motherhood, though at times she was attracted to the social status of the "wife" figure or else saw it as inevitable. Her first extant poem, also dated 1850, is a comic valentine in properly rhymed couplets which she sent to her father's law clerk, Elbridge Gerry Bowdoin. Bowdoin was a confirmed bachelor, so no one was likely to take her offer of herself and her friends seriously: "Seize the one thou lovest, nor care for *space*, or *time!*" (Fr 1). Dickinson was especially adept at imitating sermons and in the early 1850s, she wrote other comic valentines that ironized gender stereotypes and fuzzy clerical thinking.

Her seriousness of purpose was fostered and promoted by friends such as Benjamin Franklin Newton, who was another of her father's law clerks. Newton, who suffered from tuberculosis, moved to Worcester in 1849 and in 1850 sent her Ralph Waldo Emerson's poems, "a beautiful copy," which formed part of the gift-exchange of their friendship (L 30). His premature death in March 1853 unsettled her and ten months later, she wrote a letter to his clergyman Edward Everett Hale, also of Worcester, in which she described Newton as "a gentle, yet grave Preceptor, teaching me what to read, what authors to admire, what was most grand or beautiful in nature, and that sublimer lesson, a faith in things unseen, and in a life again, nobler, and much more blessed" (L 153). When she described her development as a poet in her famous 1862 letter to Higginson, she explained, "My dying Tutor told me that he would like to live till I had been a poet, but Death was much of Mob as I could master—then" (L 265). It is likely that she was referring to Newton. After the fact, there was a romantic component to her feelings for him which was not apparent at the time. It is also likely that her father was discouraging the intensity and frequency of their correspondence. As she explained to her friend Jane Humphrey, "I can write him in about three weeks—and I *shall*" (L 30). But the importance Dickinson attached to this relationship after his death was characteristic of her thought structure and deeper emotional bias. Death was her crucial "almost," the limit on human power she could not control. As fact and metaphor, it worried her for all of her writing life. Like her mother, she tended to conflate death and separation and Newton's departure in 1849, marriage in 1851, and death in 1853 intensified this tendency.

Meanwhile, her letters became more and more elliptical and in certain respects, troubled. Her close friend Susan Huntington Gilbert, who was exactly her age, was the recipient of some of them. Sue was born in Old Deerfield, Massachusetts, but the family moved to Amherst in 1832, where her father owned a tavern and stagecoach stop. Unfortunately, her mother Harriet Arms Gilbert died in the winter of 1837 when Sue was six, and her mother's death effectively broke up the family. Sue and her next-older sister Martha were sent to live with Sophia Arms Van Vranken, a "jovial" maternal aunt whose husband was a merchant in Geneva, New York.[39] When Sue's father Thomas died in 1841, reportedly because of alcoholism, he was listed as an "insolvent debtor" in the county records. Understandably, Sue was sensitive about her background and eager to make the most of her wide-ranging talents, including her love for books. In 1847 she returned to Amherst and attended the Academy for a term; beginning in 1848, she was a student at the Utica Female Academy, "which boasted a stately Ionic portico and offered instruction in everything from Latin and 'Technology' to flower painting and guitar."[40] After completing her education, she came back to Amherst, where there were rumors that she and Edward Hitchcock, Jr., son of the Amherst College president, were about to become engaged. Worldly and popular, self-confident but also insecure, when offended Sue took on what Austin, her suitor, called in an 1851 letter "that unapproachable dignity, that rigid formality."[41]

That same summer, Sue decided to leave Amherst, the Dickinsons, and what seemed to her the stifling quiet of small-town life.[42] She was eager to demonstrate her independence and took up a teaching position in a girls' boarding school in Baltimore. Austin was out of town too, teaching "poor Irish boys" in an overcrowded public school in Boston (L 43), and Emily commiserated with both of them about their jobs, though Sue seems to have been more satisfied with hers. In any event, a career in teaching for one hundred and twenty-five dollars a year plus room and board and expenses was not for her, and she returned to Amherst in July 1852, having played out this experiment in feminine self-reliance to her own satisfaction.

Sue's particular combination of insecurity and aplomb struck a deeply responsive chord in Emily, and during Sue's teaching year at Mr. and Mrs. Archer's Boarding and Day School for Young Ladies, Dickinson wrote her a series of remarkable letters that indicate how desolate she felt without her. As with other letters by Emily Dickinson, it is sometimes difficult to know how much she was posing, for example when she expressed fears for her own sanity and imagined herself chained up in an insane asylum because of the intensity of her love. Some of these intensely possessive letters must have been difficult to receive. Others were more tranquil and were focused on the exquisite pleasures of an erotic sisterhood, which excluded the routine obligations represented by "the worthy pastor." Dickinson set about creating a new sacred text, known only to the members of a secret society intent on circumventing the authority of a powerful, monolithic, and boring community of elders:

> So sweet and still, and Thee, Oh Susie, what need I more, to make my heaven whole?
>
> Sweet Hour, blessed Hour, to carry me to you, and to bring you back to me, long enough to snatch one kiss, and whisper Good bye, again.
>
> I have thought of it all day, Susie, and I fear of but little else, and when I was gone to meeting it filled my mind so full, I could not find a *chink* to put the worthy pastor; when he said "Our Heavenly Father," I said "Oh Darling Sue"; when he read the 100th Psalm, I kept saying your precious letter all over to myself, and Susie, when they sang—it would have made you laugh to hear one little voice, piping to the departed. I made up words and kept singing how I loved you, and you had gone, while all the rest of the choir were singing Hallelujahs. I presume nobody heard me, because I sang so *small*, but it was a kind of a comfort to think I might put them out, singing of you. (L 88)

Historians of sexuality such as Carroll Smith-Rosenberg and Lillian Faderman have supplied further context for understanding the homoerotic and possibly protolesbian elements of Dickinsonian desire, as expressed in the letters to Sue. Romantic same-sex friendships were the norm during the antebellum era, but for Emily Dickinson, many questions remain.[43] Whereas today the word "lesbian" can describe not only sexual practice but also an essentialized category of identity, such an identity would not have been possible for Dickinson. The sexologists of the late nineteenth and early twentieth centuries pathologized erotic intimacies and practices that some women in the 1850s could still view as normal. Practically speaking, however, in Dickinson's case, the fact that she was strongly identified with her brother Austin and devoted to his welfare was a further complication in her attempt to bind Sue to herself. Seducing Sue emotionally and perhaps in some measure physically troubled her image of herself as a devoted sister, which in some measure she was.

While some biographical critics such as Paula Bennett believe that Dickinson was primarily autoerotic, others have suggested that whereas Dickinson had what we would today call bisexual desires, she probably acted on none of them, or at least not very much. In brief, cultural paradigms of acceptable intimacy for middle- and upper-middle class white women suggest that Dickinson and Sue were engaged in risk-taking behavior if they were sexually intimate.[44] As we learn more about women's sexual ideologies and practices in America in the nineteenth century, some elements of Dickinson's situation and response are likely to be clarified. But barring some sensational new discovery, the bedroom door remains locked.

After Sue's return to Amherst in July 1852, she and Austin began seeing a great deal of each other and by March 1853, they entered into a long and difficult engagement. (In later years, their marriage was famously troubled.) After Sue's return from Baltimore, Dickinson facilitated a clandestine courtship and imagined an erotic triangle that included *her*. Yet she was pursuing mutually antagonistic goals, simultaneously attempting to create an eroticized female counterculture with Sue and to integrate her beloved friend into the Amherst family circle. Although the precise chronology of many letters is uncertain, and virtually all of Sue's letters to both Austin and Emily were subsequently destroyed, it appears that Emily's interest in Sue intensified once she realized that Austin was seriously pursuing her. This combination of personalities and familial roles was more fateful than accidental. Dickinson's identification with Austin, only one and one-half years her senior and temperamentally more like her than the less complex Vinnie, had always been very strong. During the 1850s, while he was teaching in Sunderland and Boston and then studying in Cambridge, she participated vicariously in his triumphs and defeats and repeatedly expressed her willingness to shoulder his burdens, which she tended to represent as greater than her own. They laughed together at the foibles of "the folks" (their parents) and other relatives and elders. In her eyes he could do no wrong, but she worried about him excessively, often appearing *overconcerned* about his ability to negotiate a dangerous world, but also excessively deferential.[45]

As the poet Adrienne Rich has demonstrated, excessive deference was one of Dickinson's strategies for controlling and deflecting aggression throughout her career, even in the poetry of her maturity.[46] Although Dickinson loved (and resented) her brother, she performed excessive deference in her relationship with him as a way of controlling and deflecting aggression, both hers and his. This covertly hostile, self-minimizing approach is vividly on display in some of her letters, particularly in early letters such as the following:

> I like [your last letter] grandly. . . . I feel quite like retiring, in presence of one so grand, and casting my small lot among small birds, and fishes—you say you dont comprehend me, you want a simpler style. *Gratitude* indeed for all my fine philosophy! I strove to be exalted thinking I might reach you and while I pant and struggle and climb the nearest cloud, you walk out very leisurely in your slippers from Empyrean, and without the *slightest* notice request me to get down! As *simple* as you please, the *simplest* sort of simple—I'll be a little ninny—a little pussy catty, a little Red Riding Hood, I'll wear a Bee in my Bonnet, and a Rose bud in my hair, and what remains to do you shall be told hereafter. (L 45)

Here, Dickinson seems thoroughly in control of a naive pose, which she uses strategically to express resistance to a request

Austin had apparently made in a previous letter that she write in a simpler style. Striving to do more than express herself clearly in her writing, Dickinson wanted to be philosophical and exalted, to challenge herself and her reader but also to disguise erotic subtexts that were threatening to her self-esteem and to her audience. Although Dickinson represents Austin as her incomparable role model and Austin did write verse on occasion, in a subsequent letter, she insisted that *she* held the "patent" on invention and would not let him steal it from her. "Father says your letters are altogether before Shakespeare," she wrote mordantly, "and he will have them published to put in our library" (L 46).[47]

After a tryst at the Revere Hotel in Boston in March 1853, Sue and Austin became engaged. Dickinson wrote, "Sue's outwitted them all—ha-ha! just imagine me giving three cheers for American Independence" (L 109). Austin was still attending Harvard Law School, though, and Emily and Susan continued to see a great deal of each other in Amherst. For example, in 1854, when Austin, Lavinia, and their mother visited Edward in Washington, Emily preferred to stay at home, her father acceded to her wishes, and Sue moved into The Homestead. (Emily's cousin John Graves provided the necessary male protection; Edward was always concerned about his women when he was away.) Yet the loving triangle formed by Sue and Emily and Austin was unstable, and Sue and Emily quarreled in the summer of 1854, when Austin returned from Harvard. Emily was obviously upset, and the pressures on Sue were intense. She fell ill with what was diagnosed as "Nervous Fever," and when she had recuperated sufficiently, Sue left Amherst for seven months. Dickinson's letter of late August, the first since her beloved friend's departure on August 4, alludes to their falling out and conveys the bleakness of her mood. Realizing that Sue's feeling for her was unlikely to burn as brilliantly as she had once thought it might, "It's of no use to write to you—," she complained, "Far better bring dew in my thimble to quench the endless fire" (L 172).

This extravagant vocabulary was replicated in tributes to Sue in years to come. Sue was the "only Woman in the World," the "Woman whom I prefer," and "Where my Hands are cut, Her fingers will be found inside" (L 447, L 288). Although Dickinson shared more poems with Sue than with anyone and continued to count on her both emotionally and intellectually, there were tributes such as the following that she probably did not share, one of an impressive and often heartrending group of poems inspired by her in some measure unreciprocated love for Sue:

> Ourselves were wed one summer - dear -
> Your Vision - was in June -
> And when Your little Lifetime failed,
> I wearied - too - of mine -
>
> And overtaken in the Dark -
> Where You had put me down -
> By Some one carrying a Light -
> I - too - received the Sign -
>
> 'Tis true - Our Futures different lay -
> Your Cottage - faced the sun -
> While Oceans - and the North must be -
> On every side of mine
>
> 'Tis true, Your Garden led the Bloom,
> For mine - in Frosts - was sown -
> And yet, one Summer, we were Queens -
> But You - were crowned in June - (Fr 596)

After marrying Austin, Susan entered a new phase of life. As a hostess devoted to her house and its entertainments, and as a mother, beginning in 1861, when the first of her three children was born, Sue actualized herself as a social being. "A strong-minded American woman," as she characterized herself in a letter to her friends the Bartletts, Sue's identity was also contingent and interdependent. She flirted with the charming editor Samuel Bowles (1826–1878), who was Austin's friend as well, and distinguished herself in Amherst both for the elaborateness of her entertainments and for her mercurial moods. She attracted friends easily but discarded them readily. Emily, another strong-minded American woman, was forced to be more austerely self-reliant, though we catch our last glimpses of her as a social being in the house next door, the house with the blazing wood fire, rampant fun, inextinguishable laughter. Thus she wrote to Sam Bowles in 1858, "I think Jerusalem must be like Sue's Drawing Room, when we are talking and laughing there, and you and Mrs. Bowles are by" (L 189). And in 1859 she reported, "Austin and Sue went to Boston Saturday, which makes the Village very large. I find they are my crowd" (L 212).

As her friends married—Sue and Austin on July 1, 1856—Dickinson felt increasingly solitary. By 1856, she had drafted a considerable number of poems—no one knows exactly how many—and she had won second prize for her rye and Indian bread at the local Cattle Show. In 1857, however, Dickinson virtually disappears from view. There are no letters that can be conclusively attributed to that year, which in itself is curious, since her correspondence is continuous up to that point. She was appointed to a committee of the annual autumn Cattle Show to judge a bread-baking contest, but there is no proof that she ever served. Beyond that, she disappears from view. Even the rumor mill of Amherst grinds to an unaccustomed halt. An accident of historiography? Perhaps, but it seems more likely that Dickinson was turning inward. "Tis a dangerous moment for any one," she later wrote in an undated prose fragment, "when the meaning goes out of things and Life stands straight—and punctual—and yet no content . . . come[s]. Yet such moments are. If we survive them they expand us, if we do not, but that is Death, whose if is everlasting" (PF 49; *Letters* 3:919). Subsequent letters refer to a major traumatic event, as do many of her finest poems, which describe a horrifying psychological catastrophe and its aftermath:

> 'Twas like a Maelstrom, with a notch,
> That nearer, every Day,
> Kept narrowing it's boiling Wheel
> Until the Agony. . . . (Fr 425)

* * *

> It was not Death, for I stood up,
> And all the Dead, lie down -

It was not Night, for all the Bells
Put out their Tongues, for Noon. (Fr 355)

★ ★ ★

'Tis so appalling - it exhilarates -
So over Horror, it half Captivates. . . .
Terror's free -
Gay, Ghastly, Holiday! (Fr 341)

★ ★ ★

I felt a Funeral, in my Brain,
And Mourners to and fro
Kept treading - treading - till it seemed
That Sense was breaking through - (Fr 340)

★ ★ ★

After great pain, a formal feeling comes -
The nerves sit ceremonious, like Tombs (Fr 372)

★ ★ ★

Such knowledge came from somewhere—surely not from her reading alone.[48]

The supposition that Dickinson's poetic vision was associated with psychological trauma is distressing to readers who want to believe that she chose the conditions that nurtured her art, that because of her verbal intelligence and aptitude for form, she was in control of her feelings too. Dickinson's freedom was historically situated, however, and the choices she felt compelled to make were arduous indeed. While it may be difficult to celebrate the loss of coherent social identity as a strategy of female empowerment, it is nevertheless true that in turning inward, Dickinson gained unique insights into the human psyche. For her, personal pain was integral to expression, and by 1858 she had begun transcribing poems onto sheets of stationery, which she then bound with needle and thread into small booklets. Conventionally, these homemade books are called fascicles (gatherings), or manuscript books, and Dickinson continued this practice until

1865. Subsequently, she organized sheets more haphazardly and did not bind them. (These unbound collections are conventionally referred to as "sets.") Various theories have been advanced as to their purpose, but she did not share these little manuscript books, forty in all, with anyone else. When she sent her poems out to family and friends, she distributed them one by one. The poems she sent were a form of self-publication, perhaps preparing for better days, and in 1861, we see her writing to Sue, "Could I make you and Austin—proud—sometime—a great way off—'twould give me taller feet" (L 238). At that time she was engaged in using Sue as reader, critic, and mentor; *her* writings may have influenced Sue as well.

Only five poems have been conclusively identified as having been written before 1858. By the spring of 1858, however, she had also written her first letter to the man she called "Master," whose identity has been the subject of much speculation. After Dickinson's death in May 1886, three draft letters were found among her papers. Two of them address the recipient as "Master," and the third refers to "master" in the text. It is generally assumed that they were intended for the same person, and they appear to have been written in 1858, 1861, and 1862. We do not know for certain that the final versions were sent. It is possible that Dickinson saved these drafts with her poems or otherwise segregated them from the letters that she had received and which were burned by her sister after her death. (On such occasions, it was customary in the late nineteenth century either to return letters to their senders or to destroy them.) The impetuous Lavinia came to regret the burning, but since her policy was to preserve almost everything written by her sister, perhaps that principle guided her when she saved these drafts. "Dear Master," the first of them begins, "I am ill, but grieving more that you are ill, I make my stronger hand work long eno' to tell you."

> I wish that I were great, like Mr. Michael Angelo, and could paint for you. You ask me what my flowers [a metaphor for her poems] said—then they were disobedient—I gave them messages. They said what the lips in the West, say, when the sun goes down, and so says the Dawn.

Listen again, Master. I did not tell you that today had been the Sabbath Day.

Each Sabbath on the Sea, makes me count the Sabbaths, till we meet on shore—and (will the) whether the hills will look as blue as the sailors say. I cannot talk any more (stay any longer) tonight (now), for this pain denies me.

How strong when weak to recollect, and easy, quite, to love. Will you tell me, please to tell me, soon as you are well. (L 187)

Establishing a continuum of hope and despair, this letter suggests that too much pain will silence the poet, but that when the world is sufficiently distanced, when the sun goes down, some form of artistic and spiritual rebirth is possible. Even as she anticipates a reunion with "Master" in heaven or in a place on earth that, for two together, is *like* heaven, Dickinson seems to acknowledge that she did not find it "easy, quite, to love." Whoever he was, Master did not understand the "flowers," or poems, that she had sent him. He asked her what they meant. Listen again, she says. Try harder.

As the language poet Susan Howe has observed, Dickinson's Master letters are deeply influenced by literary models.[49] Nevertheless, it seems likely that "Master" was an actual man who was corresponding with Dickinson, that she was sending him poems, which he did not understand—she blames the poems, "then they were disobedient"—and that her "terror—since September" may well have been related to a traumatic change in their relationship.[50] Whereas Richard B. Sewall, Cynthia Griffin Wolff, and Judith Farr conclude that Master was Samuel Bowles, the dynamic editor of the *Springfield Republican* and one of Dickinson's most distinguished male friends, following an earlier tradition Albert Habegger has reasserted, plausibly, that Master was the Reverend Charles Wadsworth (1814–1881).[51] Of the men with whom Dickinson is known to have corresponded, Wadsworth is the only candidate who matches what we may plausibly infer about her unknown correspondent, and after his death, she referred to him as her "dearest earthly friend" (L 807).

Dickinson probably met Wadsworth during her visit to Phila-

delphia in 1855, where he was the minister of the fashionable
Arch Street Presbyterian Church, and where her cousins the
Coleman sisters, Olivia and Maria, were members of his con-
gregation. (The second "Master" letter expresses her desire to
"come nearer than presbyteries" [L 233]. A presbytery is a govern-
ing committee of the Presbyterian church.) It is certain that
Wadsworth visited Dickinson in Amherst in 1860, when he was
in mourning for his mother, and again in 1880. In April 1862, the
same month in which Dickinson first wrote to Higginson,
Wadsworth formally accepted a post at the Calvary Church in
San Francisco and on May 1 he sailed for California with his wife
and children.[52] Wadsworth and his family returned to Philadelphia in 1869, where he suffered from the vocal impediment to
which Dickinson refers, obliquely, in her eulogy for him, "The
Spirit lasts - but in what mode" (Fr 1627). No breath of scandal
ever attached itself to Wadsworth's reputation; he was not a
known womanizer like Bowles, whose marriage was strained.
After Wadsworth's death, Dickinson entered into correspondence with his close friend, James D. Clark of Northampton, and
then with his brother. Eventually she invited both Clark brothers
to visit her in Amherst, at a time when such gregariousness toward strangers was almost unprecedented for her. In all, Dickinson sent the Clark brothers twenty-one letters, many of them
tributes to Wadsworth, whom she identified as "my Shepherd
from 'Little Girl'hood." Although she referred to an "intimacy of
many years with the beloved Clergyman" (L 766), her letters ask
for basic information about his personal life, about which she
knew little, and they never mention his wife.

The single extant letter from Wadsworth to Dickinson is addressed to "My Dear Miss Dickenson" [*sic*] (L 248a). This undated
letter, possibly from the early 1860s, expresses concern about her
"affliction," whatever it is. It asks to learn more definitely of her
"trial" and expresses appropriate sympathy. There is nothing in
Wadsworth's letter that suggests a sexual relationship, although
sexual relationships between married ministers and female con-
gregants were not unprecedented. While it is conceivable that
Wadsworth's letter was written in a code that Dickinson would
have understood, there is little reason to think that Wadsworth

went to California to escape either from his temptation to seduce Emily Dickinson or from the consequences of such a seduction. It is, however, perfectly possible that he was already thinking about relocating to California in September 1861 and that he told Dickinson about his plans. Whatever happened or did not happen between them, Dickinson continued to elaborate the mythic structure she was developing in her poetry. The "Master" letters exploit stereotypes of masculinity and femininity, as a powerful older man, invested with spiritual authority, takes on sublime and demonic attributes. "Master" does not live in New England and does not depend on Dickinson as she does on him. He is probably married, certainly he is otherwise engaged and has pressing commitments that exclude her. Master is not available for ordinary companionship. The single extant letter written by Wadsworth is signed "In great haste Sincerely and most Affectionately *Yours*." We do not know why it survived Lavinia's bonfire. Many poems reinforce the personal myth that Dickinson elaborates in the "Master" letters, yet because of the intensity of her conception of love, the awe-inspiring Master figure represented in her poems and letters does not readily correspond to his historical equivalent.[53]

For four years (1878–1882), however, long after she wrote the poems of erotic triumph and despair inspired by Sue's marriage and Master's supposed incursion into her own life, Dickinson did have one documented love affair that was significantly mutual and physical. Otis Phillips Lord (1812–1884) was an Amherst College graduate, class of 1832, with a large and lucrative law practice before he was appointed to the Massachusetts Superior Court in 1859. In the 1850s, he was active in Whig politics and was known as an effective orator. He and Edward Dickinson were political allies and became close friends in the 1860s. Lord and his wife Elizabeth lived in Salem and were childless. They first visited the Dickinsons in 1860 and were regular if not frequent guests thereafter.[54] "Phil" Lord and Dickinson fell in love with each other very shortly after his wife of thirty-four years died on December 10, 1877. As Dickinson imagined him to be in the late seventies and early eighties, Lord exemplifies the distancing thematic of the "Master" letters, even though Lord was not the in-

spiration for these letters or for the poems in which Dickinson
had characterized herself as a secret wife. Dickinson could invest
Lord with majesty, but unlike "Master," he was not cruel to her
and the poet was more in charge. She was in her late forties during the flourish years of their romance, he was in his late sixties,
and while there are still power inequalities in their relationship that she underscores, Lord emerges as a sweetened "Papa"
(L 750).

With her father dead in 1874 and her mother incapacitated by
a stroke in 1875, and following the death of Lord's wife in 1877,
Dickinson and Lord entered into an unmistakably passionate
correspondence, as can be seen in the following excerpt from
Amherst (as Dickinson called herself) to her Salem (as she called
Lord):

> My lovely Salem smiles at me. I seek his Face so often—but
> I have done with guises.
>
> I confess that I love him—I rejoice that I love him— I thank
> the maker of Heaven and Earth—that gave him me to love—
> the exultation floods me. I cannot find my channel—the
> Creek turns Sea—at thought of thee—
>
> Will you punish me? "Involuntary Bankruptcy," how could
> that be Crime?
>
> Incarcerate me in yourself—rosy penalty—threading with
> you this lovely maze, which is not Life or Death—though it
> has the intangibleness of one, and the flush of the other—
> waking for your sake on Day made magical with you before I
> went (L 559)

Lord was pressing her to give him something, either her hand in
marriage, or her sexual favor, but she wrote him:

> Dont you know you are happiest while I withhold and not
> confer—dont you know that "No" is the wildest word we con-
> sign to Language?
>
> You do, for you know all things—[top of sheet cut off]
> . . . to lie so near your longing—to touch it as I passed, for I
> am but a restive sleeper and often should journey from your

Arms through the happy night, but you will lift me back, wont you, for only there I ask to be—I say, if I felt the longing nearer—than in our dear past, perhaps I could not resist to bless it, but must, because it would be right

The "Stile" is God's—My Sweet One—for your great sake—not mine—I will not let you cross—but it is all your's, and when it is right I will lift the Bars, and lay you in the Moss—You showed me the word.

I hope it has no different guise when my fingers make it. It is Anguish I long conceal from you to let you leave me, hungry, but you ask the divine Crust and that would doom the Bread. (L 562)

She evidently refused to give herself to him. Nonetheless, she continued to write love letters, fantasizing about his touch:

I do—do want you tenderly. The air is soft as Italy, but when it touches me, I spurn it with a Sigh because it is not you. (L 750)

By this time, Dickinson's letters were deeply indebted to her own past writings, so that when she spurns the air, she echoes the opening stanza of a poem written in about 1862, in which spurning figures prominently: "If you were coming in the Fall, / I'd brush the Summer by / With half a smile, and half a spurn, / As Housewives do, a Fly" (Fr 356). And when she confesses, "The trespass of my rustic Love upon your Realms of Ermine, only a Sovreign could forgive—I never knelt to other" (L 750), we hear the echo of her "Master" letter, which contains a variant on the kneeling trope: "Low at the knee that bore her once unto [royal] wordless rest [now] Daisy [stoops a] kneels a culprit" (L 248). Dickinson in love is always a writer and her letters are brilliantly intertextual; they allude to patterns of pleasure and pain, of dominance and submission, deeply imbedded in prior and future texts. With "Phil" Lord, however, Dickinson also translated words into deeds. She engaged in a gratifying sensual and emotional relationship with Lord that had the capacity to shock—

which says as much about the repressive sexual mores of the time as about her behavior. According to Mabel Loomis Todd, when she first was getting to know Sue, Sue warned her that the two sisters next door were immoral: "You will not allow your husband to go there, I hope! . . . They have not, either of them, any idea of morality. . . . I went in there one day, and in the drawing room I found Emily reclining in the arms of a man."[55]

Immoral or not, Emily dreamt of marriage with Lord:

> The celestial Vacation of writing you after an interminable Term of *four Days*, I can scarcely express. . . . Emily "Jumbo"! [he had been teasing her about having gained weight.] Sweetest name, but I know a sweeter—Emily Jumbo Lord. Have I your approval? (L 780)

Nonetheless, the two never did marry, probably from the combined pressures of Dickinson's agoraphobic attachment to her own home, the opposition of Lord's niece and heir Abbie Farley, and the illnesses of both Lord and Dickinson in the 1880s. He died of a stroke in 1884, and when Dickinson herself died two years later, the incurably romantic Lavinia put two heliotropes in the coffin, "'to take to Judge Lord.'"[56]

The loss of Lord was the second-to-last in a series of devastating deaths during the last twelve years of Dickinson's life. The death of her father in 1874 was the first and most important, though in certain respects his death also liberated her. In June 1874, Edward Dickinson became ill while speaking in the Massachusetts legislature in favor of the Hoosac Tunnel bill—again the railroad and the economic future of Amherst were favorite causes. Faintness forced Edward to stop and retire to his hotel, where the doctor whom he had summoned administered a dose of morphine or opium. (The family believed that Edward was allergic to the medication and that medical bungling had killed him.) According to legend, after his body was brought home from the train station and after the undertaker and his assistant had left, Austin leaned down and kissed his forehead, saying "There, father, I never dared do that while you were living."[57]

Emily did not attend the funeral, or greet guests, or participate in any public way in honoring the man of whom she wrote to Higginson, "His Heart was pure and terrible and I think no other like it exists" (L 418).

Because of the social and physical circumscription of Emily Dickinson's later life, subtractions from her "estate" of family and friends weighed more heavily than they might have under other circumstances. Although Lavinia Dickinson described Emily as always ready to welcome the rewarding new person, there are numerous accounts of people, including some old friends, who tried to see the poet in her later years, only to be shut out politely but firmly by Dickinson and her protective entourage. The woman of letters Helen Hunt Jackson was cordially welcomed in the 1870s, but Jackson, who asked to be Dickinson's literary executor and pressured her to publish, was one of the rare exceptions.[58] Samuel Bowles died unexpectedly in 1878, Dickinson's mother died in 1882, as did Wadsworth, her beloved nephew Gilbert in 1883, Lord in 1884, and then "H.H." (Helen Hunt Jackson) in 1885. There is no way to be sure that these losses hastened Dickinson's end, but whether she died of Bright's Disease, a kidney disorder, or whether as now seems likely the primary cause of death was heart disease and hypertension, Dickinson's final years were riven by their elegiac tenor.[59] "All but Death, Can be adjusted," she once wrote (Fr 789), and she had too many occasions on which to affirm the wisdom of her own words. "Death" itself was exempt from change; not so, despite her best efforts to the contrary, Emily Dickinson.

"My life has been too simple and stern to embarrass any," the poet had written to Higginson in 1869 (L 330), but after reading one of her most impassioned love lyrics, this urbane man of letters was not sure that he could believe her. Was it possible that the person who signed herself his "Scholar" and his "Gnome" and whom he described as "partially cracked" had had a sexual secret?[60] When she wrote him in 1885 that "Biography first convinces us of the fleeing of the Biographied" (L 972), did he think that she was calling attention to death as an inconceivable and philosophically unsettling event? Certainly, much of her poetry is concerned with death in its literal and metaphorical guises—for death can represent powerlessness and power too—but her statement also implies that biographers feed on absences. This is especially true of Dickinson's biographers, since she did so much not only to encourage but also to thwart them. Whereas Dickinson resisted being reduced to any kind of totalizing formula, including that of the romantic recluse daring to dream beautiful dreams, "dwell[ing] in Possibility - / A fairer House than Prose," she also wrote that "Each Life converges to some Centre - / Expressed - or still - / Exists in every Human Nature / A Goal" (Fr 724). How did she balance the longing for freedom implied by the idea of dwelling in possibility and the longing for fixity implied by the idea of a center? Put somewhat differently, what ambivalences narrowed Dickinson's original ambition to publish her letter(s) to the world? She wanted to make her family proud and she wanted to select "her own Society." How could the need to be true to herself and to seek social validation be reconciled? As a young woman she remarked, "When I die, they'll have to remember me."[61] History has justified the claim.

By now, at the start of the twenty-first century, Dickinson's intellectual development, social experience, and psychological logic have been the subject of a formidable quantity of biographical research, as well as a vast quantity of idle speculation. In writings about her as a person, there has been drama and there has been melodrama, but it is well known that many of the actual facts of her life, including the exact dating of her manuscripts, have continued to elude us. There are some advantages in our belated recognition that the "real" Emily Dickinson can never be finally located, that "'It is finished' can never be said of us" (L 555), so long as we recognize that some Emily Dickinsons are more real than others. The historical frustrations she encountered help to make her real, as does the undeniable power of her language. In voicing her own contradictions, Dickinson imagined reaching out to others, including all those future poets who have wondered what she means and in some instances seen her as a problematic prototype of female genius. But this imagination of herself as available to literary histories of the future was inconsistent, as are accounts of what she wanted to happen to her poems after her death. "If fame belonged to me, I could not escape her," she wrote to Higginson in June 1862, "if she did not, the longest day would pass me on the chase—and the approbation of my Dog, would forsake me—then—My Barefoot-Rank is better" (L 265). She would not pander to the public, and as an artist, there were compromises she refused to make.

Granted that women in her time were conditioned to subordinate their own needs to those of others, we must recognize that there was a tremendously lively community of published women poets whom Dickinson chose not to join. Some of her poems suggest that she was attracted to the idea of martyrdom and that she conceived of herself as a martyr poet, sacrificing and sublimating her immediate desires so that others might live more fully. Overall, though, Dickinson's verbal inventions depend on a more complicated negotiation with desire and a stronger sense of entitlement. Turning briefly to S. P. Rosenbaum's excellent concordance, which presents us with her words, neatly arranged dictionary-fashion in alphabetical order,[62] we discover not one but many possible roads to "glory," including "Night's possibility" and "Time's possibility," to say nothing of all those *im*possibilities that she compares to wine. Why is impossibility stimulating and alternatively why is "A load" "first impossible, when you have put it down?" What kind of opportunities and burdens inspired these insights, this cost-benefit analysis, this capitalist despair? To describe Emily Dickinson's language as in certain respects representative of her socioeconomic and sexual class is not to confine her to the house of prose or to deny the larger value of her vision. Rather, Dickinson's famously indeterminate lines inspire curiosity about those personal and social histories that shaped her imagination of "heaven," including the various heavens she renounced, some of them more finally than others. Marked by its intellectual and emotional range, Emily Dickinson's writing is full of self-confidence and of secrets; the richness of her language emerges out of a narratival impulse that is fragmented and incomplete. Reminding us of "internal difference - / Where the Meanings, are" (Fr 320), her poetry also reminds us of our need to reconcile differences, in ordinary terms, to love. Whatever the limitations of her social experience, her legacy is capacious, as was her heart. "Step lightly on this narrow Spot," she wrote, gesturing toward the grave but refusing to be confined by it,

> The Broadest Land that grows
> Is not so ample as the Breast
> These Emerald Seams enclose -
>
> Step lofty for this name be told
> As far as cannon dwell,
> Or Flag subsist, or Fame export
> Her deathless Syllable (Fr 1227D)

NOTES

1. Dickinson's letters are quoted from *The Letters of Emily Dickinson*, ed. Thomas H. Johnson and Theodora Ward, 3 vols. (Cambridge, Mass.: Harvard University Press, 1958). Subsequent references are cited as (L) in the text.

2. For Higginson's military career, see *The Complete Civil War Journal and Selected Letters of Thomas Wentworth Higginson*, ed. Christopher Looby (Chicago: University of Chicago Press, 2000). See also Tilden G. Edelstein, *Strange Enthusiasm: A Life of Thomas Wentworth Higginson* (New Haven: Yale University Press, 1968).

3. Dickinson's poems are quoted from *The Poems of Emily Dickinson: Variorum Edition*, ed. R. W. Franklin, 3 vols. (Cambridge, Mass.: Harvard University Press, 1998). Subsequent references are cited as (Fr) in the text. Designations such as "A," "B," "C," etc., are Franklin's and identify different versions of poems as printed in the variorum.

4. For a more detailed discussion, see Barbara Antonina Clarke Mossberg, *Emily Dickinson: When a Writer Is a Daughter* (Bloomington: Indiana University Press, 1982).

5. On the quest motif, see Vivian R. Pollak, *Dickinson: The Anxiety of Gender* (Ithaca: Cornell University Press, 1984), chapters 4, 5, and passim.

6. Cynthia Griffin Wolff, *Emily Dickinson* (New York: Alfred A. Knopf, 1986), 16–17.

7. Frederick Clayton Waite, *Western Reserve University, the Hudson Era: A History of Western Reserve College and Academy at Hudson, Ohio,*

from 1826 to 1882 (Cleveland: Western Reserve University Press, 1943), quoted in Richard B. Sewall, *The Life of Emily Dickinson*, 2 vols. (New York: Farrar, Straus, and Giroux, 1974), 1:37.

8. Quoted in Alfred Habegger, *My Wars Are Laid Away in Books: The Life of Emily Dickinson* (New York: Random House, 2001), 27.

9. Rev. Alfred Ely, quoted in Habegger, *My Wars*, 31.

10. "What shall I call her?" Lavinia inquired about her soon-to-be stepmother Sarah Vaill, "Can I say Mother. O that I could be far away from here." Lavinia Norcross to Emily Norcross Dickinson, December 6, 1830, quoted in Wolff, *Emily Dickinson*, 51.

11. On Austin Dickinson and Mabel Loomis Todd, see Polly Longsworth, *Austin and Mabel: The Amherst Affair and Love Letters of Austin Dickinson and Mabel Loomis Todd* (New York: Farrar, Straus and Giroux, 1984), and Peter Gay, *The Bourgeois Experience Victoria to Freud: Education of the Senses* (New York: Oxford University Press, 1984), 1:71-108. (William) Austin Dickinson was called Austin after one of his mother's dead brothers.

12. On Edward Dickinson's political career, see Betsy Erkkila, pp. 133–34 and passim in this volume.

13. Habegger, *My Wars*, 344.

14. In 1860, Emily and Lavinia went to Middletown, Connecticut, where they visited their second cousin Eliza Coleman. The Coleman family had introduced Dickinson to the Rev. Charles Wadsworth in Philadelphia in 1855.

15. See Norbert Hirschhorn and Polly Longsworth, "'Medicine Posthumous': A New Look at Emily Dickinson's Medical Conditions," *New England Quarterly* 69 (June 1996): 299–316. Posthumous medicine evidently has its limitations and many theories have been advanced over the years, both about the nature and effect of Dickinson's problem. For example, some readers link her "terror—since September" to fears of blindness, but her letters do not suggest that in September 1861 her eyes were distressing her. Whatever the cause, the effect was to take her out of Amherst and away from her home. It took something extreme, and potentially self-destructive, to do it.

16. Jay Leyda, *The Years and Hours of Emily Dickinson*, 2 vols. (New Haven: Yale University Press, 1960), 2:133.

17. See Mariette Jameson, quoted in ibid., 2:406. For Jameson family context, see Morey Rothberg and Vivian R. Pollak, "An Emily

Dickinson Manuscript (Re)Identified at the Library of Congress,"
The Emily Dickinson Journal 10, no. 2 (Fall 2001): 43–51.

18. On Dickinson's logic of deprivation, see Vivian R. Pollak,
"Thirst and Starvation in Emily Dickinson's Poetry" (1979),
reprinted in *Emily Dickinson: A Collection of Critical Essays*, ed. Judith
Farr (Upper Saddle River, N.J.: Prentice-Hall, 1996), 62–75.

19. Amy Lowell, "Emily Dickinson" (1918), reprinted in *Poets and
Poetry: Essays* (Boston: Houghton Mifflin, 1930), 88, 93, 89–90.

20. On Amy Lowell's biographical ambitions, see S. Foster
Damon, *Amy Lowell: A Chronicle with Extracts from Her Correspondence*
(Boston: Houghton Mifflin, 1935), 611.

21. For a succinct discussion of Dickinson's tendency toward
panic attacks, beginning apparently in 1854, see Polly Longsworth,
"The 'Latitude of Home': Life in the Homestead and the Evergreens," in *The Dickinsons of Amherst* (Hanover, N.H.: University
Press of New England, 2001), 31–36. Longsworth emphasizes the 1854
onset of the condition and believes that "Sue [Gilbert] was one of a
few persons outside her immediate family aware that Emily was
coping with increasing anxieties that made her social behavior mys-
tifying and erratic." On agoraphobia as symptomatic of various
anxiety disorders, see John F. McDermott, M.D., "Emily Dickinson's
'Nervous Prostration' and its Possible Relationship to Her Work,"
The Emily Dickinson Journal 9 (Spring 2000): 71–80.

22. Ellen E. Emerson, quoted in Leyda, *Years and Hours of Emily
Dickinson*, 2:482.

23. Leyda, *Years and Hours*, 2:179.

24. Despite Edward's reputation for financial probity and order,
some recent scholarship indicates that there were problems.
Longsworth, "'Latitude,'" describes him as juggling a trust account
in the 1850s and then resigning suddenly as Amherst College treasurer in 1872, "frightened by an inability to balance the books" (37,
56). On the trust account for his orphaned nieces, Clara and Anna
Newman, Longsworth's "juggling" seems to capture the spirit of
the matter and Habegger argues cogently that "at no time did the
Newman heirs or their husbands register dissatisfaction with his
oversight of their affairs" (346–47). For an earlier, more dire account,
see Barton Levi St. Armand, *Emily Dickinson and Her Culture: The
Soul's Society* (Cambridge: Cambridge University Press, 1984), 307–09.

25. James M. McPherson, *Battle Cry of Freedom: The Civil War Era*

(New York: Ballantine, 1989), 121. The Kansas-Nebraska Act opened the way for slavery in territories hitherto protected by the Missouri Compromise and was unanimously opposed by northern Whigs. For more on Edward's politics and rhetoric, see Habegger, *My Wars*, 296–99.

26. On the railroad, see Domhnall Mitchell, *Emily Dickinson: Monarch of Perception* (Amherst: University of Massachusetts Press, 2000), chap. 1. See also Dickinson's poem, "I like to see it lap the Miles" (Fr 383).

27. Tutor Howland was Vinnie's beau.

28. Dickinson, quoted in *The Lyman Letters: New Light on Emily Dickinson and Her Family*, ed. Richard B. Sewall (Amherst: University of Massachusetts Press, 1965), 70.

29. *A Poet's Parents: The Courtship Letters of Emily Norcross and Edward Dickinson*, ed. Vivian R. Pollak (Chapel Hill: University of North Carolina Press, 1988), xviii.

30. Ibid., 3.

31. Ibid., 19, 18.

32. Ibid., 206, 208.

33. Leyda, *Years and Hours*, 1:81.

34. Daniel Taggard Fiske, quoted in Sewall, *Life of Emily Dickinson*, 2:342.

35. Helen Hunt Jackson, quoted in Ruth Odell, *Helen Hunt Jackson* (New York: D. Appleton-Century, 1939), 36.

36. Cousin Emily Norcross, quoted in Sewall, *Life of Emily Dickinson*, 2:360.

37. Mary Lyon, quoted in ibid., 2:366.

38. On Edward's five essays, written under the pseudonym "Coelebs" (a bachelor), and published in the *New-England Inquirer*, an Amherst paper, see *Poet's Parents*, 93 n 1 and 104–05 n 1, and passim. On February 16, 1827, "A Lady" compared his sentiments to those of an "eastern Sultan or bashaw" before concluding, "If as he professes, he is resolved to die a martyr to our cause, not unlikely he will fall as thousands before him have done, who for the want of holier motives have passed into oblivion unknown, unpitied, unlamented." Edward probably abandoned the "Coelebs" project because of the controversy it generated and a sixth essay remains unpublished.

39. Sue's biography remains to be written. The most detailed ac-

count of her early years is in Longsworth, *Austin and Mabel*. See also Ellen Louise Hart and Martha Nell Smith, eds., *Open Me Carefully: Emily Dickinson's Intimate Letters to Susan Huntington Dickinson* (Ashfield, Mass.: Paris Press, 1998), and Habegger, *My Wars*. See also Dickinson Electronic Archives, ed. Martha Nell Smith and others, www://http: dickinson/virginia.edu. This site provides published and unpublished writings by Susan in prose and verse, including her memoir "Annals of the Evergreens" and her 1886 *Springfield Republican* obituary for Dickinson.

40. See Habegger, *My Wars*, 266. Habegger emphasizes that Sue had "several well-educated and prosperous aunts, uncles, and older brothers to admire and emulate" (265). In particular, her brothers Dwight and Frank, who prospered in Michigan, provided Sue with a dowry of five thousand dollars on her marriage. She was especially fond of Dwight, who was some fifteen years her senior and whom she turned to as a father substitute, a role he seems to have enjoyed. Thomas Dwight Gilbert (1815–1894) made a fortune in lumber and shipping and eventually settled in Grand Rapids, where he became president of the local bank. The city erected a monument to him on his death. See *Ceremonies at the Dedication and Unveiling of the Thomas D. Gilbert Memorial* (Grand Rapids: Loomis & Onderdonk, 1896).

41. Austin Dickinson, letter to Sue, quoted in Habegger, *My Wars*, 269.

42. Sue lived with her sister Harriet and brother-in-law William Cutler, a prosperous merchant whom she actively disliked. On the restrictions of the Cutler household, with its sententiousness and overheated rooms, see Habegger, *My Wars*, 267.

43. See Carroll Smith-Rosenberg, "The Female World of Love and Ritual: Relations Between Women in Nineteenth-Century America" (1975), reprinted in *Disorderly Conduct: Visions of Gender in Victorian America* (New York: Alfred A. Knopf, 1985), 53–76. Smith-Rosenberg famously concludes that the supposedly repressive Victorian era may actually have encouraged a wider range of sexual practices than we do today. Lillian Faderman, in "Emily Dickinson's Letters to Sue Gilbert," *Massachusetts Review* 28 (Summer 1977): 197–225, argues that Dickinson's letters to Sue are clearly distinguishable from those intended for women "with whom she was merely good friends" (205). Some of this material is excerpted in Faderman, *Surpassing the Love of Men: Romantic Friendship and Love*

Between Women from the Renaissance to the Present (New York: Morrow, 1981).

44. For a fuller discussion of the erotics of Dickinson's love for Sue, see, in chronological order, Vivian R. Pollak, *Dickinson: The Anxiety of Gender*, especially chap. 5 (1984); Paula Bennett, *Emily Dickinson: Woman Poet* (Iowa City: University of Iowa Press, 1992); Martha Nell Smith, *Rowing in Eden: Rereading Emily Dickinson* (Austin: University of Texas Press, 1992); Hart and Smith, eds., *Open Me Carefully* (1998).

45. For further psychological speculation about Austin and Emily, see Pollak, *Anxiety*, 72–74.

46. Adrienne Rich, "Vesuvius at Home: The Power of Emily Dickinson," *Parnassus* 5 (Fall-Winter 1976): 49–74.

47. Dickinson's "patent" was also her purchase on Sue. On Dickinson's possessiveness, see Judith Farr, "The Narrative of Sue," *The Passion of Emily Dickinson* (Cambridge, Mass.: Harvard University Press, 1995), chap. 3.

48. For speculation that Dickinson suffered a nervous breakdown in 1857, see John Cody, *After Great Pain: The Inner Life of Emily Dickinson* (Cambridge, Mass.: Harvard University Press, 1971).

49. In *My Emily Dickinson* (Berkeley, Calif.: North Atlantic Books, 1985), the language poet Susan Howe locates Dickinson's Master letters in relation to nineteenth-century British fiction, especially Dickens and Charlotte and Emily Brontë. See 24–27 and passim.

50. Martha Nell Smith has suggested that "Master" is Sue. She argues that a subsequent "Master" letter (L 233) was altered by a hand other than Dickinson's to disguise its homoerotic content and that all three Master letters are encoded examples of lesbian desire. See *Rowing in Eden*, chapters 1, 3, and passim.

51. In *The Anxiety of Gender* (1984), Vivian Pollak also opted for Wadsworth as the distant beloved. She described the symbolic logic of the Master project and argued that he could not live in New England, a position with which Habegger concurs. Pollak suggested that the Master figure was, in part, a reaction to the loss Dickinson experienced when Sue turned toward Austin, a context that Habegger eclipses. Meanwhile, Martha Nell Smith and Ellen Louise Hart seek to demonstrate that Dickinson's love for Susan was fulfilling more or less throughout the poet's life. Smith and Hart believe that while the relationship had its ups and downs, as what relationship doesn't, Susan remained Dickinson's truest and most constant

friend. Thus, they reject narratives that describe Dickinson as punished for lesbian desire and instead present Susan as Emily's ideal companion, critic, and reader. Apart from Dickinson's audience in the mind, Sue was her main audience, in that Dickinson sent approximately a third of her poems to friends and in that Sue received more than anyone else, Higginson being the next nearest contender.

52. According to the *Springfield Republican* in October 1865, "Among the 'orthodox' preachers, Rev Dr Wadsworth . . . perhaps ranks first; and his society, a Presbyterian one, is probably the largest and richest of that order. He is more of a scholar than an orator, however; and is greatly respected and beloved." See Leyda, *Years and Hours*, 2:102. In the next year, Mark Twain also noted his presence. See ibid., 2:112.

53. For a fuller discussion of stereotypes of masculinity and femininity in the Master letters, see Marianne Noble, "The Revenge of Cato's Daughter: Emily Dickinson's Uses of Sentimental Masochism," *The Masochistic Pleasures of Sentimental Literature* (Princeton: Princeton University Press, 2000), chapter 5 and passim. Noble observes that "The letters and poetry of Emily Dickinson prominently feature sentimental scenarios that bear a striking resemblance to certain passages in evangelical sentimental works . . . in which helpless innocent females submit to the abusive domination of an extremely powerful male. Many of these scenarios are masochistic, for the victims willingly submit to and even seek to be dominated or hurt" (147).

54. In 1875, Elizabeth Lord was one of the witnesses to Dickinson's will.

55. Leyda, *Years and Hours*, 2:375–76.

56. Higginson, quoted in Sewall, *Life of Emily Dickinson*, 2:667.

57. Austin Dickinson, quoted in Leyda, *Years and Hours*, 2:224.

58. On Dickinson and Jackson, see Vivian R. Pollak, "American Women Poets Reading Dickinson: The Example of Helen Hunt Jackson," in *The Emily Dickinson Handbook*, ed. Gudrun Grabher, Roland Hagenbüchle, and Cristanne Miller (Amherst: University of Massachusetts Press, 1998), 323–41. See also Betsy Erkkila, "Dickinson, Women Writers and the Marketplace," in *The Wicked Sisters: Women Poets, Literary History, and Discord* (New York: Oxford University Press, 1992), especially 86–98. And for a valuable new biography

of Jackson, see Kate Phillips, *Helen Hunt Jackson: A Literary Life* (Berkeley: University of California Press, 2003).

59. Habegger has shown that Dickinson's physician overdiagnosed Bright's Disease as the cause of death in other patients. See *My Wars*, 622–23, and appendix 3. See also Hirschhorn and Longsworth, "'Medicine Posthumous': A New Look at Emily Dickinson's Medical Conditions."

60. When Higginson was preparing the second posthumous edition of poems in 1891, he wrote to his coeditor Mabel Loomis Todd, "One poem only I dread a little to print—that wonderful 'Wild Nights,'—lest the malignant read into it more than that virgin recluse ever dreamed of putting there." See Millicent Todd Bingham, *Ancestors' Brocades: The Literary Debut of Emily Dickinson: The Editing and Publication of her Letters and Poems* (New York: Harper & Brothers, 1945), 127.

On "partially cracked," see Higginson in 1877 to his sister Anna, also a poetess, quoted in Leyda, *Years and Hours*, 2:263. See also "half cracked" in Adrienne Rich, "'I Am in Danger—Sir,'" *Adrienne Rich's Poetry and Prose: Poems, Prose, Reviews, and Criticism*, ed. Barbara Charlesworth Gelpi and Albert Gelpi (New York: Norton, 1993), 26–27.

61. Leyda, *Years and Hours*, 2:481.

62. S. P. Rosenbaum, ed., *A Concordance to the Poems of Emily Dickinson* (Ithaca: Cornell University Press, 1964).

DICKINSON IN
HER TIME

"Is Immortality True?"

Salvaging Faith in an Age of Upheavals

Jane Donahue Eberwein

For those considering Emily Dickinson's reaction to changes in New England's religious culture in the middle and late decades of the nineteenth century, one grotesquely memorable poem becomes the almost inevitable proof-text:

> Those - dying then,
> Knew where they went -
> They went to God's Right Hand -
> That Hand is amputated now
> And God cannot be found -
>
> The abdication of Belief
> Makes the Behavior small -
> Better an ignis fatuus
> Than no illume at all - (Fr 1581)[1]

Editors Thomas Johnson and R. W. Franklin date this poem to 1882, though it calls to mind Dickinson images from the mid-1860s envisaging "The Funeral of God" (Fr 1112) when he would be "borne away / From Mansion of the Universe / A lifeless Deity" (Fr 795). "The death of God" may seem a modern concept, but it is one Emily Dickinson anticipated and to which she responded with concern over losing the omnipotent arm "Who laid the Rainbow's piers" (Fr 140).

Biographers read "Those - dying then" as her response to losses Dickinson shared with others of her time. James McIntosh situates the poem in the context of "the undoing of Amherst orthodoxy," while Cynthia Griffin Wolff argues that "the drift away from God was generational, the phenomenon of an increasingly secular America." Roger Lundin extends this perspective to embrace thinkers and creative artists generally, linking Dickinson with Melville, Dostoevsky, and Nietzsche among "the first to trace the trajectory of God's decline" throughout the Western world.[2]

Yet few belief systems could have seemed more stable than Calvinist Christianity in the Connecticut Valley of Dickinson's youth. At her birth in 1830, Congregationalism was still legally established in Massachusetts and all four Amherst churches traced their roots in that tradition to the Puritans who settled New England two centuries before. The Second Great Awakening spurred wave after wave of revivals that aroused America's cities and frontier campgrounds along with decorous New England parishes like Amherst's First Church, which Dickinsons had helped to found and which her family attended. The American Bible Society had launched its first two-year campaign to put a Bible in every American home. When she was two, Noah Webster, the great lexicographer and her family's Amherst neighbor for several years, published his Americanized translation of the Bible. The three children of Edward and Emily Norcross Dickinson grew up with constant reinforcement of church teachings at home, in school, and in peer relationships. Emily Dickinson knew from childhood that she was expected to emulate the sainted neighbor who "relyed wholly upon the arm of God & he did not forsake her" (L 11).[3]

Who or what, then, lopped that saving arm? Dickinson's phrase "is amputated now" ignores issues of agency. Culprits usually arraigned include romanticism in both its Transcendental and sentimental manifestations, a scientific revolution spurred by Charles Lyell and Charles Darwin, and theological rethinking unleashed by the European biblical scholarship known as the

Higher Criticism. Another crisis unsettling belief was the Civil War. Even America's growing diversity and the mobility of its native-born and immigrant populations came to undermine the sense of religious uniformity that would have been taken for granted by a child growing up in Emily Dickinson's Connecticut Valley milieu. In her childhood, belief seemed all but inevitable; by the time she died in 1886, agnosticism and even atheism had become easier positions to justify intellectually. If Dickinson were to cling to faith, it had to be in a wounded God.

Dickinson shared this dilemma with other artists and thinkers. Like Herman Melville, she coped with a disposition that "could neither believe, nor be comfortable in . . . unbelief." Yet she had certainly not "made up [her] mind to be annihilated."[4] At times, her attitude toward uncertainty could even be buoyantly playful, as when she wrote in an 1882 letter to Otis Phillips Lord that "on subjects of which we know nothing, or should I say *Beings* . . . we both believe, and disbelieve a hundred times an Hour, which keeps Believing nimble" (L 750). Yet the playfulness sometimes collapsed into desperation, as in "I know that He exists" (Fr 365), an 1862 poem that treats the soul's relationship with God as an increasingly worrisome game of hide-and-seek. In the poem following this in Fascicle 18, "He strained my faith" (Fr 366), the speaker recounts an anguishing experience of being tormented by Jesus yet avows a bewildered, indestructible devotion. Verbs relating to Christ ("strained," "Shook," "Hurled," "Wrung," and "Stabbed") remind us that God's arm could be a dreadful force as well as a saving one.

Dickinson's writing, then, brilliantly expresses tensions between doubt and faith in the nineteenth-century Western world, as evangelical Protestant orthodoxy shook when subjected to unsettling intellectual and cultural pressures. Yet she was a lyric poet rather than a systematic philosopher and a letter-writer rather than an essayist. Her poems articulate dramatically varying and ephemeral moods. Often, as in "He strained my faith," they employ personae to distance speaker from author. Or she grouped them in fascicles with companion poems that modify their impact. Her letters, though self-revealing, are always subtly attuned to audience. The comment she made to Judge Lord about the nimbleness of belief came from a love letter that wittily blended belief, doubt, and hope about both her lover and the Lord above; she never would have written about faith in such a tone to one of her pious correspondents. One can make whatever case one wants about Dickinson's beliefs or disbelief by selecting individual poems, letters, or even lines, but the way to reach insight is to look for long-term patterns in her religious references. Despite variations in tone and imagery, religion remained a centering concern for Dickinson from her first valentine with its comic references to Eden (Fr 1) to her last letter: "Little Cousins, / Called back. / Emily" (L 1046). Love, death, nature, and the many themes suffusing her work all relate to what she called her "Flood subject" of immortality (L 319). The question she probed throughout life was the one raised in an 1882 letter to the Reverend Washington Gladden: "Is immortality true?" (L 752a).

Religious in What Ways?

Before assuming that "Those - dying then" reflects the poet's own trajectory from youthful trust in God's promises to skeptical maturity—nicely synchronized with America's transition from the pietistic fervor of the Second Great Awakening to post-Darwinian skepticism—we should recall that Emily Dickinson was not "dying then" but *living* then and living in ways that sometimes deviated from stereotypes of religiosity. If we judge by her letters before 1858, the year when she began systematically recording her poems, this young woman was already distancing herself from certain aspects of religion while intensifying her focus on others.

For many people, regular church-going serves as a prime indicator of religious practice, and their assumptions certainly reflect those of the community that was Dickinson's extended home. With Sabbath-keeping still very much the norm in New England and workaday tasks set aside for a day of quiet devotion, her family typically participated in both morning and afternoon meetings of the First Church, then occupying the Meeting

House that was later assimilated into the Amherst College campus. That building had opened for worship in time for the 1829 college commencement the year before her birth. There they heard Bible-based sermons preached by their pastor, Aaron Colton, heard visiting clergymen, witnessed rituals, and—after 1839, when a double bass viol was introduced as the church's first musical instrument—sang hymns that long resonated in their memories. Her brother, Austin, recalled years later how "the tones [Josiah Ayres] drew from its lower chords in his accompaniment to the singing of some of Watts' Favorite Hymns, haunt me even now."⁵ Obviously, images and cadences of hymns, sermons, and biblical texts found their way into Emily Dickinson's poems. Her early letters, especially those to Austin and to Susan Gilbert whom he later married, were generally written on Sundays and often featured reports on Colton's "enlivening preaching" (L 46) or the efforts of other preachers, including Colton's successor, Edward Dwight, of whom she wrote "I never heard a minister I loved half so well" (L 123).

Yet this is the woman who opened one of her poems with the declaration "Some keep the Sabbath going to Church - / I keep it, staying at Home" (Fr 236), and her letters document gradual withdrawal from Sunday meetings. In that poem, her alternative to church worship was informal communion with God and nature in her garden. Letters show her welcoming minor indispositions and threatening weather as excuses to stay home and write. "They will all go but me," she wrote to Susan in 1852, "to the usual meetinghouse, to hear the usual sermon; the inclemency of the storm so kindly detaining me"(L 77). Her reasons for staying home certainly included desire to snatch time for correspondence and boredom with rituals she once summed up to Austin as "a couple of Baptisms, three admissions to church, a Supper of the Lord, and some other minor transactions time fails me to record" (L 46). It is well to remember, though, that she had earlier turned down the opportunity to join most of her Mount Holyoke classmates in an excursion to see a traveling menagerie, and that several years later she continued to visit her minister and his wife regularly, even after she ceased attending church. Avoiding crowded situations may not have signaled infidelity.

There is evidence in several letters, especially one to Sue in January 1854, that she grew frightened of appearing alone at meeting and alarmed by the social encounters inevitable at church (L 154). Another factor in withdrawal from church might be awareness that neighbors watching her were speculating on the state of her soul. Although she was expected to go to Sunday meetings, only church members could join in the Lord's Supper. For admission to the church, a candidate must satisfy the minister and deacons of her or his "experimental acquaintance with the grace of God"—at least in the poet's youth.[6] By the time the Reverend Jonathan Jenkins conferred with her in the early 1870s at her anxious father's request, she could have been admitted to the First Church readily at the minister's finding her "sound."[7]

In church and elsewhere, Dickinson was methodically introduced to Congregational doctrines. Letters and poems refer to dogmas held by virtually all Christians, such as creation, the fall, and Jesus' saving role, and she displayed awareness of characteristically Protestant stresses on scriptural revelation and salvation by faith. Although she claimed once that "I do not respect 'doctrines'" and therefore ignored a sermon on predestination (L 200), her work bespeaks intimate familiarity with church teachings. With regard to doctrines emphasized within her Calvinist culture, she seems to have strained out most of the alarming beliefs in total depravity, limited atonement, and predestination, so far as it ensured damnation of those not among the elect. In a letter to Elizabeth and Josiah Holland, whose kindlier Christianity afforded her welcome relief from severity, she recounted a troubling incident in which "the minister to-day, not our own minister, preached about death and judgment, and what would become of those, meaning Austin and me, who behaved improperly." She admitted that "somehow the sermon scared me," especially as family members already in full communion "looked very solemn as if the whole was true" (L 175). In sifting out fearsome aspects of Calvinism, however, she retained and distinctively reapplied two happier dogmas celebrating God's glory and transforming grace.

Fundamental to Protestantism is the conviction that sinful humans are saved by God's grace alone, and Calvin stressed that

Christ's atonement applied exclusively to those granted the gift of faith. No action performed in a person's natural state of depravity contributed toward salvation. Yet good works had been recognized even by New England's Puritan founders as likely signs of the sanctification effected by grace among the elect. Although nobody could earn God's favor by doing good, authentic conversion would bear fruit in selfless acts. As fourteen-year-old Emily wrote to Abiah Root, "my knowledge of housekeeping is about of as much use as faith without works, which you know we are told is dead" (L 8). Her comment reflects the emphasis of her religious culture on all sorts of charities and institutional good works, especially those that were socially useful. Her grandfather, conflating his town's prosperity with the advancement of Christ's kingdom, had bankrupted himself through business ventures intended to launch Amherst College as a center for orthodox education of young men from New England farms. Her father, similarly Whiggish in his piety though more prudent in his choices, labored for the college, the First Church, and moral reforms. Mary Lyon at Mount Holyoke challenged students to lives of active service, preferably in the missions. Emily's friend Abby Wood Bliss joined her husband in founding the Syrian Protestant College in Beirut. Around the United States, the reformist impulse expressed itself in efforts for abolition of slavery, for reform of criminals, for women's rights, and for establishment of utopian communities. Nonetheless, Dickinson recoiled from community pressure for an unmarried young lady to devote herself to charity. "The Sewing Society has commenced again," she reported to Jane Humphrey soon after returning from college, "now all the poor will be helped—the cold warmed—the warm cooled—the hungry fed—the thirsty attended to—the ragged clothed—and this suffering—tumbled down world will be helped to it's feet again—which will be quite pleasant to all. I dont attend—notwithstanding my high approbation—which must puzzle the public exceedingly" (L 30). Reference to "the public" suggests a parallel with fear of exposure keeping her home from church. At home, by writing notes and dispatching gifts to neighbors and friends, Dickinson reached out lovingly to comfort those contending with trouble. She was probably on target, though, in guessing her neighbors' judgment of her odd behavior: "I am already set down as one of those brands almost consumed—and my hardheartedness gets me many prayers" (L 30).

Prayers suggest personal piety. In this, as in matters of church-going, doctrine, and good works, Dickinson proved selective. Clearly, however, she inhabited a social environment heavily suffused with everyday pious habits. At home, her father led the family in morning prayer. At school, even spelling books and dictionaries reinforced dogma and encouraged moral formation.[8] When young Emily joked to her cousin about how they would improve themselves through conversation, she declared "we will talk over what we have learned in our geographies, and listened to from the pulpit, the press and the Sabbath School" (L 34). Like their friends, the Dickinson girls explored the popular literature being widely produced to adapt Christian instruction to the tastes of young ladies sentimentally attuned to stories of self-sacrifice in the name of loving service. Apparently, Emily found such reading less gratifying than others did. When Sue was teaching in Baltimore, Emily wrote that "I have just read three little books, not great, not thrilling—but sweet and true . . . I know you would love them all—yet they dont *bewitch* me any" (L 85).

Bewitchment, of course, set a standard of literary effectiveness not easily reached, the kind of "Conversion of the Mind" she celebrated in a poem on her joyous response to Elizabeth Barrett Browning's poems (Fr 627). The book that most stimulated her imagination, however, was the Bible, to which she alluded constantly. At a time when virtually every American Protestant had a copy of the King James Version, the Bible linked her to friends as well as to God, who revealed himself in its stories and poems.[9] Also linking Dickinson to God was prayer, though sometimes she felt she was addressing an absentee. "If prayers had any answers to them," she confided to the Hollands, "you were all here to-night, but I seek and I don't find, and knock and it is not opened. Wonder if God is just - presume he is, however, and t'was only a blunder of Matthew's" (L 133). Superior to prayers, but rarer, were those epiphanies of direct encounter with the infinite that occasionally inspired poems like "Better - than Music! / For I - who heard it" (Fr 378), which ebulliently concluded the fascicle mentioned earlier, in which she had paired "I know that He exists" (Fr 365) with "He strained my faith" (Fr 366).

Although offering no definitive proof of her spiritual condition, such ecstatic experiences support conjecture that Dickinson herself experienced the transition from fallen humanity's state of natural depravity to a state of grace; but she never formally declared conversion nor applied for church membership. Conversion, in the sense of experimental, tangible transformation remained the life-defining and essential experience of evangelical Christians. If Calvin was right in denying any merit to man or woman in the state of nature, then the soul must be justified, renewed, and empowered to move along the path of sanctification that would culminate in heavenly glory. It was only by Christ's atonement on the cross that those predestined as the elect could be saved; the vast majority of the human race faced damnation. Although Arminian and romantic developments, to be considered later in this essay, softened some of the harshness of Calvin's doctrine, nineteenth-century evangelical Christians of many denominations and throughout the country experienced intense religious excitement, as revivals ushered in seasons of awakening in which multitudes testified to the joyous relief they found in liberation from burdens of sin while they professed their love for Jesus and gratitude for his mercy. In southern and western states, the Second Great Awakening reached people through boisterously emotional camp meetings. In the cities, evangelists like Charles Grandison Finney reached uprooted and restless urban populations and even quickened evangelical fervor among Unitarians and other liberal Protestants.

The Connecticut Valley had long been a center of Congregational revivalism, though revivals there tended to be orderly, solemn events. Emily Dickinson lived through the greatest period of such excitement in Amherst. The First Church recorded revivals in 1831 (when Emily Norcross Dickinson experienced conversion and had her children baptized), 1834, 1841, 1845, 1850 (when her father, sister, and several close friends entered the

church), 1857, 1858, 1869, and 1870.[10] There were even more seasons of awakening at Amherst College and Mount Holyoke, and
the proliferation of religious periodicals throughout the country
ensured that local readers learned about successful revivals
everywhere else in America. Why, then, did Emily Dickinson fail
to respond to such occasions of grace? Her holding back seems
to have been as much a mystery to her as to the friends who
prayed for her conversion.

Her letters testify to a fascination with "the all important subject" (L 13), and she acknowledged her wish to share in the transformation virtually every force in her environment pressured her
to expect. At fifteen, she related a bit of personal history while
congratulating a converted friend: "I have had the same feelings
myself Dear A. I was almost persuaded to be a christian. I
thought I never again could be thoughtless and worldly—and I
can say that I never enjoyed such perfect peace and happiness as
the short time in which I felt I had found my savior" (L 10). But
that "short time" was soon followed by backsliding. Two years
later, she reported "there is a great deal of religious interest here
and many are flocking to the ark of safety. I have not yet given up
to the claims of Christ, but trust I am not entirely thoughtless on
so important & serious a subject" (L 20). Yet she was candid
about holding back, confessing that—instead of being encouraged by her earlier near-conversion, she had been frightened to
discover her susceptibility to the pressure she felt at church and
in conversations with saved friends, who exhorted her to yield
"to the claims of He who is greater than I" (L 10).

She had avoided attending any of the 1845 revival meetings,
just as at Mount Holyoke she resisted pressures for conversion.
When teachers there divided students into groups of those who
(like her cousin-roommate Emily Norcross) had already been
saved, those who had "hope" of conversion (meaning direct experience of what might be the stirring of grace), and those still
without hope, Dickinson was in the third group and remained a
no-hoper even after most classmates had responded to the
earnest ministrations of Mary Lyon, their evangelically zealous
college foundress.[11] On her return to Amherst, she encountered
another season of grace in the 1850 revival that drew her father,

sister, and Sue into the church. Austin joined after his engagement to Sue, apparently because his conversion mattered greatly to her. Yet in Emily's harshest letter to the friend who would become her sister-in-law, written about 1854, she slammed the door against such interference: "Sue—I have lived by this. It is the lingering emblem of the Heaven I once dreamed, and though if this is taken, I shall remain alone, and though in that last day, the Jesus Christ you love, remark he does not know me—there is a darker spirit will not disown it's child" (L 173).

Despite the attractions of conversion, some combination of things held her back. The reason she gave Abiah seems especially ironic in light of her eventual choice of a nearly conventual hidden life: "it is hard for me to give up the world" (L 23). Evidently, while conscious of the way others were observing and judging her, Dickinson drew her own conclusions about them. Early letters refer often to the transformations friends experienced under the influence of grace. "Those on whom *change* has passed," she observed, "seem so very tranquil, and their voices are kind, and gentle, and the tears fill their eyes so often, I really think I envy them" (L 35). Of Abby Wood she reported "she makes a sweet, girl christian" (L 36). Perhaps Dickinson intuited the connection between submissive behavior fostered by religion and the docility that would soon be expected of these young women as wives in patriarchally ordered Christian homes.[12] If so, her resistance presaged a parallel withdrawal from realistic prospects of marriage. She reserved her erotic passion for unattainable lovers and her spiritual passion for a savior who might or might not ever reciprocate her love. Vigilant, too, against false hopes, she must have witnessed relapses into worldliness among the self-proclaimed elect that reinforced her awareness that "Our Best Moment" seldom lasts (Fr 560). Neither did her interest in friends' conversion experiences; letters from the late 1850s on ignore this topic that had been so absorbing to her early in that decade.

Basing their case on close reading of groups of poems, several Dickinson scholars have made strong arguments for the likelihood that she did, indeed, experience the kind of conversion her culture primed her to expect.[13] Others are content to rest in un-

certainty. What we know, however, is that she underwent a transforming experience of artistic empowerment in the 1850s that
paralleled the religious experiences of her companions. Two letters written in 1850, the year of her first valentine and perhaps of
her tentative identification of herself as a poet, contrast the direction her life was taking with her friends' choices. "You are
growing wiser than I am, and nipping in the bud fancies which I
let blossom," she observed to Abiah before venturing into
metaphors of braving a storm at sea (L 39). To Jane, she confessed "I have dared to do strange things—bold things, and have
asked no advice from any—I have heeded beautiful tempters, yet
do not think I am wrong" (L 35). Perhaps it was no coincidence
that the year she began arranging her poems in fascicles was
1858, the last great revival year across the United States before the
Civil War. As with other aspects of religiosity, Dickinson dis-
pensed with the life-defining ritual of conversion in any way her
neighbors would recognize, yet she somehow distilled from cultural convention a visionary and life-renewing creative energy.

One reason why Emily Dickinson proved resistant to conversion pressures was that, aside from picking up pulpit rhetoric
(often for comic effect), her writings reveal little consciousness of
sin; she seems never to have accepted the fundamental premise
of the fall. When she reproached herself for misbehavior, it was
usually to lament failures to "improve the opportunity" of free
time, and her typical way of improving such opportunity was to
write (L 1). A dominant theme from her earliest letter to last
poems was the evanescence of time and all the fragile human
ties that are vulnerable to loss through death. What drew her to
religion, therefore, was hope for immortality rather than for for-
giveness. As a teenager, she displayed some anxiety about the
hellfire threatened for sinners, commenting to Abiah with regard
to their circle of Amherst Academy girlfriends "how sad would it
be for one of our number to go to the dark realms of wo, where
is the never dying worm and the fire which no water can quench,
and how happy if we may be one unbroken company in heaven"
(L 10). Apprehensions of the inferno soon disappeared from her
letters, though not the goal of preserving earthly friendship. A
letter to the Reverend Edward Everett Hale after Benjamin New-

ton's death beseeches, "I should love so much to know certainly, that he was today in Heaven" (L 153). She enjoyed fantasizing about the delights of an afterlife, in which "the people singing songs were those who in their *lifetimes* were parted and separated, and their joy was because they should never be so any more" (L 62). Heaven, as she figured it to the Hollands, was "a large, blue sky, bluer and larger than the *biggest* I have seen in June, and in it are my friends—all of them" (L 185), or, as she suggested to Samuel Bowles, it "must be like Sue's Drawing Room, when we are talking and laughing there" (L 189). Fittingly, her favorite biblical book was Revelation with its symbolic vision of the mysteries on the other side of death, which (to borrow Dickinson's own symbol) sets the circumference of earthly life, the boundary between all she prized in this life but could not hold (loves, nature, consciousness, moments of ecstasy) and all that the Bible promised beyond (God, awe, perpetual empowerment, love unthreatened by loss).[14] *If* she could trust those promises. The alternative beyond death was annihilation. For Emily Dickinson, then, the essence of religious experience remained in that haunting question, "Is immortality true?" (L 752a).

Descent from the Puritans

When asking how someone born in the pietistic environment of the Connecticut Valley during the Second Great Awakening could have come to imagine the grotesquely mutilated God of "Those - dying then," anyone familiar with the writings of the seventeenth- and eighteenth-century Puritans in New England must wonder what happened to the mighty arm that "in this Bowling Alley bowld the Sun," sifted a whole nation for choice grain to quicken the new world's desert, shook sinners like spiders over the pit of hell, and from his celestial eminence overturned "Heav'ns whelm'd-down Chrystall meele Bowle" to flood his elect with grace.[15] Yet if the memory Dickinson recalled in an 1877 letter to Thomas Wentworth Higginson can be trusted, we learn that her anxieties about faith preceded awareness of romantic and scientific challenges to faith, that the metaphors by which devout people around her depicted God ironically prompted fears. "When a few years old," she reported, "I was taken to a Funeral which I now know was of peculiar distress, and the Clergyman asked 'Is the Arm of the Lord shortened that it cannot save?' / / He italicized the 'cannot.' I mistook the accent for a doubt of Immortality and not daring to ask, it besets me still" (L 503). A girl small in everything but a tendency to grasp imaginatively at language had fastened her mind on what she mistook to be a nonrhetorical question. The answer the preacher assumed was surely a decisive "No!" He was alluding quite explicitly to Isaiah 59:1, which reads "Behold, the Lord's hand is not shortened, that it cannot save." It was a passage to which her pastor alluded elsewhere as evidence of divine mercy in rescuing sinners and one that abolitionist writers liked to cite in prophesying how God's arm would reach out to save the oppressed.[16] Little Emily, sitting in the rigid pew, would not have been thinking about slaves or even of the soul's rescue from its naturally depraved condition; this was a funeral, and the minister's rhetoric raised an awful pair of questions: Had, indeed, God's arm been shortened so that he could not save anybody, or could he have rescued the deceased from death but withheld his hand?[17] Perhaps the comment Dickinson later made about George Eliot reflected her own sense of deprivation also: "As childhood is earth's confiding time, perhaps having no childhood, she lost her way to the early trust, and no later came. Amazing human heart, a syllable can make to quake like jostled tree, what infinite for thee?" (L 710). The ironic possibility that Dickinson's fears may have been implanted in her home and church and her doubts ignited by words directly quoted from the Good Book prompts me to take seriously James Turner's thesis that "religion caused unbelief. . . . If anyone is to be arraigned for deicide, it is not Charles Darwin but his adversary Bishop Samuel Wilberforce, not the godless Robert Ingersoll but the godly Beecher family."[18]

In considering this indictment, we must remember that the teaching of Lyman Beecher and Aaron Colton was not exactly the faith once delivered to the saints in the early days of New England. Although the poet's father echoed William Stoughton's 1668 election sermon cited above to declare "We should render devout thanks to Almighty God . . . that the kingdoms of the Old World were sifted to procure the seed to plant this continent; that the purest of that seed was sown in this beautiful valley; that the blood of the Puritans flows in our veins," he belonged to a later time and strongly believed in progress. Austin Dickinson identified their parent as "of the sixth generation born within sound of the old meeting-house bell, all earnest, God-fearing men, doing their part in their day toward the evolution of the Amherst we live in."[19] That Amherst, they assumed, had evolved in intellectual and moral ways as well as materially. When they sought parallels with Puritan founders, it was to honor a tradition of rectitude and public service rather than fidelity to doctrines that had come to seem embarrassing by the nineteenth century. When the Dickinson family descended upon the Edwards Church in neighboring Northampton, named in honor of the Connecticut Valley's most redoubtable Puritan theologian, it was to attend a Jenny Lind concert.

The Great Awakening of the 1740s, led by George Whitefield and Jonathan Edwards, had lasted about four years and stirred revivals up and down the Atlantic seaboard. The Second, which continued for decades, is generally traced to the 1801 Great Revival at Yale, initiated by Edwards's grandson Timothy Dwight as part of his crusade to marshal Calvinist spiritual and intellectual forces against the threat posed by deism to the new republic. Among the evangelists Dwight inspired were Lyman Beecher and Amherst College's Heman Humphrey. The poet's father graduated from Yale during Dwight's influential presidency, though he had to wait several decades before experiencing the conversion that qualified him for full sacramental membership in the church to which he had long contributed legal and fiscal leadership. Such support proved especially needful after 1833, when Massachusetts became the last state to disestablish the churches that, since colonial times, had enjoyed privileged status in terms of public support. Congregational churches now had to rely on voluntary contributions, which made the influx of converts recruited through revivals all the more needful. The period of dynamic church growth that followed disestablishment seemed to confirm the lasting vigor of the religious culture nineteenth-century Yankees inherited from Puritan ancestors, but their version of that culture differed in key ways: more democratic, more pragmatic, less orthodox. Even as the National Council of the Congregationalist churches gathered at Plymouth Rock in 1865 to signify continuity of faith, it deleted the word "Calvinism" from its revised statement of doctrinal beliefs.[20] Emily Dickinson's mocking rebuke to her brother on his liaison with Sue in a Boston hotel at the time of their engagement could have had broader application than she thought: "Am glad our Pilgrim Fathers got safely out of the way, before such shocking times!" (L 110).

One effect of the Great Awakening had been division of churches within most Protestant denominations. Old Light Christians tended to be antirevivalist, focused on morality rather than conversion, and liberal in their views. In New England, Unitarians came to prominence in the seaboard cities and at Harvard Divinity School. New Light Christians took their name, not from the novelty of their beliefs (more traditionally Calvinistic than those of their liberal rivals), but from their loyalty to the conviction that sinners could be saved only through the new light of grace by which the Holy Spirit guided those saved by Jesus. In New England, most New Light Christians in Emily Dickinson's early years were Congregationalists. Their clergymen, who prepared at Yale or Andover, followed in an Edwardsean theological tradition. Trinitarian rather than Unitarian, they stressed the need for conversion and encouraged revivals, even as they gradually modified stern Calvinistic doctrine to accommodate nineteenth-century romantic sensibilities and emerging scientific perspectives.

This tradition, rooted in Puritanism but already evolved into a more progressive religion, derived authority from the general assent of the community (a formidable force in a democratic nation) and from two kinds of revelation: that of scripture and that of nature. Emily Dickinson's education stressed both, even as her questioning mind intuited some weaknesses in the church's intellectual armament that would become evident in coming decades.

Protestant piety relies on Bible-reading, and the nineteenth century was a time of unprecedented printing and distribution of scriptural texts in editions that often featured illustrations, maps, glossaries, and other apparatus to assist the reader. Although sermons and religious tracts remained popular reading, lay people were encouraged to respond to the Bible on their own despite inevitably conflicting interpretations. Dickinson, fond as she was of the Bible, nonetheless recognized that it was being read increasingly as a literary work in competition with novels and that this "antique Volume - / Written by faded Men / At the suggestion of Holy Spectres" (Fr 1577) needed artful retelling to attract restless readers of her nephew's generation. That she could imagine fresh renderings and even reached the point of referring to Bible narratives as myth not only reflected the tendencies of her time, no doubt, but also the approach to scripture taken at Amherst College, where the Bible was honored as the authoritative word of God but not assumed to be literally true.

Nature, the second source of revelation, manifested the Creator's glory in ways that bridged Enlightenment with romantic modes of understanding. A foundational text in Connecticut Valley colleges was William Paley's *Natural Theology* (1802), which demonstrated how knowledge of nature promotes reverence for the power who manifests himself in creation.[21] Assumptions that natural revelation reinforced scripture came into question in Dickinson's earliest years, however, when Charles Lyell's *Principles of Geology* (1830–1833) demolished biblical chronologies by proving from evidence of the earth itself that this planet must be millions of years old rather than six thousand. Except for fundamentalists, most Christian thinkers of the time came to accept the Genesis account as metaphorically true, in that it established God as the originating force in creation, even if one learned to think of that process as occurring over millennia of evolution rather than seven miraculous days. Connecticut Valley believers found particular assurance in taking this approach because the Reverend Edward Hitchcock, president of Amherst College from 1845–1854, demonstrated in his *Elementary Geology* (1840), *The Religion of Geology* (1851), and frequent lectures how sciences reinforce the Bible. The butterfly emerging from its cocoon in the lithographed frontispiece to Hitchcock's *Religious Lectures on*

Peculiar Phenomena in the Four Seasons (1850) served as an emblem of resurrection that stimulated Dickinson's excitement over metaphor—especially when figurative language pointed toward triumph over death. Right in her home area, dinosaur tracks and fossils offered clues into the geological and zoological past that could be paralleled with botanical cycles in her own garden to sustain the poet's hopes:

> A science - so the Savans say,
> "Comparative Anatomy" -
> By which a single bone -
> Is made a secret to unfold
> Of some rare tenant of the mold -
> Else perished in the stone -
>
> So to the eye prospective led,
> This meekest flower of the mead
> Opon a winter's day,
> Stands representative in gold
> Of Rose and Lily, manifold,
> And countless Butterfly! (Fr 147)

Although not itself a source of revelation, history (or the eye retrospective) was another area of knowledge descendants of the Puritans interpreted in scriptural terms. The Bible provides an ordered assemblage of readings that begin chronologically with the Genesis account of creation and end with prophecies of the last days and heavenly kingdom. Jonathan Edwards's *A History of the Work of Redemption* (1808), a posthumous arrangement of sermons, taught collegians like Dickinson to read world history as carrying on God's saving work in preparation for the millennium.[22] Missionaries and other travelers who visited the Holy Land confirmed the historical reality of places they had read about in Holy Writ. When Helen Hunt Jackson died a few months before Emily Dickinson, her Amherst friend remembered how Jackson's father had died on such a pilgrimage in a way understood to validate hopes for immortality: "'From Mount Zion below to Mount Zion above'!, said President Humphrey of her Father" (L 1042). Many of her contemporaries (notably Shakers, Millerites, and Adventists) awaited imminent fulfillment of revelation with Christ's second coming. Even more Americans applied Puritan typology to interpret their country's history as fulfilling God's covenant with Israel. Given the progressive flavor of nineteenth-century America, it was tempting to anticipate a perfected world of a sort Dickinson parodied in the mock-millennial rhetoric of her exhortation to George Gould: "We'll build Alms-houses, and transcendental State prisons, and scaffolds—we will blow out the sun, and the moon, and encourage invention. Alpha shall kiss Omega—we will ride up the hill of glory—Hallelujah, all hail!" (L 34).

One area in which evangelical Protestants of her time supposed themselves to have progressed beyond both the Puritans and the neo-Edwardsean Calvinists, who came to prominence in New England divinity around the time of the Revolution, was theology. In the name of progress, they cast off the harshest Calvinist doctrines that repelled sensitivities of a more humane generation. Aaron Colton, who served Amherst's First Church from Dickinson's childhood into early adulthood, stoutly denied ever hearing any New England divine preach those terrifying doctrines, often cited as alienating kindly people from a God who used arbitrary yet invincible power in ways that alarmed nineteenth-century Christians: "men of the present *punished* for Adam's sin; glorified saints in ecstasies over the suffering of the lost; willingness to be a castaway a prime evidence of piety."[23] Colton characterized the doctrines actively taught as gospel teaching that confronted sinners with their depravity while holding out hope for redemption. It was a conversion-oriented theology but one that rejected Calvinist orthodoxy as the Puritans understood it: the belief that grace is Christ's freely given but wholly unmerited gift to the relatively few elect, a transformation that no person in the state of nature could do anything to initiate.

In fact, what was being taught in the Congregational strongholds of Dickinson's day was the heresy of Arminianism (named for the Renaissance Dutch theologian Jacobus Arminius) against which the Pilgrims' pastor, John Robinson, had argued at Leyden before the *Mayflower* sailed for Plymouth and against which Jonathan Edwards dedicated his whole ministry as he battled the smug confidence of the Valley's prosperous "river gods." After disestablishment, however, well-to-do laymen like Edward Dickinson exercised tremendous influence over the churches; like most Americans, they held to democratic, progressive, optimistic views of religion. Denominations like the Congregational, Episcopalian, and Presbyterian that had long enjoyed government-mandated support now competed with rapidly growing Methodist and Baptist churches and a proliferation of new sects. Those winning the most converts were the Arminianized evangelical churches that maintained the need for conversion but exhorted aspirants to contribute to their salvation through exercise of free will. The New Haven theology of Yale's Nathaniel Taylor replaced the doctrine of total human depravity with the ideas that "sin is in the sinning" rather than inherent in human nature after the fall, and that sanctification is a cooperative process involving both man and God.[24] Lyman Beecher, Charles Grandison Finney, and Amherst-area ministers promoted this belief, which opened the possibility for everyone to obey the call to conversion.

It was largely because conversion had become a matter of individual choice that Dickinson felt pressures to accept Christ and not simply prepare herself for an experience of grace that might never come. Sometimes her writing echoes Arminian views, especially when imitating rhetoric familiar to pious correspondents. Otherwise, however, she wondered "How strange is this sanctification, that works such a marvellous change, that sows in such corruption, and rises in golden glory, that brings Christ down, and shews him, and lets him select his friends!" (L 35). Lets *him* select. As with human love and marriage, she apprehended that her role was to wait and perhaps be passed over: even while trying to attract this celestial lover's attention, still deferring to his choice or failure to choose. One of the characteristic features of Dickinson's love poems, in fact, is the frequent ambiguity that leaves the reader perplexed as to whether she writes about a human or divine lover. "He touched me, so I live to know" (Fr 349), for instance, celebrates a life-changing, ennobling experience that could well be conversion, and "Mine - by the Right of the White Election!" (Fr 411) leaves us to speculate on who has elected the rapturous speaker. While many Christians of her day looked for the fruits of conversion in public morality and benevolence, Dickinson still probed for inward transformation. One of the ways in which her Puritan heritage reinforced the romantic sensibility of her time was emphasis on one's inner life and personal response to occasions of supernatural or natural grace.[25]

Imperiled Faith

Evangelicalism, which linked Amherst Congregationalism with vibrant religious movements throughout the country, has been identified as "a religious expression of romantic sensibility" because of its reliance on emotion and intuition.[26] Yet romanticism also challenged the system of belief espoused by the churches, sometimes directly (as in Emerson's "Divinity School Address") but more often indirectly, and Dickinson responded with characteristically alert sensitivity to ways in which romantic "heart religion" sustained or threatened hopes for immortality.

"I had a letter—and Ralph Emerson's Poems—a beautiful copy—from Newton the other day. I should love to read you them both—they are very pleasant to me" (L 30). Dickinson wrote this to Jane Humphrey at the start of 1850, the revival year that would leave her isolated in her "no-hope" condition when most of those she loved best chose Christ. But the gift of Emerson's poems, linked as it was to friendship, helped to shore her up through the ordeal ahead. Emerson and other Transcendentalists like Theodore Parker and Henry David Thoreau offered an alternative perspective derived from Samuel Taylor Coleridge and German philosophy. Calling for self-reliant trust in a person's intuitive response to nature and in the creative energy he named the Oversoul, Emerson defied orthodoxies that prevented people from seeing nature freshly and tapping into the universal spiritual force he preferred not to identify with any personal deity. Dickinson's poems bear witness to the stimulus she found in this philosopher-poet; yet there is no evidence that she attended any of Emerson's lectures on his visits to town in 1857 or 1865 or ventured next door to meet him when he was Sue's and Austin's guest. She subjected Transcendental promises to the same tests she applied to church ones, sometimes finding the visionary empowerment Emerson taught her to expect from nature but often encountering an unbridgeable divide between it and her consciousness:

> But nature is a stranger yet;
> The ones that cite her most
> Have never passed her haunted house,
> Nor simplified her ghost. (Fr 1433)

Although her circumference symbol derives in good measure from Emerson's dynamic circle imagery, Dickinson applied this geometric metaphor to the limiting boundary of death and the mysteries beyond that. She would not have found in him support for her dreams of personal immortality with God; yet when he died, Dickinson trusted that "the Ralph Waldo Emerson—whose name my Father's Law Student taught me, has touched the secret Spring" (L 750). Emerson's challenge to the churches was leveled directly at rationalistic Unitarianism, but he also threatened Congregational churches that traced their heritage to the same Puritan roots. Transcendentalism, for them, was the latest eruption of the Antinomian heresy identified with Anne Hutchinson and the Quakers: belief in inner light, private revelation, and a spirituality relatively independent of churches. Yet evangelical preachers tapped into Emersonian rhetoric and assimilated many of his ideas in ways that helped young people from backgrounds like hers detach themselves from their parents' religious practices.

When that young person was a woman, however, it was the sentimental side of romanticism that she could most readily share with others. Whereas there was an element of rebellion in Dickinson's aligning herself with Emerson, there was a quality of submissive acceptance to her engagement in the sisterly culture of mutual affective support that linked her to female friends. Emphasis placed on the heart, on tender sympathies, on self-sacrificing love, and on the home as the center of human values sustained a social structure that restricted women's sphere to the domestic arena and to aspects of religion other than ordained ministry. Women enjoyed increased influence in churches, however, if only because their numbers dominated. About two-thirds of those converted during the Second Great Awakening were women, as were almost 70 percent of Congregational communicants.[27] Preachers adapted their approaches to the sensitivities of this influential majority, easing harsh Calvinist doctrines like predestination or simply neglecting to mention them. When women demurred against God's apparent cruelty toward his children, as Dickinson did in complaining that "God is rather stern with his 'little ones.' 'A cup of cold water in my name' is a shivering legacy February mornings" (L 670), clergymen shifted focus to Jesus as a suffering brother. One of the qualities that drew the Dickinson sisters to Elizabeth and Josiah Holland was their experience of domestic worship while visiting the Hollands' Springfield home. Instead of hearing their father's emphatic "'I say unto you'" (L 432), they appreciated "the Doctor's prayer . . . so simple, so believing. *That* God must be a friend—*that* was a different God" (L 731). Still, the poet tested sentimental notions of religion also, often adopting the persona of a naive child for the ironic critique of religion we find in "What is - 'Paradise'," with its bitter conclusion that "Maybe - 'Eden' a'nt so lonesome / As New England used to be!" (Fr 241). Her refuge became her home, "a holy thing . . . a bit of Eden which not the sin of *any* can utterly destroy" (L 59), and there she pursued the art that romanticism opened to her as an instrument of religious probing. With ministers drawing connections between art and faith,[28] women of her time found writing an opportunity for evangelical service that ranged from Susan Warner's *The Wide, Wide World*, through Harriet Beecher Stowe's *Uncle Tom's Cabin*, to Elizabeth Stuart Phelps's *The Gates Ajar*, all tremendously popular books.[29] The nineteenth century was also a great age of hymnody, again substantially produced by women, and it seems fitting that Dickinson adapted hymn tunes to create strikingly less orthodox poems.[30]

Although the moderating impact of romanticism on American religion was gradual and often felt to be beneficial, the Civil War struck with immediate destructive force. Given the typological linkage widely drawn between the United States and the biblical Israel, Americans tended to read scripture as reinforcing patriotism. In the North, especially, the revival of 1858 raised hopes that history was advancing rapidly toward perfection. Timothy Smith describes that awakening as a national movement engaging many Protestant denominations "to precipitate a national Pentecost which they hoped would baptize America in the Holy Spirit and in some mystic manner destroy the evils of slavery, poverty, and greed."[31] When war erupted, it was greeted as a holy cause. But there was nothing "mystic" about the four years of slaughter that brought a rescued union and emancipation at great cost, actually fostering greed and flinging families north and south into worse poverty through loss of breadwinners even as it massively escalated the number of economically desperate former slaves. Millennial hopes perished with the war as did the redemptive view of history that had connected religion to progress. War's horrors fostered doubts about divine mercy; deaths of unconverted sons, lovers, husbands, and brothers evoked crises of faith that prompted widespread rejection of Calvinist beliefs. For Dickinson and her neighbors, the first great trial came with the death of Frazar Stearns, the son of Amherst College's president, her brother's dear friend, and a spiritual searcher who apparently never reached assurance.[32]

Just two years before that fighting began, Charles Darwin initiated a different war with *The Origin of Species* (1859), which undermined the natural theology underlying Hitchcock's claims for mutual supportive revelations from science and scripture. The English biologist's theory of evolution through natural selection explained the origin of animal species without reference to God or the time-hallowed argument from design. Later, in *The Descent of Man* (1871), he raised the probability that, instead of being personally formed by God as the capstone of creation, man had evolved from apes or some shared bestial ancestor. This line of thinking, applied by social and natural scientists, threatened even metaphoric readings of Genesis. If species were inexorably evolving through survival of the fittest, then what became of the doctrine of Christ's atonement once science cast Adam out of the picture as the capstone of creation and all mankind's sinful ancestor? Fundamentalist scripture readers held their ground by denying Darwin's premise, but more intellectually venturesome religious thinkers like those at Amherst College, Andover, and Yale, having always assumed congruence between the two revelations, generally tried to assimilate these unsettling theories and found themselves mightily puzzled to find any way of harmonizing Darwin with the Bible.[33] Defending the faith meant diminishing it.

One of Dickinson's responses to this crisis was to adopt her ironic little-girl voice in a tone of complaint about scientific terminology and systems of classification. At first, "'Arcturus' is his other name" (Fr 117) reads like her version of one of Poe's laments about scientific encroachments on romantic fancy, but then Dickinson characteristically shifts focus to her centering interest in immortality: "What once was 'Heaven' / Is 'Zenith' now! / Where I proposed to go / . . . Perhaps the 'kingdom of Heaven's' changed." Yet she ends with hope that "the Father in the skies / Will lift his little girl - / 'Old fashioned'! naughty! everything! / Over the stile of 'pearl'!" Another response was a kind of droll bemusement, as she commented that "we thought Darwin had thrown 'the Redeemer' away" (L 750). Striving to maintain a hope that was not childishly naive in its repudiation of intellectual developments, the poet located the weakness of sciences in the questions they made no effort to resolve: "Why the Thief ingredient accompanies all Sweetness Darwin does not tell us" (L 359). Whatever it might discover about the origins of man, science revealed nothing about his destiny.

Christian hopes rely on God's biblical promises. When Dickinson asked Washington Gladden "Is immortality true," she evidently demanded reasons she could use to convince a doubting friend. Gladden responded: "I believe in the life everlasting, because Jesus Christ taught it. Say what you will about him, no one can deny that he knew the human soul, its nature, its laws, its destinies, better than any other being who ever trod this earth; and he testifies, and his testimony is more clear, more definite,

more positive on this than on any other subject, that there is
life beyond the grave" (L 752a). What made this declaration less
reassuring than it would have been a few decades before was the
impact of the Higher Criticism, European scholarship that employed evidence from linguistics, stylistics, history, and comparative religion to represent the Bible as something very much different and less sacred than divine inspiration. It was, instead, a
product of human authorship with multiple anonymous writers
and amenders. This research discredited the notion of Moses's
authorship of the Pentateuch, as David Friedrich Strauss's *Das
Leben Jesu* (1835–1836; translated into English by Mary Ann
Evans / George Eliot, 1846) and Ernest Renan's *Vie de Jésus* (1863)
linked Christian mysteries to pagan fertility myths while even
questioning the historical existence of Jesus. Dickinson accustomed herself to losses, admitting that "No Moses there can be"
(Fr 521) and "Ararat's a Legend - now - / And no one credits
Noah" (Fr 532).

Even without pursuing the study of comparative religions
that turned out to be one of the offshoots of the nineteenth century's linkage of missionary work to colonization, Dickinson
found herself in a much more diverse world of belief than she
would have guessed as the child of a Congregationalist household in the Connecticut Valley. The New England rupture
between Old Light and New Light factions within churches that
resulted in separation of Unitarian and Congregational denominations touched her own family when her cousins, Louisa and
Frances Norcross, became Unitarians. Among her closest friends,
Samuel Bowles, the Hollands, and Thomas Wentworth Higginson also opted for liberal Christianity.[34] Episcopal and Baptist
churches formed in Amherst, and people close to the poet dab-
bled with Christian Spiritualism.[35] New sects kept emerging in
her America (Mormon, African-American Episcopal, and Christian Science churches among the largest), while the Holiness
Movement linked worshipers in disparate conservative churches.
The culture of revivalism, like that of sentimentalism, fore-
grounded a shared evangelical style while disregarding doctrinal
disputes among sects so that cooperation was encouraged in
benevolent societies, temperance efforts, and Bible distribution.

Movement between denominations became easier. Austin's friend Frederic Dan Huntington began his ministry as a Congregationalist, became an evangelically oriented Unitarian on the Harvard faculty, and ended his career as an Episcopal bishop. Dickinson's letters accommodate their tone to the sensitivities of friends at various points along the continuum from belief to disbelief; with death more steadily in her mind with every passing year, she respected whatever beliefs sustained others as they confronted the challenges facing finite, suffering, yet hopeful creatures living in the shadow of death.

One cause that united American Protestants of Dickinson's time, especially before the Civil War, was a strident anti-Catholicism rooted in the Reformation and exacerbated by the arrival of multitudinous impoverished immigrants. In 1834, a mob of Yankee workmen burned down the Ursuline convent-school in Charlestown, Massachusetts. Other riots resulted from conflicts over King James or Douay Bibles in public schools, job access, and the Civil War draft.[36] Such hate was part of the poet's milieu. She commented wryly in an 1852 letter about the minister's "announcing several facts which were usually startling" about "the Roman Catholic system" (L 96), as though the topic were commonplace; and she gleefully encouraged her brother to thrash the Irish boys he taught in a Boston public school, joking that "Vinnie and I say masses for poor Irish boys souls" (L 43). In attacking Catholics, Protestants saw themselves championing an American way of life that promoted morality and public order. By the 1860 census, however, Roman Catholicism had established itself as the most populous American church. When a parish formed in Amherst, Edward Dickinson contributed to the building campaign. Irish Catholic domestic workers became essential members of the Dickinson household. Meanwhile, American Protestants who traveled in Catholic Europe brought back surprisingly appreciative reports about liturgical rites and arts. The poet, always sensitive to absences, seems to have felt some attraction to the way Catholics turned to Mary as mediatress between sinners and Jesus and occasionally referred to a kind of prayer quite out of keeping with her Congregational formation: "Mine to supplicate Madonna - / If Madonna be / Could behold so far a

Creature - / Christ - omitted - Me" (Fr 762). The breakdown of syntax here betrays her discomfort, yet the lines convey a vulnerable sense of loss for which her own tradition offered no recompense.

What Happened to God's Arm?

It is easy enough to discern in hindsight the crushing weight of intellectual and societal pressures that overwhelmed the structure of belief that had given confident energy to America's evangelical Protestants before the Civil War and to identify tendencies within the churches as well as outside them that prompted Dickinson to imagine God with his arm lopped off. But people survive amputations, and so may Deity—especially since God's bodily features are purely metonymic.

Several details of our proof-text poem merit attention in light of this discussion. First is that anthropomorphic image of God, based on Isaiah and other biblical passages, admittedly, yet still an image graven with pen and subject to Puritan critiques of such idolatry. That a god limited to human imagination is subject to mutilation proves nothing about the immortal, immutable, unknowable lord of creation as envisaged by Calvin. Second, if we think of this poem as a response to the implosion of the traditional argument for God's existence based on orderly design evident throughout the universe, is its surprising degree of metrical regularity. There are variants in its iambic beat, of course: trochaic feet at the start of several lines and an opening spondee, all of which could be interpreted as reinforcing the assurance that existed back "then." The iambic smoothness of "They went to God's Right Hand" accords with tone, but equal regularity in the two most devastating lines ("That Hand is amputated now / And God cannot be found") hints that the poet senses more order in the universe than the poem directly acknowledges.

The third textual feature I find striking is the poem's assertively Latinate diction in key words ("amputated," "abdication," "illume," and, most obviously, "ignis fatuus"). This Latin phrase refers to the eerie light sometimes seen over grassy marshlands at night. It gives a false illumination if mistaken for sun or moon yet has its own authenticity and might serve as a somewhat unreliable guide in darkness. Science can only guess its origin, and popular observations of this will-o'-the-wisp have given rise to many superstitions. Linking the idea of superstition to the Latin language turns thoughts toward the Church of Rome and the possibility that the time frame of this poem may be more extensive than is generally understood. Perhaps it refers, not simply to the contrast between those dying in Dickinson's youth and those facing mortality in her later years, but to a starker contrast between the doubts of post–Civil War America and an age of faith before the Reformation.

The last textual element that calls for attention is the word "Behavior" in "The abdication of Belief / Makes the Behavior small." It accords with her father's piety that valued faith as an impetus to those virtues that promoted personal prosperity while advancing Christ's kingdom. For Emily Dickinson, however, morality (often confused then, as now, with social convention) had never been the essence of religious experience, and she clearly resented the tendency of pious folk to judge their neighbors. Heroic sanctity might be less likely in America's postbellum religious culture when even so prominent a minister as Henry Ward Beecher (an Amherst College graduate) could be implicated in a messy sex scandal. Still, if behavior grows smaller in time of doubt, might not something else, specifically, hope for immortality, loom larger?

In part because Dickinson focused her imaginative energy on that "Flood subject" (L 319) rather than dogmas or practices directly challenged by these cultural upheavals, she managed to cope and even to take some pleasure in the nimble balancing act she sustained between belief and doubt. Churches coped also. Although wounded by romanticism, Darwin, the Higher Criticism, and the Civil War, they enjoyed a period of renewed vigor with considerably increased membership.[37] In the Gilded Age, Dwight L. Moody picked up the mantle dropped by Finney and Beecher to become the country's most successful revivalist. Henry Ward Beecher, Lyman Beecher's son and the novelist's brother, claimed to reconcile Christian truth with Darwin's findings. Washington Gladden, the Congregational minister to whom Dickinson directed her question about immortality, emerged as a leader of the Social Gospel movement, by which liberal Protestants applied Christian principles to political and economic advocacy for the working poor. Lew Wallace's *Ben-Hur* (1880), a sensational work of historical fiction set in Palestine in the early years of the Roman Empire and somewhat misleadingly subtitled "A Tale of the Christ," became the century's best-selling novel in America.[38] In Amherst, Austin Dickinson spearheaded the building campaign for the handsome First Church structure that went up within sight of The Homestead.

Even while questioning, Emily Dickinson continued to hope for immortality, especially as death's depredations struck closer and closer. Though she could not know for sure where the dead went, she still trusted in their journey. When her mother died in 1882, she wrote, "I believe we shall in some manner be cherished by our Maker—that the One who gave us this remarkable earth has the power still farther to surprise that which He has caused. Beyond that all is silence" (L 785). Like amputation, abdication requires an agent. One must set aside whatever is being abdicated by an effort of will, and Dickinson never abdicated hope. She even laughed at the folly of those who did: "The Fop - the Carp - the Atheist," ephemeral creatures who cling to each passing moment even as, by God's sublime joke, "their commuted Feet / The Torrents of Eternity / Do all but inundate" (Fr 1420). It is as though "Heav'ns whelm'd-down Chrystall meele Bowle," punningly imaged by the Puritan Edward Taylor, was drenching fashionable doubters of the declining nineteenth century with the wholly unexpected gift of endless life.[39] Even if the right arm Christians had earlier relied on for salvation had been amputated, the left one somehow pulled the sluice to release the flow of grace that sustained Emily Dickinson in "the Balm of that Religion / That doubts - as fervently as it believes" (Fr 1449).

NOTES

1. Quotations from Dickinson's poems in this essay refer to *The Poems of Emily Dickinson, Reading Edition*, ed. R. W. Franklin (Cam-

bridge, Mass.: Belknap Press of Harvard University Press, 1999); they will be identified parenthetically within the text with numbers preceded by (Fr). Citations from Letters (L) refer to *The Letters of Emily Dickinson*, ed. Thomas H. Johnson and Theodora Ward, 3 vols. (Cambridge: Belknap Press of Harvard University Press, 1958). I have also consulted Franklin's 1998 Variorum Edition of *The Poems*.

2. James McIntosh, *Nimble Believing: Dickinson and the Unknown* (Ann Arbor: University of Michigan Press, 2000), 3; Cynthia Griffin Wolff, *Emily Dickinson* (New York: Knopf, 1986), 451; Roger Lundin, *Emily Dickinson and the Art of Belief* (Grand Rapids, Mich.: Eerdmans, 1998), 4.

3. Books useful for establishing historical background for this period in American religious culture include Sydney E. Ahlstrom, *A Religious History of the American People* (New Haven: Yale University Press, 1972); Robert T. Handy, *A Christian America: Protestant Hopes and Historical Realities* (New York: Oxford University Press, 1971); Nathan O. Hatch, *The Democratization of American Christianity* (New Haven: Yale University Press, 1989); Charles H. Lippy, *Being Religious, American Style: A History of Popular Religiosity in the United States* (Westport, Conn.: Greenwood Press, 1994); Rosemary Radford Ruether and Rosemary Skinner Keller, eds. *Women and Religion in America*, vol. 1, *The Nineteenth Century* (San Francisco: Harper & Row, 1981); Timothy L. Smith, *Revivalism and Social Reform in Mid-Nineteenth-Century America* (New York: Abingdon Press, 1957); Donald C. Swift, *Religion and the American Experience* (Armonk, N.Y.: M. E. Sharpe, 1998); and Peter W. Williams, ed., *Perspectives on American Religion and Culture* (Oxford: Blackwell, 1999).

4. Melville's depressed state of mind while visiting England at the start of his journey to the Middle East is known to us through Nathaniel Hawthorne's account, perhaps ironically exaggerated, in *The English Notebooks*, ed. Randall Stewart (New York: Russell & Russell, 1962), 432–33.

5. W. A. Dickinson, "Address," *An Historical Review: One Hundred and Fiftieth Anniversary of the First Church of Christ in Amherst, Massachusetts* (Amherst, 1890), 56–57.

6. First Church, *The Articles of Faith and Government* (Amherst, 1834), 7.

7. MacGregor Jenkins, *Emily Dickinson: Friend and Neighbor* (Boston: Little, Brown, 1930), 80–82. Another account of this inter-

view appears in Martha Dickinson Bianchi's introduction to *Further Poems of Emily Dickinson* (Boston: Little, Brown, 1929).

8. Rowena Revis Jones, "The Preparation of a Poet: Puritan Directions in Emily Dickinson's Education," *Studies in the American Renaissance* (1982): 285–324.

9. See Paul C. Gutjahr, *An American Bible: A History of the Good Book in the United States, 1777-1880* (Stanford, Calif.: Stanford University Press, 1999), and Nathan O. Hatch and Mark A. Noll, eds., *The Bible in America: Essays in Cultural History* (New York: Oxford University Press, 1982).

10. A chapter detailing revival activity in the parish appears in Sister Regina Siegfried, A.S.C., "Conspicuous by Her Absence: Amherst's Religious Tradition and Emily Dickinson's Own Growth in Faith" (Ph.D. diss., St. Louis University, 1982), 85.

11. Lyon is one of the evangelical leaders featured in Joseph A. Conforti's *Jonathan Edwards, Religious Tradition, & American Culture* (Chapel Hill: University of North Carolina Press, 1995), chapter 4.

12. Martha Tomhave Blauvelt writes in "Women and Revivalism" that "the marital home was indeed a cloister, and conversion helped women take their vows," in *Women and Religion*, ed. Ruether and Keller, 4.

13. William R. Sherwood, strongly influenced by Thomas Johnson's chronology for the poems, locates that conversion in 1862, the year Johnson thought to be the poet's most productive. "In 1862," he argues, "Emily Dickinson did not have a crack-up . . . but a conversion, and . . . it was precisely the variety of conversion that both her inclinations and her traditions had prepared her for and against which she had fought so vigorously at Mary Lyon's Seminary in Mount Holyoke in 1848": *Circumference and Circumstance: Stages in the Mind and Art of Emily Dickinson* (New York: Columbia University Press, 1968), 138. Dorothy Huff Oberhaus reads Fascicle 40 (dated 1864) as "a three-part meditation" that reveals itself as "a simple conversion narrative" confirming the poet's developing relationship with Jesus: *Emily Dickinson's Fascicles: Method and Meaning* (University Park: Pennsylvania State University Press, 1995), 4, 14. Although Cynthia Griffin Wolff organizes her critical biography around the motif of Dickinson as a Jacob figure wrestling with God, she finds evidence of midlife experience validating early flickers of hope. "By the mid-1860s or early 1870s," Wolff declares, "well before

Father's death, a new poetry of faith had emerged": *Emily Dickinson*, 504.

14. I have elaborated more fully on this interpretation of Dickinson's "Circumference" in *Dickinson: Strategies of Limitation* (Amherst: University of Massachusetts Press, 1985), chapters 7–10.

15. Edward Taylor is my source for the bowling alley and punchbowl references, taken from "The Preface" to *Gods Determinations Touching His Elect* and *Preparatory Meditations: First Series, number* 8. It was William Stoughton who introduced the grain-sifting metaphor in "New England's True Interest," and Jonathan Edwards is famous or infamous for the spider image in "Sinners in the Hands of an Angry God."

16. William Lloyd Garrison, in his "Preface" to Frederick Douglass's 1845 *Narrative*, warned that "He who can peruse it . . . without trembling for the fate of this country in the hands of a righteous God, who is ever on the side of the oppressed, and whose arm is not shortened that it cannot save,—must have a flinty heart, and be qualified to act the part of a trafficker 'in slaves and the souls of men.'" *Narrative of the Life of Frederick Douglass, An American Slave* (New York: Viking Penguin, 1982), 38.

17. Alfred Habegger, noting 1844 as the year in which the future poet first experienced a wave of bereavements, speculates that this letter may refer to the funeral of Martha Dwight Strong, who committed suicide. If so, she (not uncharacteristically) misrepresented herself to Higginson as having been much younger at the time than was really the case: *My Wars Are Laid Away in Books: The Life of Emily Dickinson* (New York: Random House, 2001), 173–74.

18. James Turner, *Without God, Without Creed: The Origins of Unbelief in America* (Baltimore: Johns Hopkins University Press, 1985), xiii.

19. In *The Only Kangaroo Among the Beauty: Emily Dickinson and America* (Baltimore: Johns Hopkins University Press, 1979), 99, Karl Keller quotes this passage from Edward Dickinson's contribution to *Celebration of the Two Hundredth Anniversary of the Settlement of Hadley, Massachusetts* (Northampton, 1859), 77. Amherst traced its origins to Hadley. His son's statement comes from a similar commemorative work, *An Historical Review*, 58.

20. Ann Douglas, *The Feminization of American Culture* (New York: Knopf, 1977), 151.

21. Carlton Lowenberg, *Emily Dickinson's Textbooks* (Lafayette, Calif.: Lowenberg, 1986).

22. Although Edwards is known today chiefly for the oft-anthologized revival sermon, "Sinners in the Hands of an Angry God," general readers of Dickinson's generation were more likely to know him through this book and the account he wrote of David Brainerd's missionary work among the Indians. In seminaries, scholars wrestled with the theological and philosophical challenges of his treatises on *Freedom of the Will* and *Original Sin*. See Conforti, *Jonathan Edwards*.

23. Colton, *The Old Meeting House and Vacation Papers, Humorous and Other* (New York: 1890), 69–70. Such notably "hard doctrines" had, indeed, been preached earlier in New England Congregational churches. The doctrine of Original Sin as cause of human depravity was widely held before the beginning of the nineteenth century, and Michael Wigglesworth's dismayingly popular poem, "The Day of Doom" (1662), represented saints in heaven celebrating God's justice despite the horrendous fate of those condemned to hell. The idea that "willingness to be damned" (acceptance of God's ineffable will as right, even if it meant one's own eternal condemnation) was itself evidence of a converted mind emerged in the late eighteenth century among neo-Edwardsean theologians. Harriet Beecher Stowe's *The Minister's Wooing* (1859) critiques such thinking from a sentimental fictional perspective solidly grounded in knowledge of the New England Calvinist tradition.

24. Taylor—one of Timothy Dwight's protegés, minister of New Haven's First Church, and a professor at Yale Divinity School—was the principal exponent of the New Haven Theology. Sydney Ahlstrom summarizes his positions: "Taylor's fundamental insistence was that no man becomes depraved but by his own act, for the sinfulness of the human race does not pertain to human nature as such. 'Sin is in the sinning,' and hence 'original' only in the sense that it is universal. Though inevitable, it is not—as with Edwards—causally necessary. Man always had, in Taylor's famous phrase, 'power to the contrary.' As a free, rational, moral, creative cause, man is not part of the system of nature, at least not a passive or determined part": *A Religious History of the American People*, 420.

25. According to Turner, "For all the social ritual surrounding revivalism, the end of the exercise was to put the individual alone and

face-to-face with his God": *Without God*, 209. See also Amanda Porterfield, "The Puritan Legacy in American Religion and Culture," in *Perspectives*, ed. Williams, 82–83.

26. Turner, *Without God*, 105.

27. Swift, *Religion and the American Experience*, 106. See also Douglas, *The Feminization*.

28. Habegger identifies Edwards Amasa Park, whom we know Dickinson admired as a preacher, along with Horace Bushnell as nationally prominent Congregational ministers of the 1850s whose aestheticized "religion of the heart" may have "helped make feasible Dickinson's work as a poet" (*My Wars*, 310).

29. David S. Reynolds, *Faith in Fiction: The Emergence of Religious Literature in America* (Cambridge, Mass.: Harvard University Press, 1981), chapters 3–4.

30. According to Ann Douglas in *The Feminization of American Culture*, "There are several points to be noted about the hymns which proliferated and were welcomed in American homes and churches during this period: first, their relative novelty as an important part of American Protestant worship; second, their largely non-evangelical and feminine authorship; and last, their liberalized theology, poeticized form, and growing obsession with heavenly life" (217). See also two articles by Mary DeJong: "'Theirs the Sweetest Songs': Women Hymn Writers in the Nineteenth-Century United States," in *A Mighty Baptism: Race, Gender, and the Creation of American Protestantism*, ed. Susan Juster and Lisa MacFarlane (Ithaca, N.Y.: Cornell University Press, 1996), 141–67; "'With My Burden I Begin': The (Im)Personal 'I' of Nineteenth-Century Hymnody," *Studies in Puritan American Spirituality* 4 (1993): 185–223.

31. Smith, *Revivalism and Social Reform*, 62.

32. Valuable perspective on how the Civil War challenged religious faith appears in Shira Wolosky's book, *Emily Dickinson: A Voice of War* (New Haven: Yale University Press, 1984), and in Barton Levi St. Armand's *Emily Dickinson and Her Culture: The Soul's Society* (Cambridge: Cambridge University Press, 1984), chapters 3 and 4. See also Wolosky's essay in this book.

33. Paul A. Carter, *The Spiritual Crisis of the Gilded Age* (DeKalb: Northern Illinois University Press, 1971), chapter 3; Turner, *Without God*, chapter 6.

34. Helpful perspective on Dickinson's contact with liberal

Christian influences and the effect of such thinking on her relationship with Christ appears in Rowena Revis Jones's article, "A Taste for 'Poison': Dickinson's Departure from Orthodoxy," *The Emily Dickinson Journal* 2, no. 1 (1993): 47–64.

35. Benjamin Lease, *Emily Dickinson's Readings of Men and Books: Sacred Soundings* (New York: St. Martin's Press, 1990), chapter 4.

36. Lippy, *Being Religious*, 85–86; Handy, *A Christian America*, 58–59; Gutjahr, *An American Bible*, 113–18.

37. In "Religion and Modernity, 1865–1914," Stow Persons indicates that church membership grew markedly in post–Civil War America. Whereas the 1860 census showed only 23% of the U.S. population as belonging to churches, in 1910, the figure had risen to 43%: *The Shaping of American Religion*, ed. James Ward Smith and A. Leland Jamison (Princeton: Princeton University Press, 1961), 372. Easier standards for admission probably influenced these figures, as did growth in churches not existing or only slightly represented in census data from the start of the nineteenth century.

38. Paul Gutjahr attributes the tremendous popularity of *Ben-Hur* among Christians to the effect of historical accuracy that Wallace achieved as a result of extensive research and to the novel's validation of feeling over reason in matters of faith. Harper and Brothers was still selling millions of copies into the 1920s; like *Uncle Tom's Cabin*, *Ben-Hur* also inspired a long-running dramatic adaptation that toured the country for decades. Situating this publishing phenomenon within the context of responses to Darwin and Comte, Gutjahr argues that "Wallace's painstaking historical research resonated with religious readers who saw in the book a means of answering the call for scientific validation for the existence and authority of Christ and his teachings": *An American Bible*, 169.

39. A possible interpretation of variant words in the manuscript version of this poem ("the dog," "the tramp") is that Dickinson experimented with shifting perspective away from people who neglect faith by affecting fashionable doubts to those often scorned by church members and assumed to have forfeited God's grace by their degraded lives.

Public and Private in Dickinson's War Poetry

Shira Wolosky

R alph Waldo Emerson, in his essay "The Poet," declared that "the poet is representative. He stands among partial men for the complete man, and apprises us not of his wealth, but of the common wealth."[1] Within the norms of the nineteenth century, this would seem to relegate women poets to the status of "partial men." In the much accepted division of life into separate spheres, women were barred access to the "common wealth" as public space. Instead, women remained officially restricted to the domestic sphere—what Tocqueville describes as "the narrow circle of domestic interests and duties"—while men found their places in the "public" world.[2] Women thus could seemingly never achieve Emerson's representative stance—neither in its often overlooked sense (but the one most fully realized by Whitman) of the poet as public figure, nor in the more familiar sense of a rich and powerful autonomous subjectivity, which, however, finds and asserts itself in speaking for and to the wider community. In contrast, women seem at most to reflect in their work their own domestic imprisonment and its costs. In this circumscribed state, the woman poet seems cut off from history, more or less idle and more or less impotent with regard to the public course of events. She thus seems unable to address herself, as poets should, to a surrounding community, representing its true nature and direction while also lacking that strong sense of self and of identity which gives the poet his authority—what makes him, in Harold Bloom's quite conscious phrase, the central man, whose words can represent his world.[3]

In the case of Emily Dickinson, these assignments seem almost hyperbolically justified. If ever there were a private poet, surely it is she—a woman famous in her own lifetime for reclusion: accompanied by a full array of seductive, eccentric concealments and retractions: refusing to go out, dressing in white, refusing to see guests, or even to address her own envelopes. Dickinson seems the ultimate emblem of that modest retreat so urged on American girls and women, rigorously restricting them to the privacy of their own homes. Yet Dickinson's modesty, even while it conforms in many aspects with expected and prescribed female behavior, does so with such extremity as to expose and radicalize gendered norms. Dickinson's is modesty with a vengeance, more explosive than obedient, more challenging than conforming. As to the sequestering of Dickinson from public life, the reading of her work as hermetically private—a mode of self-investigation at its most interior—is in many ways an imposition on her of this gendered paradigm rather than evidence for it. It is a view of her work through the geographies of public and private which are highly gendered and which block from sight her full engagement, and address, to the central concerns of her culture. This decisively includes the Civil War—that crucible of American claims and counterclaims, of violent cultural crossings and transformations, whose implications penetrate every sphere of American cultural identity.

To begin with biography, despite her peculiar behavior, every circumstance of Dickinson's social existence argues against severe detachment from public affairs. Her family had a tradition of involvement in civic life. Her father, after many years of prominence in town meetings, at Amherst College, in the Home Mission Society, and the railroad project, was elected representative to the General Court of Massachusetts in 1838 (where he came to know Herman Melville's politically controversial father-in-law, Judge Lemuel Shaw. This seems to be the reference in Dickinson's poem "I had some things that I called mine - / And God, that he called his" [J 116 / Fr 101] where she retains him in her quarrel with God: "Jove! Choose your counsel - I retain 'Shaw'!") Edward Dickinson was twice elected Massachusetts State Senator in 1842 and 1843; was delegate to the Whig National Convention in 1852; and in the same year was elected to the United States Congress. His term in Congress spanned the period of the Kansas-Nebraska Act, the Fugitive Slave Act, and the first attempts to found the new Republican Party (with meetings to discuss this issue taking place in rooms he shared with Thomas D. Eliot, granduncle to a later American poet).[4] Both her father, Edward, and her brother, Austin, were active recruiters and outfitters of Amherst soldiers, involved in raising both funds and morale.

Many of Dickinson's other acquaintances were directly involved in political reporting and public affairs. Samuel Bowles, a long-time intimate of the family and herself, was editor of the *Springfield Republican*—which published soldiers' letters home and a column on "Piety and Patriotism." (Among the few Dickinson poems published anonymously in her lifetime are those which appeared in publications that aided the war effort.) Dr. Josiah Holland, another close friend, was a columnist for the *Springfield Republican* and editor of *Scribner's Magazine*. He also wrote one of the first biographies of Lincoln. And Thomas Wentworth Higginson, so central in the drama of Dickinson's own unpublication history, was a radical abolitionist (even to the point of supporting the John Brown conspiracy), an activist in women's rights, and colonel to the first black regiment of the Union army when Dickinson first wrote to him. As Hawthorne wrote in "Chiefly About War Matters": "There is no remoteness of life and thought, no hermetically sealed seclusion, except, perhaps, that of the grave, into which the disturbing influences of this war do not penetrate."

This is not to claim that Dickinson was herself a public activist, as many women indeed were. Despite the rigors of the ideology of the separate spheres, the boundaries between public and private were, in fact, extremely volatile, with women not only active but also in many ways the central actors in a variety of public-sphere ventures. These included education, religion, and many forms of what would be today called social services, such as hospital work, work with the poor, with orphans, with immigrants; urban planning, sanitation; abolition, temperance; purity reform and women's rights. Such activity generally belies the relegation of women to a "private" and "domestic" sphere— terms that were nevertheless applied to their community activities as seen to be continuous with the sorts of things women did inside the home. Many of these commitments, however, are neither domestic nor particularly like what women do in houses: urban planning, for example, or preaching. Some activities are political according to any imaginable criteria, even when, as in the case of abolition, the campaigns were (also) conducted in the name of the sanctity and integrity of family life against the constant assault of sexual slavery and the slave market's very denial of family existence. Nor were most of these ventures undertaken within the confines of the household. Domesticity, in fact, is only figurally geographic, since many women's activities took place outside the domicile. The geography of domesticity, so powerful in ascribing women to the private sphere, proves to be a gendered rubric applied to activities not because of their location but exactly because women performed them (when men performed such activities, they were not considered private but public).[5]

Among these central areas for this women's activism, Dickinson directly experienced only the new realm of education— albeit with a strong exposure to the religious-civic sphere with which it was so forcefully intertwined. Her headmistress at Mount Holyoke Female Seminary, Mary Lyon, had founded the college in dedication to mission work and civic activism in the context of the enormous revivalism sweeping through Dickinson's religiously quite conservative home-county through much of her girlhood and indeed her lifetime. Even publication, a major and immensely consequential new venture for women, remains tensely ambiguous in Dickinson's case. Publication offered many women an avenue into public discourse. This emergence into publicity Dickinson declined, lacking both the economic contexts (most women moved into publication by way of either financial motive or financial excuse) and, apparently, the desire. Her fascicle nonpublication remains ambiguously poised between textual inscription and its own effacement and certainly evades publicity—although the circulation of her poems in letters to friends suggests something close to the coterie circles of shared poetry in earlier, Renaissance, courtly worlds.

Despite these almost unique removals from the mainstreams of American women's poetic lives, Dickinson's own writing career remarkably aligns with the enormous and traumatic political events surrounding her. More than half of her poetic production coincides with the years of the Civil War, 1861–1865. The years immediately preceding the war, when the possibility and rhetoric of conflict ominously intensified, were also the years which Thomas Johnson identifies with "the rising flood of her talent," as well as with the beginning of her reclusive practices. Her correspondence is similarly marked by public consciousness, with at least fifteen references to the war in the seventy-five letters she wrote between 1861–1865. Some are passing mentions, some are concerned with the fate of Amherst boys who had gone off to fight, including, notably, Frazar Stearns, over whose death Dickinson especially and personally grieved. But some letters are more general. Thus, to Louise and Frances Norcross, she wrote that "Since the war began" she has an increasing sense that "Tis dangerous to value, for only the precious can alarm. I noticed that Robert Browning had made another poem, and was astonished—till I remembered that I myself, in my smaller way, sang off charnel steps" (L 298).

Dickinson here places many of her most deeply felt poetic impulses into the wider context of the national agony enveloping her world. Dickinson's sense of the precariousness of possession, of the assault of time, contingency, and above all death on all that is precious and valuable, only acquired dire confirmation in the assaults of war. One might say that Emily Dickinson disapproved of reality, and for excellent reasons. What has long seemed a merely eccentric and highly gendered withdrawal from exposures to the world, takes on both motive and defiance once historical context is admitted.

Poetry in the nineteenth century directly participated in the discussions, arguments, claims, and counterclaims of the most pressing questions facing America. For women, it provided a par-

ticularly powerful avenue for engagement in issues of public concern and entry into public debate. Dickinson's case is certainly
most oblique. Yet her poetic engagement with her wider culture,
and the importance of her work as a major response to the issues
most central to nineteenth-century American cultural definition,
can be investigated through a variety of methods—and without
reducing the texts to mere historical document, ideological program, or political tract. Recent work, for example, has begun to
probe how Dickinson uses the words of her culture, and how
they import, into the arena of her texts, the associations, implications, often contested meanings of their general usage. This can
involve her uses of various kinds of political language, or her images of whiteness against the backgrounds of their racial meanings.[6] One moving poem of desperation and appeal, "At least -
to pray - is left - is left" concludes: "Thou settest Earthquake in
the South - / And Maelstrom, in the Sea - / Say, Jesus Christ of
Nazareth - / Hast thou no arm for Me?" (J 502 / Fr 377). "South"
here is surely a political-geographic marker, no less than "south"
is in Whitman's "Out of the Cradle Endlessly Rocking." There
are scattered through the verse references to emigrants and settlers, showing Dickinson's awareness of contemporary demo-
graphic movement. Death is described as democratic in a poem
which meticulously lists the demarcations of social division -
"Color - Caste - Denomination" that "He" so equably ignores (J
970 / Fr 836). Another poem firmly declares that "Not any higher
stands the Grave / For Heroes than for Men -." In a radical assertion of the unique worth of every individual, Dickinson brushes
aside all conditions, whether historical heroism or economic status—the poem goes on to equate "The Beggar and his Queen"—
before the "Democrat" death (J 1256 / Fr 1214).

A quite interesting set of poems use canny electoral puns.
These include the famously isolating "Soul selects her own Society," which figures self-selection as a "Majority" chosen from
"an ample nation"(J 303 / Fr 409). Another poem declares "The
Heart is the Capital of the Mind / The Mind is a single State,"
with "One" a "Population - / Numerous enough" for the "ecstatic Nation" of the self (J 1354 / Fr 1381). There is the pervasive yet
almost unnoticed use of economic imagery—of stocks and

options and properties and ownerships—that weaves Dickinson's work into the volatile and increasingly defining American commitment to money ("Myself can read the Telegrams" reports Dickinson as following "The Stock's advance and retrograde / And what the Markets say" [J 1089 / Fr 1049], to take one example.) The vicissitudes of her own family fortunes—her father's financial reversals and then recovery—is of course a matter of biographical record (and altogether common in a period with little financial regulation). Still another avenue toward a historical Dickinsonian poetics is her position in the gendered distributions of her society, as, for example, through the representations in her work (and indeed in her life) of modesty—including the obscurities and obfuscations of her "slant" poetic truths—which so powerfully defined femininity in her period.[7] There is, as well, Dickinson's continued and intensive engagement with contemporary religious culture, then undergoing volatile and explosive transformation. Finally, there is the exploration of Dickinson's notions of selfhood in relation to models emerging in nineteenth-century America, with enormous consequences for American political, social, economic, and cultural life.

In all these cases, Dickinson's poetry becomes not only the powerful expression of her personal sensibility but also a centrally important representation of her society and her culture—a dimension which has been repeatedly neglected due, not least, to assumptions about gender. Through her work as a whole, I will argue, at stake in Dickinson's poetry is the possibility of interpreting her world at all, within her given paradigms of understanding and their promises of intelligibility and coherence. These the Civil War directly tested and contested. The trauma of the war put extraordinary pressure on the norms, and fundamental faiths, that had promised to structure Dickinson's world and render it meaningful. The result is a work deeply marked by the strains of reality around her and their implications for poetic expression and, specifically, for poetic language.

The question of war penetrates Dickinson's work both through specific historical events and, more hauntingly, as a general, framing context (which of course it unquestionably was). In terms of specific references, there are numerous poems that invoke war, either indirectly or directly.[8] Indirect imagery of war takes many forms. Nature is represented in battle imagery as "martial Trees" that "Barrricade against the Sky . . . with a Flag at every turn" (J 1471 / Fr 1505). Soldiers drop "like flakes" (J 409 / Fr 545) and sunsets spread in the uniform colors of blue and gray (J 204 / Fr 233) or as "Gulfs - of Red, and Fleets - of Red / And Crews - of solid Blood" (J 658 / Fr 468). Or war becomes a figure for Dickinson's contested interior life, a "Battle fought between the Soul / And No Man" (J 595 / Fr 629), a "Campaign inscrutable / Of the Interior" (J 1188 / Fr 1230), a soul "Garrisoned . . . In the Front of Trouble" (J 1243 / Fr 1196). "To fight aloud, is very brave" but it is still *"gallanter"* to "charge within the bosom / The Cavalry of Wo" (J 126 / Fr 138). Or "My Wars are laid away in Books" (J 1549 / Fr 1579).

There are, however, poems that directly treat the Civil War in imagery and still others that are fully structured around it (as well as poems that may or may not be). For example, in one poem of equivocal consolation—"If any sink, assure that this, now standing -" (J 358 / Fr 616)—"the Worst" presumably gives way to some positive attainment or at least endurance, which, however, turns out to be death itself: "Dying - annuls the power to kill." The ultimate image of such "Dread" is "the Whizzing, before the [cannon] Ball." Then there are the elegies on specific war-dead. These include "It dont sound so terrible" (J 426 / Fr 384, probably); "It feels a shame to be alive" (J 444 / Fr 524); "He gave away his Life" (J 567 / Fr 530, probably); "Robbed by Death" (J 971 / Fr 838, probably); "Victory comes late" (J 690 / Fr 195). These are poems mainly in connection with the death of Frazar Stearns, the son of Amherst College's president. "When I was small, a Woman died" (J 596 / Fr 518) stands at least partly in memory of Francis H. Dickinson, the first of Amherst's war-dead (the poem may be a composite memorium). More general war memorials (as far as we know) are "Some we see no more" (J 1221 / Fr 1210), "My Portion is Defeat - today" (J 639 / Fr 704), "My Triumph lasted till the Drums" (J 1227 / Fr 1212). "My country need not change her gown" compares the present with the Revolutionary War (J 1511 / Fr 1540). Other poems no doubt remain to be detected; still other poems change in aspect once the context of war is admitted. Among these, notably, is "My Life had stood - a Loaded Gun," a poem that figures violence as firearms, and concludes with an ambiguous measuring of the power to kill against the power to die. There is also the wonderful and apparently early "Success is counted sweetest" (of course, martial language was already current right before the war) which carefully weighs gain against loss, deeply identifying with defeat in battle. Success itself becomes defined through its loss, to one

> defeated - dying -
> On whose forbidden ear
> The distant strains of triumph
> Burst agonized and clear! (J 67 / Fr 112)

The first striking feature of these war poems is the fundamental and commanding place they give to the problem of theodicy. Dickinson's war poems are persistently structured around the problem of justifying evil or suffering, or rather, of justifying a God who permits, at the very least, so much evil and suffering to pervade his world. The war seemed to her an agony of suffering and love. As she wrote to her Norcross cousins (cited above) announcing the death of Amherst's Frazar Stearns: "Let us love better, children, it's most that's left to do" (L 255, 1862). In her next letter to her Norcross cousins, she remarks: "I wish 'twas plainer, the anguish in this world. I wish one could be sure the suffering had a loving side" (L 263). In 1864, she writes the cousins again: "Sorrow seems to me more general than it did, and not the estate of a few persons, since the war began; and if the anguish of others helped with one's own, now would be many medicines (L 298).

Dickinson's war poems generally attempt to make out "the anguish in this world" and to decipher whether it has "a loving side." This would mean its fitting into some wider schema, some purpose that would justify the suffering, giving it place and hence significance. Yet in text after text, Dickinson marshals her own forces, ranging positive against negative, gain against loss, good against evil. In text after text, she assesses whether good triumphs over and justifies evil, whether gain outweighs loss, such that all find their place in a coherent, meaningful, and hence ultimately positive pattern which places and thus redeems the negative. And yet, in text after text, such measures do not come out. In, for example, "If any sink, assure that this, now standing" (J 358 / Fr 616), the apparently consoling terms prove, as we have seen, to be only death, as the cancellation rather than the redemption of dread. The answer to "Dread" as "the whizzing, before the ball" is nothing other than a death that "annuls the power to kill." In "Success is counted sweetest," the fullest appreciation of victory is granted to one denied it—an intensified negative rather than a positive claim. Dickinson's elegy for Francis Dickinson, "When I was small, a Woman died" (J 596 / Fr 518) imagines the mother's reunion with her son in "Paradise." Yet, while she has sympathy for the mother and admiration for the son, the conditions of heaven remain something the poet "cannot decide" and in uncertain relation to the all too certain "Scarlet Maryland." Other war poems focus on the accidental nature of winning or losing, dying or living. "He fought like those Who've nought to lose" (J 759 / Fr 480) portrays a soldier who, though courting death, is somehow denied it; while other soldiers, "Coy of Death," somehow suffer the "Doom" which eludes him. A paradigmatic "After Horror" is nevertheless represented through warfare, where uncertain death, or uncertainty in general, is figured as looking down a gun-barrel:

> Is like a Face of Steel -
> That suddenly looks into our's
> With a metallic grin -
> The Cordiality of Death -
> Who drills his Welcome in - (J 286 / Fr 243)

Far from fitting into an ordained and significant plan, war shows death to be arbitrary and recalcitrant.

Some texts give elaborate and immediate consideration to the challenges of war, to its meaning—or, dreadfully—its meaninglessness. "My Portion is Defeat - today -" (J 639 / Fr 704) vividly represents war's violence, in deeply felt distress and despair at consolation. Dated 1862, the poem was written during the long and disheartening years of Northern defeat in battle. For Dickinson, picturing herself walking among scraps of body—and, significantly, of "Prayer"—on the battlefield, the vision of "Victory" is something remote—"somewhat prouder, Over there -." This delusive image of victory only makes worse the pain of defeat. But Dickinson is equally disturbed and dissatisfied by victory when it is achieved. "My Triumph lasted till the Drums" progressively erases any consoling or atoning value to victory, in distress for the "finished Faces" (of either side?) it cost: "And then I hated Glory / And wished myself were They" (J 1227 / Fr 1212).

This poem very significantly then opens into a general meditation on patterns of time and perspectives that promise to place, integrate, and hence redeem chaotic moments:

> What is to be is best descried
> When it has also been -
> Could Prospect taste of Retrospect
> The Tyrannies of Men
> Were Tenderer, diviner
> The Transitive toward -
> A Bayonet's contrition
> Is nothing to the Dead - (J 1227 / Fr 1212)

In a pun on "diviner," Dickinson intersects foresight with Godhead, divining with divinity. Julia Ward Howe, in her "Battle Hymn of the Republic," claims to "have seen" the glory of God and to "read" a fiery gospel in the scenes of war she witnesses. Dickinson too seeks to descry, to witness current events as placed within a larger vision of time's whole, as in God's eternal perspective. This is in faith that the "Transitive" so seen becomes "Tenderer," that time's motion finds its pattern and hence meaning in a visionary and encompassing "Retrospect." Yet Dickinson eschews such a visionary grasp of the whole, remaining caught instead in a fragmentary present. And her ultimate image of repudiation is a "Bayonet," whose contrition offers "nothing" to the dead it neither redeems nor restores.

Dickinson's work brings to awareness the importance of

theodicy as a core literary (as well as philosophical and religious) structure, in, for example, Aeschylus, Augustine, and Milton, Herbert and Donne, or, closer to Dickinson, Melville and Hopkins. In Dickinson, the problem of theodicy is at once personal, historical, metaphysical, and textual. In Dickinson's war poetry, what emerges is the way the problem of suffering is at once most acutely personal and yet also broadly and fundamentally historical. The theodicean questions about suffering and its justification are surely Dickinson's private ones, but they are not private only. They belong to her wider community. Indeed, it is, oddly, just where poems are most personal in terms of Dickinson's suffering, that they are also most culturally engaged. For the problem of suffering is essentially the problem of history. This is expressly and centrally the case in Christian terms, whose metaphysics continued to frame Dickinson's own experience and understanding. In this model, earthly events find their place and their meaning in a providential history that is both comprehensive and redemptive. Each experience is thought to find its corollary, and hence its significant place in a meaningful order, eternally present to divine vision. This divine order was specifically revealed through biblical pattern, focused in the life of Christ. In Christ, and especially in his suffering, death, and resurrection, earthly travail gained its full significance and justification—justification exactly in its significant reference to Christ's own suffering as the path and means of redemption.

This biblical and providential vision, encoding events in nature, history, and the self in an overarching divine pattern, continued to be strongly felt in the habits of orthodox, antebellum Amherst. Here was Jonathan Edwards country, a land of religious revivals, where, as Dickinson puts it in one poetic reference to Edwards, a "Martial Hand" urges "Conscience" (J 1598 / Fr 1640).[9] For Dickinson, the problem of suffering remains deeply tied to the paradigms of her religious inheritance (with Thomas à Kempis's "Imitation of Christ" a favorite text). But this was no less the case for her broader cultural world and not only in conservative Amherst. Very generally and normatively, the Civil War itself was interpreted through religious reference directly and potently felt, indeed vigorously invoked. The war was widely seen in the North as enacting apocalyptic scenes of punishment and retribution, whereby the nation would be judged and cleansed of the sin of slavery.[10] The war witnessed incredible outbursts of organized missionary activity. It was the object of intense prayer in churches throughout the nation. As Dickinson wrote to Thomas Wentworth Higginson, then serving in the South as colonel to the first black regiment: "I trust you may pass the limit of War, and though not reared to prayer—when service is had in Church, for Our Arms, I include yourself" (L 280). The rhetoric of contest itself resonated with the language of holy war and religious drama. Dickinson's father put it thus in a published plea of 1855: "By the help of Almighty God, not another inch of our soil heretofore consecrated to freedom, shall hereafter be polluted by the advancing tread of slavery."[11] Even Lincoln, with his exquisite restraint, could speak on one of the many days of fasting and Thanksgiving, which made up a public religious ritual throughout the war, of Union victories as "the gracious gifts of the most high God, who, while dealing with us in anger for our sins, hath nevertheless remembered mercy."[12]

Although not all of the numerous references to war in Dickinson's letters and poems can be certainly and directly related to immediate historical events, there is a continuity between martial imagery in political and religious contexts that makes them impossible entirely to separate in her work. But the same is true for her historical world. Attempts to find redemptive responses to the most daunting, violent, historical events would have been, in Dickinson's context, completely current. It is more than a coincidental curiosity that Dickinson began writing intensively, and wrote over half of her poems, during the American Civil War. The Civil War reached levels of carnage before unknown, made possible both by new technology and new strategies of total warfare, in combination with a profound ideological challenge to American national claims and self-identity, political and religious.[13]

With regard to the latter, the war represents a crucial, although by no means unique, arena in which Dickinson enacted her ongoing and intensive religious anguish. Emily Dickinson's is very much a poetry of the religious imagination. Religion continues to be a fundamental paradigm through which she interpreted her world. This is not to claim that Dickinson is an orthodox religious poet. On the contrary, her work offers a forceful and original critique of traditional metaphysics in ways that recall her near contemporary Friedrich Nietzsche. Religion in many ways is a paradigm that fails Dickinson, and yet, she never completely discards it. If she is not devout, she is also not secular. Dickinson's work repeatedly rehearses her reasons for both asserting and denying a divine order, in constant countertension. In this sense, Dickinson's work does not take shape as a quest. Rather, it engages in endless disputation, which is endlessly inconclusive. There is a perpetual clash in which different positions challenge each other, with each one found ultimately wanting. In this disputation, religious questions confront religious answers, which do not, however, adequately resolve them. The result is a world that remains unsatisfactory without God, but equally unsatisfactory with the God of her fathers. In this light, readings of Dickinson as though she had comfortably settled into a post-Christian enlightenment, substituting art and the powers of her own mind for faith in divine orders and meanings, are both historically anachronistic and untrue to her verse. Historians underscore how religious institutions, hermeneutics, and sensibility continued forcefully to frame nineteenth-century life, especially the lives of women. As the century advanced, religious norms may have been boiling away, but they had by no means evaporated. Across America—in the North, and, differently, in the South—providential histories continued in strong, if also in transformed ways, marking not only American Romanticism with its demons of analogy but also the historical culture at large. The events of America continued to be understood as moments in a universal drama of redemption, even if such redemption was increasingly claimed for history rather than eternity. Dickinson's poems repeatedly operate within this framework and its promise of transcendent reference. In her terms, time should represent eternity; earthly experience, even or rather especially when involving loss and death, should find transfigured meaning within a structure of transcendence.

In certain moods, Dickinson's poems declare just such transfigurations, making hers a "Compound Vision . . . The Finite - furnished / With the Infinite. . . . Back - toward Time - / And forward - Toward the God of Him -" (J 906 / Fr 830). More often, however, Dickinson exhibits difficulties with her inherited metaphysical system, which prevent her from enjoying its promises. Readings of Dickinson that see her poetry as converting limitation to infinity, pain to joy, suffering to redemption, and death to poetic immortality replicate and transfer fundamentally Christian structures to the realm of art. But these basic structures of conversion, whether in religion or in art, appear to her to be faulty. In this regard, the claim that Dickinson freed herself from Christian orthodoxy while transposing many of its most constitutive structures into aesthetic experience and activity remains very problematic. On the contrary, Dickinson's work exactly explores just how problematic such transpositions can be. She questions to what extent art can indeed serve as figure for faith and, conversely, exposes how religious assumptions persist even beyond specific dogmas, to continue to exert pressure on both social and aesthetic ideologies. Her poetry repeatedly and painfully attests to misgivings that prevent her from reading her world as signs for any redemptive meaning whatsoever. It traces her resistance to making experiences types for each other in a chain of transferred meanings that point ultimately to some redemptive realm. This does not, however, make transcendent meaning dispensable. In text after text, she returns again to religious premises and promises; again finding them wanting; again finding them necessary.

Dickinson thus shares with her wider culture the imperative to make sense of suffering, disorder, disruption, through reference to coherent, overarching, redemptive patterns. The war focused her pressing need for interpretive transfiguration, in order to put together a world that was breaking apart—quite literally, in the American sectional strife and ideological warfare. And yet the war also pressingly and gravely ruptured the very paradigms needed for such justification. Dickinson in one letter presents her war effort as a poetic one, in contrast to the extensive and activist provisioning of soldiers most women engaged in: "I shall have no winter this year—on account of the soldiers—Since I cannot

weave Blankets, or Boots—I thought it best to omit the season—
Shall present a 'Memorial' to God—when the Maples turn"
(L 235). Instead of blankets and boots, she offers poems. But
Dickinson's poetic "Memorial" remains deeply equivocal. In this,
Dickinson remains a rare case among her contemporaries
in withstanding the impulse to defend and explicate suffering
in terms that claimed for it metaphysical justification and redemptive value. Only Melville seems comparable, and even he,
in "Battle Pieces," seems (slightly) more palliative, on the political grounds of the evil of slavery and the good of the Union.[14]
(Whitman's case is multiply complex, with brave affirmation offered across stark qualms.) Dickinson, in fact, is rarely political in
the sense of engaging directly in issues of public policy.

Yet there is another sense in which Dickinson's war writing
engages with the political, and that is in the sense of the polis—
of public space and the life of the community within it. War is
proposed not only as a historical-metaphysical problem—where
metaphysics and history intersect—but also as a problem of selfhood, of the place of the self in the culture and community
which surrounds it. For, as Sacvan Bercovitch has shown, it is in
the life of the community that historical experience as providential pattern unfolds.[15] This was explicitly and dramatically the
case for the original Puritan settlers, who conceived themselves
as a federal people in covenant to God, whose fulfillment (and
chastisement) would be directly revealed and experienced in the
course of a divinely ordained providential history. This American
habit of regarding itself as a chosen nation, a beacon on the hill,
whose historical events resound with cosmic and divinely ordained significance, evolved through the Colonial and Revolutionary periods, into the nineteenth century. It then emerged
with a vengeance in the ideologies, and the rhetoric, preceding
and exploding in the Civil War. The course of the community, its
ultimate test and ultimate vindication, comes through as a history deeply imbued with transformed religious significance.

Dickinson is acutely conscious of this public and communal-
historical dimension. And, as with religion and religious histories, she is deeply disturbed and conflicted regarding it. For in
war, not only the status of the community and its historical

course is ultimately tested, but also the status and claims of the
individual self are equally so tested. In war, above all, the self is
called upon to place life second to, or in service of, community,
in the name of a greater purpose. War is above all the time when
community commands and supersedes the self, for and within
larger historical ends. At issue are not only the claims of the community but also the definitions of selfhood itself. These topics are
engaged in one of Dickinson's specific war elegies, "It feels a
shame to be Alive - / When Men so brave - are dead," written for
Frazar Stearns, who had himself written to his father, Amherst
College's president: "How can you terrify one who can look
death in the face and has made up his mind that his life is his
country's and expects it at any time? If I can serve my country
better by dying now than living I am ready to do it."[16]

> The Stone - that tells defending Whom
> This Spartan put away
> What little of Him we - possessed
> In Pawn for Liberty
>
> The price is great - Sublimely paid -
> Do we deserve - a Thing -
> That lives - like Dollars - must be piled
> Before we may obtain?
>
> Are we that wait - sufficient worth -
> That such Enormous Pearl
> As life - dissolved be - for Us -
> In Battle's - horrid Bowl?
>
> It may be - a Renown to live -
> I think the Men who die -
> Those unsustained - Saviors -
> Present Divinity - (J 444 / Fr 524)

On the one hand, Dickinson pays great tribute to individual
value and sacrifice. On the other, there is great tension between
the self and the community for whom self-sacrifice is made.
These variant senses of the self, and its very definition, emerge as

contested, complex, under scrutiny. The soldiers themselves are honored and even exalted, as "unsustained - Saviors" who "Present," and in whom is made present, divinity in this world. Yet the soldier stands in strained relation to the community for whom his sacrifice has been made. The structure of justification is again invoked and again refused. "It feels a shame to be Alive," the poem opens, "When Men so brave - are dead." And it then asks: "Are we that wait - sufficient worth." It is noteworthy that Dickinson here brings herself in, at least as a member of the community at war. And, despite women's removal from direct participation in warfare, she efffectively combines the domestic world with the public conflict in the striking image of "Battle's - horrid Bowl."[17]

Noteworthy as well is the measure of value in units of money—the importance of economic and indeed monetary terms. Such economic imagery is surprisingly pervasive in Dickinson. Here it is elaborate. The soldier is a "Pawn for Liberty," where pawn is both a sacrificial piece in a chess game and a property ceded but not yet sold. His sacrifice is a "price" that is "Sublimely paid." More abrasively, the men's lives are likened to "Dollars" in piles (a macabre reference to the piles of dead and wounded in the newly circulating war-photographs?). Dickinson here engages the emerging ascendancy and power of money in defining value and the self in America.

This overlay of economy, theodicy, and war is prominent in other war poems. "He gave away his Life" describes the sacrifice of self in war as "Gigantic Sum." This poem again concludes with a tribute to heroism and the infinite value of the transfigured individual (J 567/ Fr 530). The community, however, is in a compromised position: "Tis Our's - to wince - and weep - / And wonder - and decay." "Victory comes late" is less generous still. In this poem, even if victory is achieved or granted, it comes too late for the dead who suffered for it. One of Dickinson's few poems in free verse, the text is an outcry for those dead, without consolation from whatever the community has gained. Above all, it is an indictment of the divine, whose penury refuses the grace and love, care and charity inherent in the very notion of divinity:

Was God so economical?
His Table's spread too high for Us -
Unless We dine on Tiptoe -
Crumbs - fit such little mouths -
Cherries - suit Robins -
The Eagle's Golden Breakfast strangles - Them -
God keep His Oath to Sparrows -
Who of little Love - know how to starve - (J 690 / Fr 195)

Victory, rather than enclosing the event of suffering in its re-
deeming pattern, remains disjoined from the experience of sacrifice. Instead of serving as a sign of divine intention and intervention, it stands as a sign of divine denial, not only of his creatures
but also of his own promised nature: a God of parsimony rather
than of constant providence, who betrays, rather than rescuing, a
sparrow in its fall. The bird emblems here are suggestive. The
robin Dickinson had associated with herself as seeing "New
Englandly" (J 285 / Fr 256). Here, it is excluded from the divine,
communion table, while the Eagle—perhaps the American
emblem?—who is apparently served is instead strangled. Providence becomes perverse economy.

Economic language was, to be sure, part and parcel of the
rhetoric of American religion since its Puritan foundings. Dickinson registers this in many poems, where God appears as "Burglar!
Banker" (J 49 / Fr 39); as "Mighty Merchant" (J 621 / Fr 687) and
Swindler (J 476 / Fr 711); as "Exchequer" (J 1270 / Fr 1260) and
"Auctioneer of Parting" (J 1612 / Fr 1646). "Paradise" is an "Op-
tion" one can "Own in Eden" (J 1069 / Fr 1125). The language of
covenant and the notion of heavenly reward serve to represent
spiritual matters in human language and human terms. But as
Dickinson's work almost mercilessly exploits, analogies are dis-
concertingly unstable and can ultimately be converted in either
direction, toward either term of comparison. Money may be an
image of divine things, but divine things may conversely be reduced to money.

Money also, with accelerating power, is coming in Dickinson's
century to define the individual as well—as Thoreau, for example,
laments long in *Walden*. "Pawn for Liberty," Dickinson writes

with complex punning (J 444 / Fr 524). The soldier-self as sacrifice for liberty is the Union's ideology. But liberty also—as is quite explicit in the original Lockean formula that underwrote Jefferson's *Declaration*—means possessions. The liberal contract in Locke's terms pledged itself to uphold life, liberty, and property—which is to say liberty as property. Jefferson opened this Lockean term to a more multiply constituted "pursuit of happiness"; but liberty itself retains a basic sense of the individual's right to what he owns against tyrannical attempts to take it from him without his consent, with the self itself a kind of property, proper to itself, determined by the self.[18] (Here it is necessary to remark that the gender is purposely male. Women were not accorded such liberal rights to property or the individuality it constituted, but rather were incorporated into the property of the male individual.)[19] Here further tensions emerge within the liberal polity. The self thus self-determined stands in strained relation with the community constituted by it precisely in order to protect and uphold just such individual rights and liberties. For absolute assertion of individual interests against any communal commitment would lead to endless centripetal forces unto dissolution. This, of course, is exactly the issue which exploded as civil war—with the South and North each claiming "liberty." In the Southern case, liberty is each individual state's right to secede against the tyranny of centralized power, but in the second, Northern case, liberty is the right to self-determination for each individual, which slavery was increasingly felt to betray.[20] That defense of this Northern claim nevertheless necessitated constraining individuals to a common cause was acutely grasped by Lincoln. In a Special Session of Congress, in 1861, he spoke:

> And this issue embraces more than the fate of these United States. It presents to the whole family of man, the question, whether a constitutional republic, or a democracy—a government of the people, by the same people—can, or cannot, maintain its territorial integrity, against its own domestic foes. It presents the question, whether discontented individuals, too few in numbers to control administration, according to organic law, in any case, can always . . . break up their Gov-

ernment, and thus practically put an end to free government upon the earth. It forces us to ask: "Is there in all republics, this inherent, and fatal weakness?" "Must a government, of necessity, be too strong for the liberties of its own people, or too weak to maintain its own existence?"[21]

Can government maintain or grant such liberty to the individual as to fulfill its promise of self-government, yet not thereby dissolve into fractured chaos? Can the pull to each self be prevented from becoming a mere pulling apart of the community? This, of course, is a core question of the Gettysburg Address, where Lincoln asks whether a nation "conceived in liberty . . . can long endure."

Emily Dickinson's poetry, like the Civil War itself, can be said to show the strains of these potent, intimate, and conflicting impulses and claims of American cultural life. The poem "Robbed by Death" describes dying in war as being "Robbed by Liberty / For her Jugular Defences" (J 971 / Fr 838).[22] Here the curious, if subtle use of a legal and economic term—robbery—verges into oxymoron: liberty quintessentially involves the protection from being robbed, the assertion of self-possession and its rights at the heart of individualism. (One more often thinks of being robbed *of*, not *by*, liberty). It is as if Americans' basic premises are consuming themselves, shown to be at odds within or between poems. "I'm ceded - I've stopped being Their's - " (J 508 / Fr 353) turns on a political pun, asserting selfhood radically against the authority of society. In the language of secession, the poet claims the right of withdrawal and independence from normative social-religious claims. In this defiant and solitary selfhood, she takes possession of a "Crown" of Queenship as self-sovereignty. Yet absolute selfhood can also leave the self isolated and frozen. In another poem with reference to war, "The Soul has Bandaged moments," the soul is wounded (J 512 / Fr 360). Its movement toward some complete "Liberty" of "escape" is fraught with danger, when the soul "dances like a Bomb," only to plunge back into "Horror."

The Civil War thus emerges as stage, motive, and image for Dickinson's deeply conflicted relationships to her cultural world, in religious, historical, as well as personal senses of the self. The consequences for her art and its language are momentous and profound. One poem very curiously stakes out these connections.

> Step lightly on this narrow Spot -
> The Broadest Land that grows
> Is not so ample as the Breast
> These Emerald Seams enclose.
>
> Step lofty, for this name be told
> As far as cannon dwell,
> Or Flag subsist, or Fame export
> Her deathless Syllable (J 1183 / Fr 1227)

In this poem of homage to the war-dead, what is absent defines and dwarfs what is present. The "narrow" grave is ampler than the "broadest Land," which however takes shape through it. The hero's sacrificial death, in turn, is significantly made into a trope for poetry itself. The image of "Seams" which enclose the hero's burial place recalls Dickinson's own sewn fascicles. And this death, like poetry and art, bestows a "name" that is lofty and immortal. "Cannon," "Flag," and "Fame" become mutual reflections, all gathered into the final enduring image of poetics itself as "deathless Syllable."

This poem offers a number of arresting alignments. The self is, on the one hand, invested with great significance. Yet this significance is tied to, and measured by, its relation to others and the sacrifices made for them. The value of the self emerges not simply in itself but in terms of others. Dickinson here situates herself at the very clash of contending impulses. Her self, on the one hand, remains independent, even defiant, of society's claims, with a courage of judgment that is unwavering. On the other hand, she is also skeptical of selves that are invested only in themselves, without reference, or devotion, to anything beyond the self. She is critical, that is, of both social authority and also of absolute selfhood. This contention ultimately informs her sense of her own vocation, of poetry and of herself as poet, as can be seen in one text with arresting conjunctions with her war poetry:

> The Martyr Poets - did not tell -
> But wrought their Pang in syllable -
> That when their mortal name be numb -
> Their mortal fate - encourage Some -
>
> The Martyr Painters - never spoke -
> Bequeathing - rather - to their Work -
> That when their conscious fingers cease -
> Some seek in Art - the Art of Peace - (J 544 / Fr 665)

The poet here, like the heroes in many Dickinson war-elegies, is a sacrificial figure. As in many war poems, the self is at once granted enormous value, and yet a value that emerges in self-effacement—indeed, in martyrdom, as witness to others at the cost of the self. Here Dickinson verges toward gendered senses of selfhood as self-denial. Indeed, the self in this poem is deeply strained, as is the poem's poetic, stretching tensely between declaring and denying its own poetic venture. Here are poets who do not tell, painters who do not speak. The self is at once affirmed and negated, with a painfully high cost to the self in both its assertion and renunciation—a strain Dickinson dramatically enacted in her own refusals to publish, even while circulating and preserving her poems in letters and fascicles.[23] There is a terrible burden in these denials, a severe disjunction from the audience the poem yearningly addresses. Yet, for all Dickinson's solitude and self-veiling, the poem is placed resolutely in a place of exchange, addressing and bequeathing to others. Even the immortality of poetic fame remains grounded in the limited mortal self, in an art undertaken in service to others: to "encourage Some," to bequeath "their Work."

This poem does not speak of war but rather of peace, which emerges as a strange trope for or strangely implicating art. It seems a kind of space standing beyond the turmoil of the historical world, yet also in close relation to it.[24] As an "Art of Peace," poetry does not escape suffering but rather renders it "in syllable." Here a certain relation between art and war, between language and rupture, becomes suggested. At issue is the strained and extraordinarily disrupted textuality of Dickinson's poetry, which, as in "The Martyr Poets," so often stretches between utterance and revocation, assertion and denial, claim and disclaimer, in ways that penetrate every poetic element and indeed basic linguistic structure such as grammar and punctuation. These textual ruptures, I would venture, suggest a final implication of Dickinson's war poetry. Many have been struck by Dickinson's apparent modernity; by how her strained and difficult forms—at once contained within and yet strenuously recasting hymnal meters and modes—seem to foreshadow the radical experimentation of twentieth-century poetics.[25] This homology seems to me rooted in the ways Dickinson's work represents an intersection between historical, metaphysical, and aesthetic forces when these are under extraordinary pressure, and specifically, when long-standing, traditional assumptions regarding the basic frameworks for interpreting the world are challenged to the point of breakage. Dickinson's work is among the first directly to register the effects on poetic language of such breakdown. Articulate language depends on, even as it expresses and projects, the ability to conceive reality as coherent and meaningful. Dickinson, like Nietzsche and increasing numbers of poets and writers from the late nineteenth into the twentieth century, makes this power of language to assert order, and this vulnerability to disorder, central to her aesthetic. As one critic writes of Gerard Manley Hopkins, when reality and paradigms for interpreting it seem secure, "language need not carry a very heavy burden. The greater encompassing harmony is preestablished, as it were. Call this harmony into question . . . and the burden on language immediately becomes greater. It has to exert itself to hold things together."[26] Such "splitting apart of the communion" between paradigm and world, metaphysics and history, marks modern experience.[27] It deeply penetrates Emily Dickinson's poetic language, where disjunction penetrates grammar and line, word and image, often setting each against the other in strained and contested utterance. The breaking apart of metaphysical confidence and model, as interpretive framework for explosive historical events, and in conditions of radically changing senses of society and self: all these come together in the exquisite, painful, and proleptic register of Dickinson's language and poetics.

This certainly was the impression of one of the twentieth century's most radical experimental poets, Paul Celan. Celan, a Jewish, German-speaking Holocaust poet, is removed from Dickinson in place, religion, gender, and historical moment. Nevertheless, he deeply recognized himself in her, as attested by his translations of her work. His renderings propose and disclose the mutual implication and dependence of metaphysical, historical, and linguistic experience projected in her writing. For Dickinson, the Civil War raised problems not unlike those Theodor Adorno ascribes to the Second World War: "Our metaphysical faculty is paralyzed because actual events have shattered the basis on which speculative metaphysical thought could be reconciled with experience."[28] What Dickinson's work reveals and dramatizes are the consequences of such paralysis and assault on the very structure and language of poetry.

Emily Dickinson's texts are battlefields between contesting claims of self and community, private and public interest, event and design, metaphysics and history, with each asserted, often against the other. The contest finally penetrates the very construction of her poems, in their contentious image systems, their ambivalent and conflicting stances, their complicating grammar, and strained, often disjunctive language. And it penetrates into her sense of herself as poet, her role and vocation, and the very possibility of expression. Sequestered in her home, refusing to publish, bounded by gender roles that conventionally forbade her a direct representative or public position (although also under contest during her period), Dickinson nevertheless not only explores her world in her work but also addresses it. Dickinson's poems of war are never poems only about a specific historical event. They always reach into figural spaces beyond any immediate referent. At the same time, to deny them historical reference is to deny them, and to deny her, that representative status of speaking to and for others in a mere poetic of isolation. In the context of war, her poetry emerges as scenes not only of personal conflict but also confronting the most imperative concerns of her—and our—culture, in a poetics of contest and strain and concealment, but also of address and courage and revelation.

NOTES

Dickinson's poems are quoted from *The Poems of Emily Dickinson: Variorum Edition*, ed. R. W. Franklin, 3 vols. (Cambridge, Mass.: Harvard University Press, 1998). I also supply their Johnson numbers from *The Poems of Emily Dickinson, Including Variant Readings Critically Compared with All Known Manuscripts*, ed. Thomas H. Johnson (Cambridge, Mass.: Harvard University Press, 1955). Subsequent references are cited as (J) and (Fr) in the text.

Dickinson's letters are quoted from *The Letters of Emily Dickinson*, ed. Thomas H. Johnson and Theodora Ward, 3 vols. (Cambridge, Mass.: Harvard University Press, 1958). Subsequent references are cited as (L) in the text.

1. Emerson, "The Poet," in *Selections from Ralph Waldo Emerson*, ed. Stephen Whicher (New York: Riverside, 1957), 222–40, 223.

2. For discussion of Tocqueville's image and an overview of the separate spheres, see Linda Kerber, "Separate Spheres, Female Worlds, Woman's Place: The Rhetoric of Women's History," *Journal of American History* 75, no. 1 (June 1988): 9–39.

3. Harold Bloom, "The Central Man: Emerson, Whitman, Stevens," *The Ringers in the Tower* (Chicago: University of Chicago Press, 1971), 217–34. Bloom, of course, is quite conscious of the gender-implications of central manhood, and purposively includes Dickinson in the category.

4. I review these and other historical connections more fully in *Emily Dickinson: A Voice of War* (New Haven: Yale University Press, 1984).

5. For fuller discussion, see Wolosky, "Public Women, Private Men," *Signs* 28, no. 2 (Winter 2003): 665–94.

6. See, for example, Vivian Pollak, "Dickinson and the Poetics of Whiteness," *The Emily Dickinson Journal* 9, no. 2 (2000): 84–95; Daneen Wardrop, "'That Minute Domingo': Dickinson's Cooptation of Abolitionist Diction and Franklin's Variorum Edition," *The Emily Dickinson Journal* 8, no. 2 (1999): 72–86; Domhnall Mitchell, "Northern Lights: Class, Color, Culture, and Emily Dickinson," *The*

Emily Dickinson Journal 9, no. 2 (2000): 75–84. See also below note 22 on Cristanne Miller.

7. See Wolosky, *Poetry and Public Discourse*, vol. 4 of *The Cambridge History of American Literature*, ed. Sacvan Bercovitch (New York: Cambridge University Press, forthcoming).

8. This is in contrast with, for example, Thomas Ford's early, and for long unique, article on "Emily Dickinson and the Civil War," *University Review of Kansas City* 31 (Spring 1965), which estimates four poems as directly deriving from the war (199).

9. Cf. Letter 712, in (L 3:701).

10. For one treatment, see Ernest Lee Tuveson, *Redeemer Nation* (Chicago: University of Chicago Press, 1968).

11. Jay Leyda, *The Years and Hours of Emily Dickinson*, 2 vols. (New Haven: Yale University Press, 1960), 1:333.

12. "Proclamation for Thanksgiving, Oct. 3, 1863," *Selected Writings and Speeches of Abraham Lincoln*, ed. T. Harry Williams (New York: Hendricks House, 1980), 228.

13. George Fredrickson, *The Inner Civil War* (New York: Harper Torchbooks, 1968), 79–80.

14. Dickinson here stands in contrast with, for example, Timrod and Lanier, James Russell Lowell and Longfellow, Julia Ward Howe and Helen Hunt Jackson, as well as the countless versifiers collected in *The Rebellion Record* or, more recently, in Alice Fahs, *The Imagined Civil War: Popular Literature of the North and South, 1861–1865* (Chapel Hill: University of North Carolina Press, 2001). Whitman reserves his skepticisms mainly for the postwar period.

15. Sacvan Bercovitch, *Puritan Origins of the American Self* (New Haven: Yale University Press, 1975), as well as his subsequent works: *The American Jeremiad* (Madison: University of Wisconsin Press, 1978) and *The Rites of Assent* (New York: Routledge, 1993).

16. Quoted in Polly Longsworth, "Brave among the Bravest: Amherst in the Civil War," *Amherst Journal* (Summer 1999): 25–31, 28.

17. See Margaret Randolph Higonnet, ed., *Behind the Lines: Gender and the Two World Wars* (New Haven: Yale University Press, 1987), for discussion of the effects and complexities of women as (seen as) removed from battle.

18. C. P. Macpherson, *The Political Theory of Possessive Individualism* (London: Oxford University Press, 1962).

19. An enormous literature exists in political theory on this topic. See especially, works by Carole Pateman and Susan Moller Okin. Also Wolosky, "Public Women, Private Men," in note 5 above.

20. See Wolosky, "North and South," in note 7 above. James McPherson's *Battle Cry of Freedom* (New York: Oxford University Press, 1988) makes the differing senses of this crucial term a broad context for discussing the war.

21. Abraham Lincoln, *The Political Thought of Abraham Lincoln*, ed. Richard Current (Indianapolis: Bobbs-Merrill, 1967), 181.

22. This poem is elaborated in Cristanne Miller's thoughtful discussion on the term "liberty" in Dickinson and her surrounding culture, "Pondering 'Liberty': Emily Dickinson and the Civil War," *American Vistas and Beyond: A Festschrift for Roland Hagenbüchle*, ed. Marietta Messmer and Josef Raab (Trier, Germany: Wissenschaftlicher Verlag, 2002).

23. In my own view, Dickinson, on the one hand, dreaded publication as an exposure that both her gender roles and her personal sensibility prohibited (and lacking, as mentioned above, both the economic reasons that motivated or allowed publishing by other women, as well as other such contexts, such as religious calling or political activism). On the other hand, I believe Dickinson believed in her gift as a poet, that she imagined her sister finding her carefully preserved texts as well as their eventual publication through the coterie she had created among highly literary correspondents such as Thomas Wentworth Higginson, as indeed occurred. Her deadline was not publication but immortality. Again, one recalls Whitman with his ventriloquist addresses to his future readers. Dickinson's relationship to audience is, I feel, deeply inscribed in her acts of writing, her self-conception as a poet and woman poet, the way her texts are constituted, even without her directly addressing an immediate concrete audience through publication.

24. There are, in fact, scattered references in Dickinson to "peace" in ways that seem to oppose it to war, as in the poem "I many times thought Peace had come" (J 739 / Fr 737), dated 1863.

25. On hymns, see Wolosky, "Rhetoric or Not: Emily Dickinson and Isaac Watts," *The New England Quarterly* 61, no. 2 (June 1988): 214–32; and Cristanne Miller, *Emily Dickinson: A Poet's Grammar* (Cambridge, Mass.: Harvard University Press, 1988).

26. Sigurd Burkhardt, "Poetry and the Language of Commu-

nion," in *Hopkins: Twentieth Century Views*, ed. Geoffrey Hartman (Englewood Cliffs, N.J.: Prentice Hall, 1966), 163.

27. J. Hillis Miller, *The Disappearance of God* (Cambridge, Mass.: Harvard University Press, 1963), 3.

28. T. W. Adorno, *Negative Dialectics* (London: Routledge & Kegan Paul, 1973), 361. I have discussed Dickinson and Celan in my unpublished dissertation, devoted to his translations of her work (Princeton University, 1982). See also Wolosky, *Language Mysticism* (Stanford: Stanford University Press, 1995); Wolosky, "Apophatics and Poetics: Paul Celan Translating Emily Dickinson," in *Language and Negativity*, ed. Henny Fiska Hagg (Oslo: Novus Press, 2000), 63–84; and Wolosky, "The Metaphysics of Language in Emily Dickinson (as Translated by Paul Celan)," in *Trajectories of Mysticism in Theory and Literature*, ed. Philip Leonard (New York: St. Martin's Press, 2000), 25–45.

Dickinson and the Art of Politics

Betsy Erkkila

Has the Mexican War terminated yet
& how? Are we beat? Do you know of
any nation about to besiege South
Hadley?
—Emily Dickinson to Austin
Dickinson, 1847

"George Washington was the Father of
his Country"—"George Who?" That
sums all Politics to me.
—Emily Dickinson to Elizabeth
Holland, 1884

In February and March 1855, Emily Dickinson and her sister Lavinia made a three-week visit to Washington, D.C., where their father, Edward Dickinson, was completing his second year as a Whig representative in the national Congress. At the time of their visit, the political "Union" was in a state of crisis, as the linked issues of race, class, gender, capital, technology, territorial expansion, and war exposed major contradictions in the ideology of the American republic. Anxious to save the Union by placating the South, Dickinson's father, like his hero Daniel Webster, had accepted the terms of the Compromise of 1850 and a more rigorous Fugitive Slave Law, which made it possible for free blacks to be captured in the North and returned to the South as slaves.

During his first year in Congress in 1854, Edward Dickinson voted with other antislavery Whigs to oppose the Kansas-Nebraska bill, which repealed the Missouri Compromise of 1820 and opened the western territories to slavery. Approved by Congress and signed into law by Democratic President Franklin Pierce in 1854, the Kansas-Nebraska bill led to a state of guerilla warfare in "Bleeding Kansas," the demise of the Whig Party, the rise of the Republican Party, and the heightened hostility between North and South that led to the Civil War.

Immediately following the passage of the Kansas-Nebraska bill, some thirty members of Congress met in the rooms of Edward Dickinson and Thomas Eliot of Massachusetts to discuss the formation of a new antislavery party that would be called the "Republican Party." But while other political representatives from Massachusetts, including most notably Charles Sumner, joined the new Republican Party that would lead to the election of Abraham Lincoln as the first Republican president in 1860, Edward Dickinson remained loyal to what he called "the true Republicanism" of the Whig Party, which had been formed in 1833–1834 to oppose Jacksonian tyranny in the name of the revolutionary ideals of republican self-government, political liberty, and public virtue.[1] When Edward left Washington, D.C., after the visit of Emily and Lavinia in 1855, his career in national politics was, in effect, over. Although he ran again as a Whig representative to Congress in 1854 and 1855, he was "swept . . . from the public scene" by "untried, unknown men," who were elected as representatives of the newly formed anti-Catholic Know-Nothing Party.[2] Over the next few years, the Whig Party would dissolve, and Dickinson would not return to public political office until 1873, when he was elected to the General Court of Massachusetts shortly before his death in 1874.

At Washington's Tomb

I begin with this detailed description of the state of the Union on the occasion of Emily Dickinson's visit to Washington, D.C., because I want to locate her work as a letter writer and poet as fully as possible within the political and social struggles that marked her time. What Dickinson most remembered about her trip to the national capital was her visit to the tomb of George Washington at Mount Vernon. Dickinson described her visit in a letter sent to Elizabeth Holland from Philadelphia, where she and Lavinia stayed for another two weeks after leaving Washington:

> I will not tell you what I saw—the elegance, the grandeur; you will not care to know the value of the diamonds my Lord and Lady wore, but if you haven't been to the sweet Mount Vernon, then I *will* tell you how on one soft spring day we glided down the Potomac in a painted boat, and jumped upon the shore—and how hand in hand we stole up a tangled pathway till we reached the tomb of General George Washington, how we paused beside it, and no one spoke a word, then hand in hand, walked on again, not less wise or sad for that marble story; how we went within the door—raised the latch he lifted when he last went home—thank the Ones in Light that he's since passed in through a brighter wicket! Oh, I could spend a long day, if it did not weary you, telling of Mount Vernon. (March 18, 1855; L 2:319)

Setting the merely material "elegance" and "grandeur" of the new economic order of money and show—signified by "the value of the diamonds my Lord and Lady wore"—against the heroic and apotheosized figure of Washington, Dickinson's idyllic and seemingly otherworldly account is a version of national pastoral. Her evocation of the "wise" and "sad" affect of Washington's "marble story" suggests the political role that the cult of Washington came to play for an elite class of disempowered Federalists and conservative Whigs, who believed that their authority, status, and power were being eroded by the new forces of democracy, party, self-interest, money, vulgarity, and demagoguery. For Dickinson, as for her paternal grandfather, Samuel Fowler, who also apotheosized a still living Washington in a fourth of July oration delivered in 1797, Washington embodied the "enlightened views and virtuous sentiments" of an elite class that Madison envisioned as the proper rulers and representatives of the people in Federalist # 10.[3] What Dickinson finds in Washington's "marble story" is the image of an older Federalist order of military heroism, virtuous republicanism, patriotic self-sacrifice, and sovereign authority—above party and faction, above "politics" as Washington had insisted in his "Farewell Address"—that was passing away amid the modernizing, democratizing, and politically diversifying forces of the time.

Like Edward's determination to remain true to the republican principles of the Whig Party amid the political confusion and "fusion" surrounding the national crisis over slavery, Dickinson's turn to the "marble story" of Washington is not an escape from politics. Rather, it is a conservative republican critique of democratic history that seeks, like Washington himself, to rise above the increasingly fractious, intrusive, and noisy politics of democracy that had come to dominate public space during the Age of Jackson. Standing reverently "hand in hand" with Lavinia before "the tomb of General George Washington" at "sweet Mount Vernon," Dickinson presents herself in the guise of a pastoral elegist, whose own "wise" and "sad" letters and poems would continue to mourn the death and entombment of a whole way of elite country life that passed away during her lifetime, between the year of Dickinson's birth in rural Amherst in 1830, through her years of greatest literary productivity during the massive carnage and death of the Civil War ("[I] sing off charnel steps," she said), to the year of her death in 1886, when even progressive thinkers were beginning to wonder if the course of American empire was not downward rather than westward or forward.

Later, in another letter to Elizabeth Holland, written during the abusive and scandalmongering presidential campaign of 1884, which resulted in the election of Grover Cleveland and the return of the Democrats to power after twenty-four years of Republican rule, Dickinson once again invoked Washington and the revolutionary heritage as a means of setting herself apart from the "Politics" of the time:

Before I write to you again, we shall have had a new
Czar—Is the Sister a Patriot?

"George Washington was the Father of his Country"—
"George Who?"

That sums all Politics to me—(L 3:849)

Although Dickinson's words have been read as a further expression of her indifference to the political culture of her time, they
might be read as a declaration of republican solidarity—"Is the
Sister a Patriot?"—amid the tawdry money-driven and boss-dom-
inated "Politics" of the Gilded Age, when violence and assassination had become the primary means of resolving political differences, and neither the politicians nor the democratic masses
appeared to remember who George Washington was. "George
Who?"

Against the traditional view of Dickinson as an essentially
"private" and isolated poet, who transcended the history and
politics of her time, I want to argue that along with John and
Abigail Adams, Dickinson was a witty and articulate spokes-
person for an essentially conservative tradition, a late Federalist
state of mind and sensibility, which passed out of favor with the
democratic "Revolution" of 1800, when Jefferson was elected
president and which has not been legible within the primarily
textual and/or national democratic frames of American literary
studies.[4] The full force of Dickinson's political wit and conser-
vatism is evident in a poem that she sent to Austin about 1862
regarding an encounter that he had with Ithamar Francis Conkey,
an Amherst lawyer and local leader who opposed the conservative Whig politics of the Dickinson family. "Father said Frank
Conkey—touched you—," Dickinson writes, comparing whatever confrontation Austin had with Conkey to being "clawed" by
"a Burdock" or splashed by a *"Bog"*:

> A *Bog* - affronts my shoe -
> What *else* have Bogs - to do -
> The only trade they *know* -
> The *splashing Men!*
> Ah, *pity - then!*

'Tis *Minnows* can despise!
The *Elephant's* - calm eyes
Look *further on!* (Fr 289A)

Dickinson's poem nicely encapsulates the historical struggle between an older elite order of New England Whigs and the advancing forces of democratic and republican liberalization that
marked the nineteenth century. Presenting the liberal views of
the opposition as a coarse weed, "a Burdock" that "clawed" her
"Gown" because she "went too near," Dickinson's high-class
speaker cautions Austin not to deign to engage Conkey's "af-
front." Whereas the speaker appears to stand for republican
virtue and principle, the opposition is a mere "Bog" that only
knows the "trade" of besmirching the settled authority of real
Men. It is only inferior beings—*Minnows*—who engage in passionate displays of public spleen. True republicans, Dickinson
concludes, in an uncanny anticipation of the political symbolism
adopted by the Republican Party in the 1870s, are like *Elephants*:
Standing above the lowly *Burdocks* and *Bogs* in their path, they
take the high road and "Look *further on!*"

House Politics

As "A Burdock - clawed my Gown -" suggests, Dickinson lived in
a political house. Some of the most powerful political figures of
the time not only visited but also spent the night at the Dickinson house, including Massachusetts Governor George N. Briggs
and Otis P. Lord, who served in the Massachusetts legislature and
Senate in the 1840s and 1850s and later in the Superior Court and
the Supreme Court of Massachusetts. In 1857, after delivering lectures in Amherst, Ralph Waldo Emerson and Wendell Phillips
were also "royal guests" at the house of Austin and Susan Dickinson, who lived next door.[5]

Like Dickinson's grandfather, Samuel Fowler Dickinson, who
was forced to move to Ohio in 1833 after losing the family house
and fortune by overcommitting his money and energy to founding Amherst College and other public projects, Edward Dickin-

son was "An Old-School-Gentleman-Whig," who believed in the civic humanist ideal of public service for the common good. Writing in support of Dickinson as the Whig candidate to the national legislature in 1852, who would best serve "the great interests of the Connecticut Valley," an editorial in *The Hampshire and Franklin Express* described him as "A true whig in every sense of the word . . . ever ready to sacrifice personal preference to the good of principle. . . . The great industrial interests of the country at large, Agriculture, Manufactures, Commerce, will find in him a staunch supporter. . . . Always a firm friend of temperance, ever first in sustaining the true principles of law and order, he always looks toward the right, and with indomitable perseverance pursues it."[6]

Although Emily Dickinson used writing, books, and literary culture as a means of setting herself apart from what she called "Fathers real life" (L 1:161), Whig political culture inhabited her house, and she expressed pride in both her family's political connections and her father's public achievements on the local, state, and national levels.[7] Following her father's service on the nine-member Governor's Council in 1845 and 1846, Dickinson indulged in a playful high-class exchange of *my political acquaintances are more powerful than yours* with her friend Abiah Root. "You don't [know] how I laughed at your description of your introduction to Daniel Webster," she wrote. "You must feel quite proud of the acquaintance & will not I hope be vain in consequence. However you don't know Gov Briggs & I do, so you are no better off than I" (L 1:56). When her father succeeded in bringing "the grand Rail Road" to Amherst in 1852, Dickinson shared some of the local "jubilee" in a letter to Austin: "Father is realy *sober* from excessive satisfaction, and bears his honors with a most becoming air. Nobody *believes* it yet, it seems like a fairy tale, a most *miraculous* event in the lives of us all" (L 1:173). A few months later, when her father was sent as a delegate to the national Whig convention in Baltimore in June 1852, she expressed pleasure that he was receiving the local and national recognition that he deserved: "I think it will do him the very most good of anything in the world," she wrote to Austin, "and I do feel happy to have father at last, among men who sympathize with him, and know what he really is" (L 1:213).

At times, however, Dickinson also expressed hostility to a masculine political order that seemed oblivious to the affairs of women. "Why cant *I* be a Delegate to the great Whig Convention?—don't I know all about Daniel Webster, and the Tariff, and the Law?" she wrote in a love letter to Susan Gilbert (who was teaching in Baltimore), imagining the possibility of a romantic tryst between sessions. Then, in an apocalyptic fantasy that aligns Dickinson with the grim political imaginings of other writers of her time—the sinking of the Pequod at the end of *Moby Dick,* the "wrath of Almighty God" at the end of *Uncle Tom's Cabin*—she concludes with a hex on the entire political order: "I don't like this country at all, and I shant stay here any longer! 'Delenda est' America, Massachusetts and all!" (L 1:212). But while Dickinson's remarks on the political doings of her father—and the nation— sometimes bristle with irony and even rage, she seems painfully aware of the fact that her father represents a set of classical republican values that were passing away in an age increasingly defined by economic self-interest rather than public virtue and self-sacrifice for the public good. When Vinnie suggests that they send Austin his slippers in a package franked by Congress, Dickinson responds with a form of house politics that comically inverts her father's Roman virtue. "I wish Vinnie could go as a member," she wrote to Austin in 1853. "She'd save something snug for us all, besides enriching herself, but Caesar is such 'an honourable man' that we may all go to the Poor House, for all the American Congress will lift a finger to help us—" (L 1:275).

Although Dickinson did not share her father's public political commitment or his faith in what Henry Clay called the "American System"—a progressive, business-oriented, and national Whig agenda grounded in a strong military, a federal tariff, a national bank, and internal improvements—as I have argued in "Emily Dickinson and Class," she shared many of his class values and social fears in response to Jacksonian democracy, the masses, foreigners, the Irish, Negroes, labor, reform, and westward expansion at a time when the aristocratic class-based values of the past were being eroded under the pressure of an increasingly democratic and industrial capitalist society of new money and new men.[8]

These political values and fears are evident in a letter she wrote to Austin from Mount Holyoke College in 1847, in which she describes a dream she had about losing the Dickinson property to Seth Nims, a Democrat, who served as the Amherst postmaster during the Democratic presidencies of Polk, Pierce, and Buchanan:

> Well, I dreamed a dream & Lo!!! Father had failed & mother said that "our rye field which she & I planted, was mortgaged to Seth Nims." I hope it is not true but do write soon & tell me for you know "I should expire with mortification" to have our rye field mortgaged, to say nothing of it's falling into the merciless hands of a loco!!! (L 1:48–49)

Here as elsewhere in her writing, the specter of Samuel Fowler's loss and departure from Amherst appears to hang over the Dickinson house, causing Dickinson to experience anxiety about a similar loss of property and status amid the rising democratic and leveling forces of the time, signified by the "locofocos"—a name associated with the radical antibank and antimonopoly faction of the Democratic Party popular with workingmen and reformers in New York.

In the same letter, Dickinson also mocks the state of political nonknowledge and removal in which girl students are kept, as she queries Austin for information about the political happenings of the time:

> Wont you please tell me when you answer my letter who the candidate for President is? I have been trying to find out ever since I came here & have not yet succeeded. I don't know anything more about affairs in the world, than if I was in a trance. . . . Has the Mexican war terminated yet & how? Are we beat? Do you know of any nation about to besiege South Hadley? (L 1:49)

Dickinson's intense engagement with "affairs in the world," especially the Mexican War (1846–1848), which many New Englanders saw as an imperialist land grab aimed at extending slavery and the "Slave Power," and the presidential campaign, which would result in the election of Zachary Taylor and a major Whig victory in 1848, suggests that one of the reasons she left Mount Holyoke after only one year is that she felt isolated and removed from a whole world of political "affairs" and dialogue to which she had grown accustomed in the Dickinson house. Written at a time when the Massachusetts legislature had resolved that the Mexican War was "unconstitutionally commenced by order of the President,"[9] Dickinson's letter mocks the politics of manifest destiny and President Polk's expansionist ambition to annex Mexico; it also registers a more local Whig fear that New England was itself under siege, not by the republic of Mexico, but by the nationalist, imperialist, and proslavery forces of Polk and the Democrats.

The arrival of the train in Amherst provoked similar antidemocratic fears. Whereas Edward Dickinson saw the Amherst and Belchertown Railroad as a means of stimulating Amherst manufacturing and production and bringing western Massachusettts into the national economy, Dickinson saw it as an intrusion from abroad of money, commerce, and the masses. "Our house is crowded daily with the members of this world," she wrote to Austin in 1853; "the high and the low, the bond and the free, the 'poor in this world's goods,' and the 'almighty dollar,['] and 'what in the world are they after' continues to be unknown—But I hope they will pass away, as insects on vegetation, and let us reap together in golden harvest time—that is you and Susie and me and our dear sister Vinnie" (L 1:257). As Leo Marx has argued, the train was "*the* revolutionary machine of the age," associated with breaking down regional and social barriers to produce a newly unified and egalitarian country.[10] Against the socially transforming and leveling effects of the train's arrival in Amherst, Dickinson imagines herself reaping in "golden harvest time" with a select community of family and friends. Like her reluctance to leave Amherst and her later refusal to "cross" what she called "my Father's ground" (L 2:460), Dickinson's desire to retreat into an older pastoral order of kinship, status, and love was not the absurd gesture of either a disturbed psyche or an eccentric poetess: it was an act of political and social resistance against the disruptive democratic, commercial, and technological forces of her time.

Dickinson also lived during a time when women were challenging their subordination and exclusion within the masculine orders of power. "We would have every arbitrary barrier thrown down. We would have every path laid open to Woman as freely as to Man," Margaret Fuller had declared in 1845 in *Woman in the Nineteenth Century*.[11] In 1848, at a women's rights convention in Seneca Falls, New York, women issued a "Declaration of Sentiments," modeled on the Declaration of Independence, that asserted women's equality and their right to vote. While Dickinson had no interest in woman's suffrage or the movement for women's rights, her status as the daughter of a socially prominent family gave her a latitude of privilege that enabled her to revolt against the orthodox sexual ideologies of her time. She resisted marriage, rebelled against domestic ideology, and saw housework as a plebeian interference with her writing. Mocking the politics of housework—"mind the house—and the food— *sweep* if the spirits were low"—and the true womanly ideals of "meekness—and patience—and submission," Dickinson declares in a letter to her friend Jane Humphrey:

> Somehow or other I incline to other things—and Satan covers them up with flowers, and I reach out to pick them. The path of duty looks very ugly indeed—and the place where *I* want to go more amiable—a great deal—it is so much easier to do wrong than right—so much pleasanter to be evil than good, I don't wonder that good angels weep—and bad ones sing songs. (L 1:82)

As Dickinson's identification of her desire to write with Satan suggests, at a time when the Calvinist orthodoxy of the fathers was breaking down, she retained the language, imagery, and conscience of New England Puritanism without the faith. "Christ is calling everyone here," she wrote to Humphrey in 1850, "and I am standing alone in rebellion" (L 1:94). While her friends and family converted to the Congregational religion during the many revivals that passed through Amherst and the surrounding community in the 1840s and 1850s, Dickinson refused to give herself up and become a Christian.

Living in a time of major political, social, religious, and epistemological breakdown, perhaps best signified by the political collapse, blood violence, and on-going social questions raised by the Civil War, Dickinson turned to writing not as a retreat into privacy but as a higher order of culture and a powerful means of talking back to, with, and against her democratic age.

The Republic of Letters

In *Emily Dickinson: Face to Face,* Dickinson's niece, Martha Dickinson Bianchi, wrote that "with her gentleness, sensitiveness, and the shyness so popularly associated with her, went a tacit and coercive will and an unconscious power of personality that imposed its own terms."[12] Like many during her time—especially women and others who had been excluded from citizenship and political being under the terms of the Constitution—Dickinson expressed her "will" and "power" not on the national but on the local level, where she made her upper-class female voice and vision heard to a select group of family, friends, and other socially and culturally prominent figures among her contemporaries.[13]

Dickinson's powerful and at times mordantly satiric voice is already evident in her first published work, a valentine that she sent—perhaps to George Gould—in February 1850. Her letter begins with a sequence of latinate nonsense—"war alarum, man reformam, life perfectum, mundum changum, all things flarum"—that mimics the political rhetorics of war, reform, perfectionism, world revolution, and apocalypse that marked her time. Requesting "an interview" with an unknown "Sir" who might be a particular man (such as George Gould) but who might also stand for a more generalized "public," with whom she would like to have a conversation—"a chat, sir, or a tete-a-tete, a confab, a mingling of opposite minds"—Dickinson imagines that together they might become "the United States of America": "We will talk over what we learned in our geographies, and listened to from the pulpit, the press and the Sabbath School." Having committed herself to "talk" about books, religion, politics, and the press, Dickinson describes their "friendship" in language that adumbrates the multiple work of her writing: "We'll be instant, in season, out of season, minister, take care of, cherish, sooth, watch, wait, doubt, refrain, reform, elevate, instruct." She concludes with a passage that satirizes the progressive religious, political, and scientific rhetoric of her time:

> But the world is sleeping in ignorance and error, sir, and we must be crowing cocks, and singing larks, and a rising sun to awake her; or else we'll pull society up to the roots, and plant it in a different place. We'll build Alms-houses, and transcendental State prisons, and scaffolds—we will blow out the sun, and the moon, and encourage invention. Alpha shall kiss Omega—we will ride up the hill of glory—Hallelujah, all hail! (L 1:92)

Ventriloquizing the language of revivalist preachers and social reformers who called upon Americans to "pull society up to the roots" and begin anew, Dickinson pokes fun at the overweening confidence and optimism of the antebellum era, signified by transcendental visionaries who imagine ridding the world of poverty and evil and by scientists and inventors whose Faustian visions of mastery lead them to imagine "blow[ing] out the sun, and the moon."

Published anonymously in February 1850 in *The Indicator*, which was edited by a group of Amherst College students, the letter was preceded by an editorial note: "I wish I knew who the author is. I think she must have some spell, by which she quickens the imagination, and causes the high blood 'run frolic through the veins'" (L 1:93). Whether "the author" was known to the editors or not—and the evidence suggests that she was—this first publication reveals that by 1850 Dickinson was already setting up in the anonymous but public guise of a local prophetess and muse. The valentine establishes an early pattern in Dickinson's relation to the "public": letters or poems that she sent signed (or not) to those with access to cultural power and print in an effort to engage in dialogue about the literary and social world.[14] This pattern, which she continued throughout her life, suggests the inadequacy of the terms "private" and "public" that have been used to read, interpret, and historically locate Dickinson's life, letters, and poems.

In *The Structural Transformation of the Public Sphere*, Habermas describes a public sphere that exists between civil society and the state, in which private persons engage in public talk about issues of common concern. Habermas's notion of the public sphere makes it possible to conceive of a public realm of politics and letters that exists apart from either the economic market or the state.[15] As defined by Habermas, the public sphere emerged in the eighteenth century out of the privacy of the bourgeois family and the "literary form" of "the letter" turned outward toward the public: "Subjectivity, as the innermost core of the private, was always already oriented to an audience (*Publikum*)," he writes.[16] Even diaries were public-oriented letters addressed to oneself. Habermas's formulation enables us to get beyond the question "did Dickinson *intend* to publish?" in order to consider more fully the alternative forms of address, publicity, and political engagement one finds in Dickinson's letters and poems.

While Dickinson did not—and could not—go to the national Whig convention in Baltimore in 1852—beginning in the early fifties, her letters and poems are engaged in dialogue with some of the most powerful cultural and social figures of her time.[17] Her network of known correspondents included Samuel Bowles, the editor of the *Springfield Daily Republican,* one of the most influential newspapers in the country, and an outspoken supporter of antislavery, woman's suffrage, the Republican Party, and Lincoln; Josiah Gilbert Holland, the literary editor of the *Springfield Daily Republican*, founding editor of *Scribner's Monthly* in 1870, and popular author of numerous novels and books, including a *Life of Abraham Lincoln* (1865); Thomas Wentworth Higginson, a well-known writer, Unitarian minister, liberal republican advocate of abolition and women's rights, and colonel, who led one of the first regiments of black troops during the Civil War; Thomas Niles, the editor of Roberts Brothers, a major publishing house in Boston; Judge Otis P. Lord, a leading figure in Massachusetts politics and law; and Helen Hunt Jackson, one of the most highly acclaimed women writers of her time.

Along with the many letters she sent to a select community of family and friends, which included her sister-in-law, Susan Dickinson, who was herself a major cultural broker in the Amherst community, her Boston Unitarian cousins Louisa and Frances Norcross, who became involved with the transcendentalists when they moved to Concord in 1874, and Elizabeth Holland, the wife of Josiah Gilbert Holland, Dickinson's network of correspondence became a kind of counter public sphere, an alternative republic of letters through which she resisted—and talked back to—the disruptive social and political forces of her time.

"*The Republican* seems to us like a letter from you, and we break the seal and read it eagerly," Dickinson wrote to the Hollands in 1853. As her comment suggests, Dickinson was an avid reader of both local and national newspapers and magazines, including the *Hampshire and Franklin Express, Harper's Magazine, Atlantic Monthly, Scribner's,* and especially the *Springfield Daily Republican,* which defined itself in its first issue as a print public sphere—"a medium for the discussion of matters of local interest"—in which readers were invited to participate as a form of republican citizenship.[18] Dickinson's letters are full of sometimes oblique references to the events, stories, publications, and accounts of her friends' lives that she read in the newspapers and magazines. In fact, she often turned to these publications to find out "news" about her socially prominent friends. At a time of massive transformation in communication technology, when traditional class relations were breaking down and literary and cultural authority was shifting from more democratic New York to more conservative Boston, newspapers and magazines such as the *Springfield Daily Republican* and *Atlantic Monthly* became a means for the New England social and political elite to maintain its class coherence and its political and cultural power.[19]

In addition to enabling her to correspond with members of her own class about local and national news, Dickinson's republic of letters served multiple functions. During an age when "letters" had become one of the standard personalizing forms in which information was published, Dickinson's letters to Austin often sound like witty accounts of local and familial "news" similar to what she might have read in the *Hampshire and Franklin Express* or *Springfield Republican*. Whereas her letters to her women friends are frequently focused on defining an alternative realm of female value against the patriarchal orders of her time,[20] her letters to Bowles and Higginson seem more cryptic and oblique, as Dickinson seeks to forge her public "private" image as "Queen Recluse" and poet. Through her letters Dickinson also engaged in talk about a shared realm of cultural and literary value. Her correspondence is full of allusions to and exchanges about the major writings of her time, including works by the Brontë sisters, Elizabeth Barrett Browning, George Eliot, and Charles Dickens, but also popular American political writings, such as Harriet Beecher Stowe's *Uncle Tom's Cabin*, Rebecca Harding Davis's *Life in the Iron Mills*, Higginson's *Army Life in a Black Regiment,* and Jackson's *Ramona* ("Pity me . . . I have finished Ramona," she wrote to Jackson in response to her 1884 novel protesting American Indian policy [L 3:866]).

Dickinson's republic of letters also became a means of resisting the debased values of the literary marketplace by circulating her poems among a select group of family, friends, editors, and high placed others. In addition to the 252 poems Dickinson sent to Susan Dickinson, she sent 103 poems to Higginson, forty to Bowles, thirty-one to Elizabeth Holland, six to her husband Josiah, eight to Thomas Niles, eleven to Jackson, and thirteen to Mabel Loomis Todd. Like the seventy-one poems that Dickinson sent to the Norcross sisters, who may have read her poems to the transcendental reading group they attended in Concord in the 1870s, the poems that Dickinson sent in her letters and as letters were read aloud to others and in some cases circulated to others either in transcribed or holograph form.[21]

Between 1858 and 1865, Dickinson gathered over 800 of her poems into forty hand-sewn booklets of about twenty poems each. In one of these booklet poems, she describes her poetry as another form of letter writing and "News" addressed to her "countrymen":

> This is my letter to the World
> That never wrote to Me -

The simple News that Nature told -
With tender Majesty

Her Message is committed
To Hands I cannot see -
For love of Her - Sweet - countrymen -
Judge tenderly - of Me (Fr 519)

Here as elsewhere in her writing, Dickinson presents her poetry
not as a "private" production but as a form of "public" address—
a "letter to the World"—whether imaginary or real. Perhaps
Dickinson addressed an imaginary community; or perhaps she
imagined her poems being passed from hand to hand among a
select republic of "country" men as some 600 of her poems were
during her lifetime. Or perhaps by publicizing the "News" of her
writing to some of the most powerful social and cultural figures
of her time, she anticipated that her poems would eventually
reach a larger "World" of "countrymen," as they did after her
death when Thomas Higginson and Mabel Loomis Todd, two of
the many public "Hands" to which Dickinson "committed" her
poems while she was alive, edited the first volumes of her poetry
and letters for print publication in the 1890s.

During her lifetime, however, with the exception of ten poems,
seven of which were published in the *Springfield Republican,* Dickinson refused to go to market. "Publication - is the Auction / Of
the Mind of Man - " she wrote in a poem that associates print publication with blackness, wage slavery, and the degradations of
both the slave auction and the capitalist marketplace:

Poverty - be justifying
For so foul a thing

Possibly - but We - would rather
From Our Garret go
White - unto the White Creator -
Than invest - Our Snow - (Fr 788)

Deploying the language of both antislavery protest and artisan
republican protest against wage labor as a new form of slavery to

constitute herself and her writing as part of an elect community of whiteness, Dickinson resists the "foul" values of the commercial marketplace: "reduce no Human Spirit / To Disgrace of Price -." Written at the time of the Emancipation Proclamation when the war to save the Union had become in the eyes of many, including Edward Dickinson, an unconstitutional executive war to abolish slavery, Dickinson's poem suggests that like her republic of letters, her refusal to publish was not so much a private act, as it was an act of social and class resistance to the commercial, democratic, and increasingly amalgamated and mass values of the national marketplace.[22]

Political Interiors

"I had a terror—since September—I could tell to none—," Dickinson wrote to Higginson in April 1862, "and so I sing as the Boy does by the Burying Ground—because I am afraid—" (L 2:404). Whatever the sources of Dickinson's "terror"—a personal love crisis, a failure of religious belief, the advent of the Civil War, the collapse of an older New England social order, the horrifying prospect of everlasting "Death," metaphysical angst, or all these together—her poems powerfully register the disintegrative psychic, emotional, and bodily effects of social transformation and political crisis that marked Dickinson's years of greatest productivity during and after the Civil War.

"To fight aloud, is very brave -," Dickinson wrote, setting the external struggles of her time against the *"gallanter"* wars of those "Who charge within the bosom / The Cavalry of Wo - ":

> Who win, and nations do not see -
> Who fall - and none observe -
> Whose dying eyes, no Country
> Regards with patriot love - (Fr 138)

Implicitly measuring those who struggle "within" against the model of republican virtue represented by the founding fathers, Dickinson suggests that her own internal "charge" against "The

Cavalry of Wo" might—like Washington's—be worthy of her Country's "patriot love." But while Dickinson is like Edgar Allan Poe one of the major poets of nineteenth-century *interiority*, it is an interiority haunted by the ghosts and spooks of ante- and postbellum American political culture.

Although Dickinson's poems allude only occasionally to public political events, her poetic landscapes—even her most interior ones—are full of "public" attitude about the political, social, religious, sexual, racial, scientific, and economic contests that marked her time. Her aristocratic sense of class consciousness and hereditary entitlement is evident in poems such as "The Soul selects her own Society - " in which Dickinson's imperial speaker "shuts the Door" on all but the select few: "I've known her - from an ample nation - / Choose One - / Then - close the Valves of her attention - / Like Stone -" (Fr 409a). Several poems register Dickinson's anxiety about the twin forces of democracy and technology that were transforming rural Amherst and moving America from the country to the city in the nineteenth century: "I'm Nobody! Who Are You?" resists the noisy "public" culture of democracy—of stump speech and camp meeting—addressed to "an admiring Bog" (Fr 260); and "I like to see it lap the Miles - " literalizes the "omnipotent" figure of the train as "iron horse" in language that subtly protests the "horrid - hooting" agent of capital and commerce that was radically altering the older country rhythms of New England life (Fr 383).

Like Harriet Beecher Stowe's *Uncle Tom's Cabin* and like Lincoln's plan to colonize blacks elsewhere once they were freed, Dickinson's poetry is shaped by the cultural presumption that the future of the American republic belongs to whites of a certain class and breeding.[23] "The Lamp burns sure - within - / Tho' Serfs - supply the Oil -" (Fr 247) she writes, in a poem that assumes the naturalness of the master/slave relation and the invisibility of slave labor—black, Irish, or working class—in the cultural production of white genius and American civilization.[24] In "Civilization - spurns - the Leopard!" Dickinson appears to identify her creative power and her difference with the African leopard—and perhaps by implication the African American—but the poem is structured by a logic of racial and national purity, in which Ethiopians belong in "Ethiop," Asians belong in "Asia," and "Civilization" belongs to whites who "spurn" the "Tawny" customs and "Spotted" nature of Africans (Fr 276).

Poems such as "Mine - by the Right of the White Election!" give voice to the ways "whiteness"—what Dickinson calls "A Whiter Gift - within - " (Fr 280) or "A Woman - white - to be - " (Fr 307)—comes to function as a form of self-possession and intellectual property in the political struggles of the nineteenth century. "The Malay - took the Pearl -," which was written at the time of the Civil War, turns on the irony that "The Swarthy fellow," who is presumed to be less worthy, "took the Pearl" that the white aristocratic speaker—"the Earl"—implicitly deserves (Fr 451). While the poem "Color - Caste - Denomination -," which was written after the Emancipation Proclamation toward the close of the war, gestures toward a "large" and essentially utopian social order in which "All Hue" will be "forgotten," the speaker's "minuter intuitions" lead her to "Deem" democracy "unplausible" and indeed rather horrifying not only within but also beyond social time (Fr 836). Although Dickinson's language of white precedence is grounded in biblical and Judeo-Christian symbolism, her poems suggest the ways religious symbolism joins with racial ideology and Western aestheticism to create a perdurable racist *mentality*—a psychology of whiteness—that remains intact despite the legal passage of constitutional amendments that abolished slavery, declared black men citizens, and provided for black male suffrage in the post–Civil War period.[25]

The relation between Dickinson's poetic interiors and the outward struggles of her time is nowhere more evident than in her poems on religion. In an 1862 letter addressed to the prominent Unitarian minister and political activist, Thomas Higginson, Dickinson described her family's faith: "They are religious—except me—and address an Eclipse, every morning—whom they call their 'Father'" (L 2:404). Despite Dickinson's seemingly "liberal" and detached pose, God continued to be a gnawing source of anguish and doubt. Her poems provide a dense social record of a broader crisis of belief at a time when the religious orthodoxies of the past were splintering into a number of competing faiths from the high-bred Unitarianism and Transcendentalism of

New England to the more populist and reformist evangelicalism of Charles Finney, the Baptists, and the Methodists in the West. In many of her poems, Dickinson's republicanism appears to short-circuit her capacity for Christian faith: like Milton's Satan she resists God's impersonality, his "supreme iniquity" (Fr 1500), his cruelty, and his tyrannical power. Declaring her independence from God in favor of life ("To be alive - is Power -"), "Liberty" ("Let Us play Yesterday -"), and happiness on earth ("The Fact that Earth is Heaven -"), Dickinson constructs a counterreligion of nature ("Some keep the Sabbath going to Church -"), pokes fun at the Puritan fetishization of "Death" ("I Heard a Fly buzz - when I died -"), urges a happier retelling of the Bible ("The Bible is an antique Volume -"), and says prayers for "Liberty" rather than salvation: "God of the Manacle / As of the Free - / Take not my Liberty / Away from Me -" (Fr 754).

But while Dickinson's poems are inflected by the more rational, humane, and secular perspective of Boston Unitarianism ("'Faith' is a fine invention / For Gentlemen who *see!* / But Microscopes are prudent / In an Emergency!" [Fr 202C]), and while she occasionally speaks the Emersonian language of self-reliance ("On a Columnar Self - / How ample to rely," [Fr 740]) or "Reels" and "Rows" in transcendental ecstasy, she did not share what Henry Adams called "the mental calm of the Unitarian clergy." If "Boston had solved the universe," as Adams wrote in *The Education of Henry Adams*, Emily Dickinson had not.[26] In a poem written toward the close of her life, she expresses the pain of living in an era of unbelief:

> Those - dying then,
> Knew where they went -
> They went to God's Right Hand -
> That Hand is amputated now
> And God cannot be found - (Fr 1581)

As someone who could not believe in either the saving Christian orthodoxy of the past or the progressive democratic ideology of the future, Dickinson gives voice in her poems to the spooked interiors of ante- and postbellum America, the specters of un-

meaning, abjection, and death that stalked the American landscape during the Civil War, and the prospect of what she called
"Miles on Miles of Nought -" (Fr 522).

In "Their Hight in Heaven comforts not -," the failure of religious belief merges with a broader social critique of an enlightenment epistemology grounded in individual reason, science, and
knowledge. "'Twas best imperfect - as it was - / I'm finite - I cant
see -," Dickinson writes, resisting the "comforts" of "Heaven" in
language that also encodes her resistance to the expansionist politics of Horace Greeley's "Go West, Young Man": "The Glimmer-
ing Frontier that / Skirts the Acres of Perhaps - / To me - shows insecure -." Against "The House of Supposition," Dickinson clings
to the "meaner size" of the "Wealth" she "had":

> Better than larger values -
> That show however true -
> This timid life of Evidence
> Keeps pleading - "I don't know" - (Fr 725)

Here as in such poems as "Surgeons must be very careful," "I reason, Earth is short -," and "Wonder - is not precisely knowing,"
Dickinson gives voice to the limits of the self, reason, sight, and
epistemological certainty upon which the scientific confidence
and the progressive ideology of her age depended. Like Melville's similarly spooked and charged symbolic narratives, Dickinson's poems are wracked by the fear of a malign power—the
"blonde Assassin" who "beheads" in the name of "an Approving
God" (Fr 1668)—or worse, a universe completely unhinged from
any meaning at all: "I cling to nowhere till I fall - / The Crash of
nothing - yet of all -" (Fr 1532).

Although Dickinson might be read as the avatar of a residual
Calvinism giving rise to an emergent liberal ideology of the self,
she continues to be haunted by the old imprisonment. In "Soto!
Explore thyself!" she urges an exploration of "The 'Undiscovered
Continent'" within (Fr 814c) that appears to affirm the infinite ca-
pacities of "the unencumbered self" at the heart of liberal political theory.[27] And yet, while Dickinson's speakers seek to enlarge
the freedom and power of the individual against the state, the

Church, and all external structures of authority—in accord with classical liberal theory—her speakers are also often "split," mad, and in pieces. The collapse of religious, political, and epistemological order is "felt" and mourned internally as a "Funeral" in the "Brain" (Fr 340). The self-divided, terrorized, and incoherent speakers in "The first Day's Night had come -," "The Brain, within it's Groove," and "I felt a Cleaving in my Mind -" suggest a problem in liberal and democratic theory with putting individuals—even elite ones—in charge.

Singing "Off Charnel Steps"

In 1860, when the newly formed Constitutional Union Party nominated John Bell and Edward Everett to run for president and vice president and Edward Dickinson to run for lieutenant governor of Massachusetts, Dickinson wrote to her cousins Louisa and Frances Norcross, with whom her father was staying while he attended the state Constitutional Union Convention in Worcester:[28]

> Won't Fanny give my respects to the "Bell and Everett party" if she passes that organization on her way to school? I hear they wish to make me Lieutenant-Governor's daughter. Were they cats I would pull their tails, but as they are only patriots, I must forego the bliss. (L 2:368)

The Constitutional Union Party was formed on the state level by what Edward called "the great Mass of the old Whig & Conservative party of Massachusetts, which contains the talent, character & property, of Massachusetts" to oppose "the depths of radicalism" through which the Know-Nothings and Republicans had "dragged" the "most deserving portion of our citizens" over "the last six years."[29] The Union Party was, in effect, the old Whig Party with a new national name formed to head off the secession of the Southern states that was about to occur with the election of Lincoln as the first Republican president in November 1860. Dickinson's gesture of respect to the "Bell and Everett

party" not only suggests her support for the values of the Constitution, the Union, and the laws endorsed by her father and the
Union Party; her seemingly dismissive observation that *they are
only patriots* once again registers an almost wistful sympathy for
an "old Whig" order and a set of "Conservative" republican values that were, in effect, passing away with the rise to state and
national power of a more radical, abolitionist, and democratic
Republican Party under the national figure of Lincoln.

Edward Dickinson ultimately turned down the nomination to
run for lieutenant governor once in 1860 and again in 1861 when
he was nominated by the Republican Party, and Emily Dickinson
was denied the opportunity of entering either Massachusetts or
Republican history as the "Lieutenant Governor's daughter." In
his October 1861 letter declining the Republican nomination,
Dickinson denounced "as subversive of all constitutional guaran-
tees, if we expect to reconstruct or restore the Union, the hereti-
cal dogma that immediate and universal emancipation of slaves
should be proclaimed by the government as the means of
putting an end to the war." He hoped that "in the good providence of God, emancipation [would] be one of the blessed re-
sults of the war." "[L]et us unitedly gird ourselves for the terrible
contest in which we are engaged," he wrote, "and resolve to
'fight on and fight ever' *under the constitution,* 'until the sway of
the constitution and the laws shall be restored to all portions of
our country.'"[30] Dickinson's words are a fair indication of his response to the Civil War: while he opposed Lincoln, the Republican Party, and government-imposed abolition, he supported the
war to save the primacy of the law and the Constitutional Union.
Whereas Edward became involved in local initiatives to fill and
provide for Amherst's quota of volunteers (YH 1:27), Austin pro-
cured a substitute for $500 when he was drafted in 1864, and
Emily Dickinson turned to writing as a kind of aesthetic *substitu-
tion,* a means of suffering the inner emotional life of the war
through writing.

When the Civil War began on April 12, 1861, it became the
larger historic ground against and through which Dickinson enacted her own form of personal and political "Calvary." The massive carnage, suffering, and death of the Civil War propelled Dick-

inson into further doubts about republican destiny, divine providence, and the nature of things, a fuller withdrawal from society, and a renewed dedication to art as a higher order of culture. In 1861, she sent "Title divine, is mine" to Samuel Bowles with the following note at the end of the poem: *"Here's* - what I had to 'tell you' - You will tell no other? Honor - is it's own pawn" - (Fr 194A). Although the poem is usually read as a personal confession of love for somebody (perhaps Bowles himself), it also reveals the interconnections among sexual resistance, religious crisis, artistic dedication, and the trauma of war in Dickinson's work:

> Title divine - is mine!
> The Wife - without the Sign!
> Acute Degree - conferred on me -
> Empress of Calvary!
> Royal - all but the Crown!
> God sends us Women -
> When you - hold - Garnet to Garnet - (Fr 194A)

What Dickinson may want "to tell" Bowles—who was himself an advocate of women's rights and a loyal supporter of the Republican Party, Lincoln, and the Union war—is that as the "Empress of Calvary" she will suffer the passion, wounding, and crucifixion of the times through art as an alternative form of religion and marriage. As in "I'm ceded - I've stopped being Their's -" and other "poet" poems composed during the war years, Dickinson enacts her artistic dedication in language that uses biblical symbolism and Church ritual to challenge the social, sexual, and religious ideologies that eclipse and shroud women's lives.

Within a week after the war began, William Seymour Tyler, a professor of Latin and Greek at Amherst College, preached a "rousing sermon" in the college chapel "intended to inspire courage, heroism, and self-sacrificing devotion."[31] In the first months of the war, Amherst residents, including many college students, were quick to respond to Lincoln's call for 75,000 militia to serve for ninety days to put down the southern "Rebellion."

But as the war began to turn against the Union with the retreat of Union forces at Bull Run in July 1861 and the massive casualties at Shiloh and Antietam in 1862, the number of volunteers in communities like Amherst began to fall off. The Emancipation Proclamation and the national Conscription Act of 1863 made it possible for Amherst to solve the problem of draft quotas "genteelly" by paying for substitutes.[32] Thus, after 1863, as the war became increasingly a site of mass butchery, in which the side that had the most bodies to sacrifice would win, it also assumed a starkly class and racial dimension, in which upper-class white men like William Austin Dickinson sent the poor, the unemployed, or recently "liberated" blacks to fight, suffer, and possibly die in their stead to preserve the traditional white class structure in place.

In February 1863, shortly after the Emancipation Proclamation had changed the meaning of the war into a war for black liberation, Dickinson wrote to Higginson, who was serving as the colonel of a regiment of black volunteers in South Carolina: "War feels to me like an oblique place . . . I found you were gone, by accident, as I find Systems are, or Seasons of the year, and obtain no cause—but suppose it a treason of Progress—that dissolves as it goes" (L 2:423). In the past, critics have emphasized Dickinson's isolation from the war and history and the merely personal sources of the crisis she suffered in the years immediately preceding and following the start of the war. And yet, of the 1,789 poems in Franklin's variorum edition, over half were written during the years of the Civil War between 1861 and 1865; and of these, almost 300 were written in 1863, a year of crisis and turning point in the war, when even Union victories such as Gettysburg had become scenes of horrific bloodletting and mass death on both sides. As poems such as " 'Tis so appalling - it exhilarates -" and "Revolution is the Pod" suggest, the war crisis appears to have set "Fright at Liberty," inspiring Dickinson to a "Bloom" of creative power in the very midst of the "over Horror," "rattle" of "Systems," and "Death" (Fr 341, Fr 1044) signified by the Civil War.[33]

For Dickinson, the Civil War became the external symbol of the war against God, church, society, and state that she began in the antebellum years and the death throes of an older conservative order that she mourns. "Sorrow seems more general than it did, and not the estate of a few persons, since the war began," she wrote the Norcross sisters during the war.[34] "I noticed that Robert Browning had made another poem, and was astonished—till I remembered that I, myself, in my smaller way, sang off charnel steps" (L 2:436). Locating her poems historically amid "the charnel steps" of the war at the same time that she suggests the role of poetry in singing "off"—or against—the blood site of democratic history, Dickinson's comment reveals the ways the internecine carnage and trauma of the war inflects and intensifies her struggle against the specters of loss, change, unmeaning, and death during the war years and after.

In at least one instance, Dickinson wrote a poem in response to the death of a local soldier, Frazar Stearns, who was killed at the battle of Newbern on March 14, 1862. The son of the president of Amherst College, Stearns was well known locally for his self-sacrificial devotion to the Union cause.[35] Dickinson described the funeral of "this young crusader—too brave that he could fear to die" in a letter to the Norcross sisters (L 2:398). She also described Austin's stunned response to Stearns's death in a letter to Bowles: "Austin is chilled—by Frazer's murder—He says—his Brain keeps saying over 'Frazer is killed'—'Frazer is killed,' just as Father told it—to Him. Two or three words of lead - that dropped so deep, they keep weighing—" (L 2:399). Dickinson's poem, "It dont sound so terrible - quite - as it did -," evokes the psychological impact of death in words that echo Austin's response to Stearns's death: "I run it over - 'Dead', Brain - 'Dead.'" Seeking to bring the "shrieking" reality of death "under rule," the speaker resolves to "Put the Thought in advance - a Year -": "How like 'a fit' - then - / Murder - wear!" (Fr 384).

"I wish 'twas plainer, Loo, the anguish in this world," Dickinson wrote to Louisa Norcross a few weeks after Stearns's funeral. "I wish one could be sure the suffering had a loving side" (L 2:407). Against the self-sacrificial patriotism of local "soldier-hearts" like Frazar Stearns—"His big heart shot away by a 'minie ball'" (L 2:398)—and against the public rhetoric of blood sacrifice for the Union cause or the sin of slavery, several of the poems

Dickinson wrote during and after the war express doubt about the larger meaning and value of war, suffering, and death. In "Victory comes late," "The Eagle's Golden Breakfast" never arrives to save the poem's starved subjects (Fr 195B). The speaker in "At least - to pray - is left - is left -" cannot find the redemptive figure, the "Jesus in the Air -," who "settest Earthquake in the South - / And Maelstrom, in the Sea" (Fr 377). In "It feels a shame to be Alive - / When Men so brave - are dead -," the speaker wonders if sacrifice of human lives "In Pawn for Liberty -," or for the United States ("for Us"), is worth the price:

> The price is great - Sublimely paid -
> Do we deserve - a Thing -
> That lives - like Dollars - must be piled
> Before we may obtain?
>
> Are we that wait - sufficient worth -
> That such Enormous Pearl
> As life - dissolved be - for Us -
> In Battle's - horrid Bowl? (Fr 524)

Similarly, in "My Portion is Defeat - today -," Dickinson presents a starkly realistic evocation of the "Bone and stain" of the battlefield—of "Moan" and "Prayer" and "Chips of Blank - in Boyish Eyes"—but the scene has no meaning beyond "Death's surprise, / Stamped visible - in stone -" (Fr 704).

Dickinson resists the redemptive democratic vision of the Gettysburg Address (1863), in which Lincoln locates the blood sacrifice of the Civil War within a consoling national narrative of "a new birth of freedom . . . that government of the people, by the people, and for the people, shall not perish from the earth." She also resists the providential reading of American history in Lincoln's Second Inaugural Address (1865), in which he presents "this terrible war" as a "mighty scourge" sent by a "true and righteous" God to rid the nation of "American Slavery."[36] Dickinson's resistance to Lincoln's war policy and his public attempts at rationalization may explain the fact that she made no comment on his assassination and death after the war's close in

April 1865. Her single possible reference to Lincoln was made when he was reelected as president: "The Drums keep on for the still Man," she wrote Lavinia, perhaps in reference to the torchlight procession held by the Lincoln Clubs of Cambridge on November 13, 1864 (L 2:436). If the allusion is indeed to Lincoln, it works against the national mythology in presenting him not as the nation's savior but as a sepulchral figure, a stone man who has presided over a national burial in the name of the higher "purposes" of democracy, equality, black empowerment, and an "Almighty" God that Dickinson cannot believe in.[37]

For Dickinson, the Civil War represented the death throes of an older order: the triumph of Northern capitalism, industry, wage labor, the city, a democratic and "mixed" electorate, mass culture, and a centralized nation state against a country order grounded in agriculture, rule by an elite white class, an artisan republic of crafts and trades, a culture of hierarchy, deference, and subordination, and local or state sovereignty. In her poems Dickinson mourns not only the war dead but also the loss of a whole way of life. "A loss of something ever felt I -," she wrote around the close of the Civil War, presenting herself as "A Mourner" and an outcast "Prince" "bemoaning" the loss of "a Dominion": "I am looking oppositely / For the Site of the Kingdom of Heaven -" (Fr 1072). Despite the fact that Charles Sumner's republican politics were more radical than her own, she responded to his death on March 11, 1874—after his long service as United States senator from Massachusetts (1852–1874) and outspoken voice of New England republicanism—as the apotheosis of a "Giant" on an expiring "Continent." "He was his Country's," she wrote in a poetic memorial following his death: "When Continents expire / The Giants they discarded - are / Promoted to endure -" (Fr 1321).[38]

For Dickinson as for many in the country, the assassination of Republican President James A. Garfield in 1881 by a disappointed office seeker, Charles J. Guiteau, appeared to confirm the national apostasy from the ideals of the past signified by the corruption, scandal, and spoils of the Gilded Age. "The Pilgrim's Empire seems to stoop - I hope it will not fall -," she wrote to Elizabeth Holland in August 1881, shortly before President

Garfield died from a bullet wound in the back. About the new "republican" order, Dickinson could only be ironic: "We have a new Black Man," she wrote in the same letter, "and are looking for a Philanthropist to direct him, because every time he presents himself, I run, and when the Head of the nation shies, it confuses the Foot -." Dickinson's words have a more than merely personal reference to a new black laborer at the Dickinson "Mansion." Her words also suggest the threat posed by the "new Black Man" to the older social order, which Dickinson naturalizes as the bodily relation of "Head" (whiteness) to "Foot" ("Black Man") and then caps with the specter of black revolt and cannibalism: "When you read in the 'Massachusetts items' that he has eaten us up, a memorial merriment will invest these preliminaries" (L 3:706).

Against the increased industrialization, urbanization, immigration, and democratization that marked the post–Civil War decades, Dickinson continued to identify with the "country" values of an earlier era. On the occasion of the centennial of the American Revolution and the unveiling of "The Minute Men" monument at Concord on April 19, 1875, she wrote the Norcross sisters: "I have only a buttercup to offer for the centennial, as an 'embattled farmer' has but little time" (L 2:539). Alluding to the lines from Emerson's "Concord Hymn"— "Here once the embattled farmers stood / And fired the shot heard round the world"—which are inscribed at the base of the statue, Dickinson identifies with the "embattled farmer" of the past ("I am a rural Man," she wrote in another poem of the 1870s [Fr 1488B]), suggesting that the revolutionary battle may be on-going in the present struggle of "embattled farmers" against corporate power and the nation-state. She expresses a similarly revolutionary "attitude" in a poem sent to the Norcross sisters:

> My country need not change her gown,
> Her triple suit as sweet
> As when 'twas cut at Lexington
> And first pronounced "a fit." (Fr 1540C)

Toward the close of her life, Dickinson's resistance to change, her allegiance to the country habits and "triple suit" of an earlier time, manifests itself in her passionate attachment to Massachusetts Supreme Court Judge Otis P. Lord, a conservative Whig who—like Dickinson's father—held fast to the older gentry values of the past against the liberal, progressive, and democratizing politics of the ante- and postbellum years. In the relationship that Dickinson formed with Judge Lord in the late 1870s or early 1880s, she seeks to create a kind of fantasy republic of love grounded in the values of patriotism, self-sacrificing virtue, and freedom that had been lost to American history: "my native Land—my Darling," she wrote in a letter drafted to Lord, "come oh *be* a patriot now—Love is a patriot now Gave her life for its (its) country Has it meaning now—Oh nation of the soul thou hast thy freedom now" (L 2:615).

"Some Work for Immortality"

"My Wars are laid away in Books -," Dickinson wrote in the final years of her life, perhaps in reference to the forty hand-sewn "Books" of poems that she stopped making in 1864, before the war's close. It was after the Civil War, and especially after the death of her father in 1874, that Dickinson's reclusive tendencies and her habit of dressing in white increased. During the war years and after she turned increasingly to her writing and to her exclusive circle of friends as a means of securing herself against what she called in a letter to Higginson "a treason of Progress—that dissolves as it goes" (L 2:423).

Dickinson's poetics is split between an older mode of literature as something embedded in the social rituals of daily life and emergent notions of art as something separate and transcendent. "If I can stop one Heart from breaking / I shall not live in vain" (Fr 982), she wrote, in words that suggest the multiple daily uses her letters and poems served—especially during and after the war—as prayer, medicine, consolation, gift, and cure. On the other hand, the vacancy that was created by what she called "the abdication of Belief" (Fr 1581) and the erosion of an older elite order under the pressure of democracy, industry, and modernity was filled for Dickinson by her turn toward a higher order of art. In "I reckon - When I count at all -," she affirms the absolute value of "Poets" above the "Sun," "Summer," and "the Heaven of God": "The Others look a needless Show - / So I write - Poets - All - / Their Summer - lasts a solid Year -" (Fr 533).

When Dickinson wrote to Higginson in the midst of the Civil War in April 1862 to ask if her "Verse" was "alive" (L 2:403), she was looking to art—to poetry writing—as a means of overcoming not only "Death" but also the lack of higher meaning, order, and value in the world. Her letter responds to Higginson's "Letter to a Young Contributor," the lead article in the April 1862 issue of the *Atlantic Monthly*, in which Higginson emphasized the absolute value of literature—its nobility and "majesty"—over such mundane concerns as politics, especially in a time of national war. Ranking "high culture" above the "present fascinating trivialities of war and diplomacy," Higginson concludes, citing Rufus Choate, "'a book is the only immortality.'"[39] As a regular contributor to the *Atlantic*, "A Magazine of Literature, Art, and Politics," which was founded in Boston in 1857 (with a portrait of John Winthrop featured on its cover), Higginson was not only well known as a supporter of women writers; he was also actively engaged in an elite effort to make New England the source and center of ethical and cultural value—what the *Atlantic* called "the American idea" in its first editorial. As Higginson argued in "A Plea for Culture," which Dickinson also read in the *Atlantic* in 1867, this new American cultural aristocracy would supply "that counterpoise to mere wealth which Europe vainly seeks to secure by aristocracies of birth."[40]

Like Thomas Carlyle and Elizabeth Barrett Browning, whose pictures hung in her room, Dickinson sought to define art as a serious form of labor, craft, and work at a time of labor struggle, when the values of craftsmanship and art were being degraded by the transformation to a new economy of wage labor. In "Myself was formed - a Carpenter - / An unpretending time," Dickinson speaks in the voice of an artisan republican laborer, resisting the forces of the market and commodification represented by "a

Builder": "Had we the Art of Boards / Sufficiently developed - He'd hire us / At Halves -." To which Dickinson's "Carpenter" responds disdainfully: "We - Temples build - / I said -" (Fr 475). Here as elsewhere, Dickinson identifies her poetic craft with the sacred and unalienated value of labor as "Art" in an older artisan system. "Dare you see a Soul at the 'White Heat?'" presents the village "Blacksmith" as a "symbol for the finer Forge / That soundless tugs - within -" (Fr 401C); and, at a time when the local Amherst economy was being pressed into production of cash crops for the national market, "The Products of my Farm are these" links poetic creation—"With Us, 'tis Harvest all the Year"—with the self-sufficiency and barter of an older agricultural economy (Fr 1036).

"Some - Work for Immortality - / The Chiefer part, for Time -," Dickinson wrote in 1863, setting the new commercial economy of money, exchange, and free-flowing cash—"The Bullion of Today"—against the "Slow Gold," "the Currency / Of Immortality -" she associates with the transcendent work of art. "One's - Money - One's - the Mine -" (Fr 536), she writes, invoking contemporary political debates about the gold standard as opposed to the free circulation of greenback notes. But Dickinson's artistic and class removal could also make her impervious to the social misery of others. In a letter written to the Norcross sisters about the economic panic of 1873, she pokes fun at the national "scare" set off by the financial failure of the banking firm of "Jay Cooke": "I am not yet 'thrown out of employment,' nor ever receiving 'wages' find them materially 'reduced'" (L 2:515), she affirms, at a time when millions, including many farmers and workers in Amherst, were hard hit by the most severe economic depression in American history. For Dickinson as for other members of her class during the war years and after, art becomes a new form of social and class distinction, a higher realm of culture, value, and truth through which an older elite order seeks to maintain its power against the rising forces of materialism, commerce, democracy, mixture, modernity, and the masses.

While Dickinson's "Work for Immortality" and the forms in which she circulated it look backward toward a set of Federalist and country values embodied in the figure of George Washington, her work also looks forward to the increasing valorization of art as an aesthetic object separate from the messiness of politics and history that came to be the dominant mythos of literary modernism and that still shapes the ways Dickinson's work is interpreted today. By reading Dickinson as a poet whose unsettled and unsettling *interiors* existed *inside* rather than *outside* the political and social struggles of her times, I have tried to move beyond the "public" and "private" frames that have too often structured past approaches to her work. I have tried to suggest some of the new social and aesthetic perspectives that might be opened by reading—or more properly rereading—Dickinson's life, letters, and poems *within* the political histories that she lived, suffered, wrote about, and resisted.

NOTES

I am indebted to Coleman Hutchison for his expert and thorough research assistance on the political contexts of Dickinson's work.

Dickinson's letters are quoted from *The Letters of Emily Dickinson*, ed. Thomas H. Johnson and Theodora Ward, 3 vols. (Cambridge, Mass.: Harvard University Press, 1958). Subsequent references are cited as (L) in the text.

Dickinson's poems are quoted from *The Poems of Emily Dickinson: Variorum Edition*, ed. R. W. Franklin, 3 vols. (Cambridge, Mass.: Harvard University Press, 1998). Subsequent references are cited as (Fr) in the text.

1. Letter to Salmon P. Chase, July 23, 1855; reprinted in *Emily Dickinson's Home: Letters of Edward Dickinson and His Family*, ed. Millicent Todd Bingham (New York: Harper, 1955), 568. For an excellent account of Whig political history, see Michael F. Holt, *The Rise and Fall of the American Whig Party: Jacksonian Politics and the Onset of the Civil War* (New York: Oxford University Press, 1999).

2. Speech of Otis P. Lord, speaker of the Massachusetts House of Representatives, at the Whig State Convention, October 2, 1855; reprinted in *Emily Dickinson's Home*, 393.

3. Alexander Hamilton, James Madison, John Jay, *The Federalist Papers*, ed. Clinton Rossiter (New York: Penguin Putnam, 1999), 52.

4. During the years when American literary studies was being constituted as a distinct national field, Lionel Trilling observed: "In

the United States at this time liberalism is not only the only dominant but even the sole intellectual tradition. For it is a plain fact that nowadays there are no conservative or reactionary ideas in general circulation": Preface, *The Liberal Imagination: Essays on Literature and Society* (New York : Harcourt Brace Jovanovich, 1950), n. p.

5. See also Martha Dickinson Bianchi's description of Edward's Commencement tea party, which was held annually for forty years: "Here one could always find Governors and Judges, interesting missionaries, famous professors from our best colleges, editors of high repute, fair women and brave men. . . . Later on in her life, Emily Dickinson forsook her usual seclusion at these times, and radiant as a flying spirit, diaphanously dressed in white, always with a flower in her hand, measured her wit and poured her wine amid much excitement and applause from those fortunate enough to get near her": *The Life and Letters of Emily Dickinson* (Boston: Houghton Mifflin, 1924), 42.

6. Cited in Richard B. Sewall, *The Life of Emily Dickinson*, 2 vols. (New York: Farrar, Straus and Giroux, 1974), 1:60. Editorial reprinted in *Emily Dickinson's Home*, 527.

7. In addition to serving as a representative to Congress in 1853–1855, Edward had a distinguished record of public service, including representative to the General Court of Massachusetts, in 1838, 1839, and 1874; state senator in 1842 and 1843; member of the Governor's Council in 1845 and 1846; delegate to the Whig National Convention in 1852; delegate to the state Whig Convention in 1855; possible candidate for governor in 1859; and nominee for lieutenant governor in 1860 and 1861, which he declined. After leaving national politics in 1855, he continued to serve in numerous local and state organizations, including lifelong trustee of Amherst College and treasurer, 1835–1873; president of Amherst and Belchertown Railroad; director of the Home Mission Society; trustee of Northampton Lunatic Asylum; chair of the annual Amherst Cattle Show; and member of the local Temperance Society and First Church Parish Committee. When he died of a heart attack in June 1874, he was delivering a speech as representative to the Massachusetts House in support of increased funding for the Massachusetts Central Railroad.

8. Betsy Erkkila, "Emily Dickinson and Class," *American Literary History* 4 (1992): 1–27.

9. Charles Sumner, "Report on the War with Mexico" (April 1847); reprinted in *Old South Leaflets*, vol. 6 (Boston: Old South Work, 1902), 30.

10. Leo Marx, *The Machine in the Garden: Technology and the Pastoral Ideal in America* (New York: Oxford University Press, 1964), 180.

11. Margaret Fuller, *Woman in the Nineteenth Century* (New York: W. W. Norton, 1971), 37.

12. Martha Dickinson Bianchi, *Emily Dickinson: Face to Face: Unpublished Letters with Notes and Reminiscences* (Boston: Houghton Mifflin, 1932), 49.

13. See Glenn C. Altschuler and Stuart Blumin, who argue that during the antebellum period the social elite retreated into what Richard L. Bushman has called "vernacular liberalism"—"an unreflective absorption in the daily routines of work, family, and social life, those private and communal domains that the small governments of the era hardly touched": "'Where is the Real America?': Politics and Popular Consciousness in the Antebellum Era," *American Quarterly* 49 (June 1997): 230.

14. Dickinson's first published poem "Sic transit gloria mundi" appeared anonymously on February 20, 1852 in the *Springfield Daily Republican*, which was edited by Samuel Bowles. The poem was prefaced by a note inviting a more direct "correspondence" between the author and the *Republican*: "The hand that wrote the following amusing medley to a gentleman friend of ours, as 'a valentine,' is capable of writing very fine things, and there is certainly no presumption in entertaining a private wish that a correspondence, more direct than this, may be established between it and the Republican" (Fr 1:53).

15. For a consideration of the ways Habermas's notion of the public sphere might be used to discuss what Nancy Fraser has called *subaltern counterpublics*, see Fraser, "Rethinking the Public Sphere: A Contribution to the Critique of Actually Existing Democracy," in *Habermas and the Public Sphere*, ed. Craig Calhoun (Cambridge, Mass.: The MIT Press, 1992), 109–42; Mary P. Ryan, "Gender and Public Access: Women's Politics in Nineteenth-Century America," in Calhoun, 259–88; and Seyla Benhabib, "Models of Public Space: Hannah Arendt, the Liberal Tradition, and Jürgen Habermas," in Calhoun, 73–98.

16. Jürgen Habermas, *The Structural Transformation of the Public*

Sphere: An Inquiry into a Category of Bourgeois Society, trans. Thomas Burger (Cambridge, Mass.: The MIT Press, 1991), 48, 49.

17. According to Mabel Loomis Todd, Lavinia told her that while she preserved Dickinson's poems, "She had burned without examination hundreds of manuscripts, and letters to Emily, *many of them from nationally known persons*": "Emily Dickinson's Literary Début," *Harper's Monthly Magazine* (March 1930): 463, my emphasis.

18. "We invite our friends to assist us by communications on such subjects as they may deem important or interesting," the editor wrote in the first issue of the *Springfield Republican* as a daily on April 4, 1844: 1. Presenting itself as politically independent after 1855 and the demise of the Whig Party, the *Republican* sought to supplement the news with items of social, political, and cultural interest.

19. On the shift of literary and cultural authority from New York to Boston see John Stafford, *The Literary Criticism of 'Young America': A Study of the Relationship of Politics and Literature, 1837–1850* (Berkeley: University of California Press, 1952), 121–22. Ryan also argues that after the Civil War there is a reversal in "the spatial ordering, if not the power relations, of public life," as the lower classes lay claim to "open public spaces" and the elite classes exert more invisible power behind the scenes ("Gender" 277–78). See also Lawrence W. Levine, *Highbrow/Lowbrow: The Emergence of Cultural Hierarchy in America* (Cambridge, Mass.: Harvard University Press, 1990). In *On Native Grounds* (New York: Harcourt, Brace and Company, 1942), Alfred Kazin observes that literary capital shifted once again to New York when William Dean Howells moved there in 1888, taking "the literary center of the country with him . . . from Boston to New York" (4).

20. For a detailed discussion of Dickinson's correspondence with women and her engagement in women's literary culture, see Betsy Erkkila, *The Wicked Sisters: Women Poets, Literary History, and Discord* (New York: Oxford University Press, 1992), 17–98.

21. For a discussion of the Norcross sisters' involvement with the Concord Saturday Club, which included among its members Bronson and Louisa May Alcott and Lydia and Ralph Waldo Emerson, see Martha Ackmann, "Biographical Sketches of Dickinson," in *The Emily Dickinson Handbook*, ed. Gudrun Grabher, Roland Hagenbüchle, and Cristanne Miller (Amherst: University of Massachusetts Press, 1998), 19–20.

22. For Edward Dickinson's opposition to government-imposed abolition, see my discussion of his October 1861 letter in this essay, 156.

23. In a public letter about the fourth of July celebration in Belchertown in 1855, Edward Dickinson expressed hope that "by the help of Almighty God, not another inch of our soil *heretofore conse-crated* to freedom, shall *hereafter* be polluted by the advancing tread of slavery": in *The Years and Hours of Emily Dickinson*, ed. Jay Leyda, 2 vols. (New Haven: Yale University Press, 1960), 1:333; subsequent references will be cited parenthetically as YH. Although Dickinson opposed the expansion of slavery into the territories, he also opposed the abolitionist goal of immediate emancipation of Southern slaves. For him as for many in the antebellum era, including Lincoln, anti-slavery zeal was underwritten by a fear that the white American republic would be "polluted" by the "advancing tread" of *blackness* into the new states. Emily Dickinson appears to have shared her father's anxiety about the pollution of the American republic by ethnic, racial, and low class others. See, for example, her 1851 recommendation that Austin "kill" some of his Irish students at Endicott School in Boston: "there are so many now, there is no room for the Americans" (L 1:113); the aristocratic speaker's sense of bereaved entitlement and loss when "The Negro" takes "the Pearl" of white civilization "Home - / Home to his Hut!" in her poem "The Malay took - the Pearl -"(Fr 451); and Dickinson's description of her flight from the "new Black Man" on the Dickinson grounds in 1881 (L 3:706).

24. Here as elsewhere in her evocation of poetic mastery, Dickinson's "The Lamp burns sure - within -" enacts Benjamin's historical materialist view of the "horror" that underlies "cultural treasures": "They owe their existence not only to the efforts of the great minds and talents who have created them, but also to the anonymous toil of their contemporaries. There is no document of civilization which is not at the same time a document of barbarism": *Illuminations: Essays and Reflections*, ed. Hannah Arendt, trans. Harry Zohn (New York: Schoken Books, 1969), 256.

25. For a more detailed analysis of the hierarchies of racial and class difference that inform Dickinson's poems, see Erkkila, "Emily Dickinson and Class," especially 9–12. In " 'The Negro never knew': Emily Dickinson and Racial Typology in the Post-Bellum Period,"

Paula Bennett discusses "The Malay - took the Pearl -" in the context of the persistent racial stereotyping in such journals as the *Springfield Republican*. (See "'The Negro Never Knew': Emily Dickinson and Racial Typology in the Post-Bellum Period," in *Legacy: A Journal of American Women Writers* 19, no. 1 (2002): 53–61. For an alternative reading see Vivian Pollak, who grants the racial stereotyping of poems such as "The Malay" at the same time that she emphasizes the positive dimensions of Dickinson's "use of race as a politically subversive form of self-definition": "Dickinson and the Poetics of Whiteness," *The Emily Dickinson Journal* 9 (2000): 90.

26. *The Education of Henry Adams* (Boston: Houghton Mifflin, 1961), 34.

27. In *A Theory of Justice* (Cambridge: Belknap Press of Harvard University Press, 1971) the liberal political theorist John Rawls writes: "Each person possesses an inviolability founded on justice that even the welfare of society as a whole cannot override" (3).

28. Johnson writes that Edward Dickinson "was in Boston for the convention" (L 2:368), but the state convention was held in Worcester, Massachusetts. Johnson is also incorrect in saying that the "Bell and Everett party" was formed on September 12, 1860 in Massachusetts. The national Constitutional Union Party was formed in Baltimore in 1859. John Bell, the presidential nominee was a slaveholder from Tennessee, who sided with the Southern rebels during the Civil War. The Massachusetts State Constitutional Union Party was formed in Boston in early 1860; the state convention took place in Worcester, Massachusetts on September 12, 1860; see *Springfield Daily Republican*, "The Bell-Everett Convention at Worcester," September 13, 1860.

29. Letter to Salmon Chase, January 23, 1860, reprinted in *Emily Dickinson's Home*, 569.

30. *Springfield Daily Republican*, October 17, 1861. Here again, Dickinson biography has been mistaken in alluding to only one nomination of Edward Dickinson as candidate for lieutenant governor. Dickinson, was in fact, nominated as a candidate for lieutenant governor on two different occasions: once by the Constitutional Union Party at their convention in Worcester in 1860 and once by the Republican Party at their convention in Worcester in 1861.

31. Mason White Tyler, *Recollections of the Civil War* (1912) in YH 2:26.

32. On May 26, 1864, at the very time when Austin had been

drafted, the *Springfield Republican* reported: "Amherst has heretofore been rather backward in filling her quotas, but . . . the people put the thing through genteelly, and in town meeting voted to [fill the quota by paying for substitutes]" (YH 2:88).

33. Of the ten poems that Dickinson is known to have published during her lifetime, seven of these were published during the Civil War, including her manifesto poem "I taste a liquor never brewed -," which was published as "The May-Wine" in the *Springfield Republican* a few weeks after the war began. In 1864, she published four poems, three of which appeared in *Drum Beat*, a fund-raising magazine for the U.S. Sanitary Commission, which was founded in 1861 to provide medical supplies and help for the Union army. Karen Dandurand has argued importantly that these poems "must be seen as [Dickinson's] contribution to the Union cause" ("New Dickinson Civil War Publications," *American Literature* 56 [1984]: 17). However, if she did contribute these poems voluntarily, and there is no evidence for this, they were more likely sent to support the sick, wounded, and dying, who were sacrificing their lives in support of a cause that was—in Dickinson's view—at best questionable. For a detailed discussion of Dickinson's poems in relation to the Civil War, see Thomas Ford, "Emily Dickinson and the Civil War," *University of Kansas City Review* 31 (Spring 1965): 199–203; and especially Shira Wolosky, *Emily Dickinson: A Voice of War* (New Haven: Yale University Press, 1984).

34. Although the exact date of this letter is unknown, Leyda suggests that it was written in late December 1862 in response to the announcement of a new long poem by Robert Browning in the *Springfield Republican*, December 20, 1862 (YH 2:72).

35. See *Adjutant Stearns* (Boston: Sabbath School Society, 1862), which was written by Stearns's father William Augustus Stearns; see also Barton Levi St. Armand, *Emily Dickinson and Her Culture: The Soul's Society* (Cambridge: Cambridge University Press, 1984), 104–15.

36. Abraham Lincoln, *The Collected Works of Abraham Lincoln*, 9 vols., ed. Roy P. Basler (New Brunswick: Rutgers University Press, 1953–55), 7:23; 8:333.

37. Dickinson's apparently negative attitude to Lincoln may have been shared by Judge Lord, who in 1866 made a controversial ruling in favor of a man who was tarred and feathered for saying that the assassination of Lincoln was a good thing and, according to the

Springfield Republican, "the best news he had heard for many a day" (cited in Sewall, *Life,* 2:648).

38. In 1871, Sumner was removed from his influential international position as chair of the Senate Foreign Relations Committee (1861–1871) when he helped to defeat President Ulysses S. Grant's proposal to annex Santo Domingo. The following year Sumner was also condemned by the Massachusetts legislature when in a conciliatory effort toward the South, he introduced a Senate resolution against putting the names of battles between American citizens on the army's regimental colors. Although Sumner was a leading figure in the radical republican fight for black emancipation, reconstruction, and civil rights, his relations with the Dickinson family appear to have remained cordial throughout his political career. In 1855, while Edward Dickinson was serving in Congress, Sumner gave him a copy of Lydia Maria Child's *Isaac T. Hopper* as a gift for Mrs. Dickinson (YH 1:330). In a letter to Sumner dated May 12, 1862, Edward expressed "high esteem" for Sumner's Senate "speech on the duty of the U.S. Govt. to recognise the Independence of Hayti & Liberia"; and in another letter to Sumner dated July 20, 1868, Edward thanks him for his speech in favor of "specie payments" on the "National debt." Efforts to repudiate the national debt will, Edward fears, "demoralise the people," destroy public "faith" in the government, and follow "in the wake of Republics that have existed & flourished & died out": reprinted in Norbert Hirschhorn, "New Finds in Dickinson Family Correspondence," *Emily Dickinson International Society Bulletin* (May/June 1995): 5.

39. Thomas Wentworth Higginson, "Letter to a Young Contributor," *Atlantic Monthly* 9 (April 1862): 410. Rufus Choate was a nationally known Massachusetts lawyer and orator, who completed Daniel Webster's unexpired term in the Senate in 1841. *The Works of Rufus Choate: with a memoir of his life* by Samuel Gilman Brown was published by Little, Brown in Boston in 1862.

40. Thomas Wentworth Higginson, "A Plea for Culture," *Atlantic Monthly* 14 (January 1867): 30. At about the same time, Whitman was calling for a more radical democratization of American literature in *Democratic Vistas* (1871), parts of which were published as "Democracy" and "Personalism" in the *The Galaxy* in 1867 and 1868. Higginson objected to the muscular masculinity and bodiliness of Whitman's democracy; he thought *Leaves of Grass* should have been

burned (see Tilden J. Edelstein, *Strange Enthusiasm: A Life of Thomas Wentworth Higginson* [New Haven: Yale University Press, 1968], 352-56). When Dickinson said that she "was told that [Whitman] was disgraceful" in a letter to Higginson (April 25, 1862; L 2:404), she may have been responding to a review entitled "'*Leaves of Grass*'—Smut in Them" in the *Springfield Republican* on June 16, 1860. The review was probably written by her friend Josiah Gilbert Holland.

Dickinson in Context

Nineteenth-Century American Women Poets

Cheryl Walker

B y now the feminist argument that Emily Dickinson should be read in the context of other nineteenth-century American women poets has a long history. To be sure, it is still a minor strain in Dickinson criticism, but what is minor, as the poet herself was fond of suggesting, can over time find a permanent place at the table. The first hint that this might happen came in 1977, when Emily Stipes Watts published her ambitious survey of American women poets and situated Dickinson among her peers, arguing that "In a variety of ways, . . . Dickinson's poetry stands firmly within the developing tendencies of [nineteenth-century] American female verse."[1] Watts also illustrated this idea by giving a great many examples, expanding considerably our sense of who was writing during Dickinson's lifetime and what they wrote.

I still remember the anxiety I felt at the publication of Watts's *The Poetry of American Women from 1632 to 1945*. At that time, I was hard at work on my own presentation of the Nightingale Tradition and wondered if there would be anything left to say. Even now, looking back at Watts's initial survey, I am impressed by the originality of its scholarship and its attempt to explore not only the subject matter of women's poetry but also the similarity of some forms of their expression. Unlike some later feminist critics, Watts studied the language of women's verse as well as its thematic content. But, of course, there was more to say after all.

In this essay I will remind readers of the arguments that made the feminist intervention important in the first place. Dickinson had usually been compared to male poets—Emerson, Whitman, Hopkins, Tennyson, Hardy, Frost, Stevens, etc.—but, as I will indicate, feminists were neither the first nor the only critics to consider Dickinson in the context of other women poets. After a brief summary of this history, I will suggest that, even within feminism, views concerning the importance of Dickinson's gender, as it impacts our understanding of her relation to other women poets, have changed over the past several decades, perhaps as our views of gender have changed. Whereas initially it seemed to us that women poets, because they were so often essentialized in public discourse, should be considered together as a disempowered group, feminist second thoughts have complicated this notion by focusing on the disparities within this group due to issues, such as race, class, ethnicity, sexual preference, and geographic location. This has contributed to a repositioning of Dickinson (and sometimes a reisolating of her as a special case). In the end, however, I will argue for a balanced appreciation of Dickinson's relationship to her contemporaries: by not only looking at the subject matter but also drawing attention to the echoes of other women poets in Dickinson's work, I will reaffirm the argument that she needs to be understood as simultaneously inside and outside the realm of nineteenth-century American women's poetry, the beneficiary of its strengths as well as our most exemplary critic of its limitations.

Putting Dickinson in Her Place

To begin with, we must remember that feminists were not the first to link Emily Dickinson to other nineteenth-century women poets. As long ago as 1948, Robert E. Spiller et al., in the long used and once highly respected *Literary History of the United States*, had this to say: "Reminding us of Christina Rossetti, of whom she was, except for five days and eight years, the exact contemporary, and of Elizabeth Barrett, without the fulfillment of love in marriage, [Emily Dickinson] lived for fifty-six years on the quiet Amherst street her thrilling life as an adventuress in eternity—and as eternity's witty critic, too."[2] After these somewhat overheated comments, however, very little is said in Spiller about what might specifically link Dickinson to other women writers of her time, and no attempt is made to connect her to *American* women poets.

For his part, Karl Keller in *The Only Kangaroo among the Beauty* (1979) tended to equate the potential influence of contemporary women writers with bluestocking feminism, "the hopeless ditch," as he called it, echoing a letter by Dickinson about her response to Elizabeth Stuart Phelps. He emphasized the repressiveness of Victorian culture, concluding, "The refinement it asked for in a woman of parts, when compared with the primitivism Emily Dickinson admitted to and was awfully self-conscious about, was a sign of deficient vitality. Distortion through awe gave her far more versions of life than they could approve of."[3] Other women poets, it seems, were not capable of "distortion through awe," so Dickinson seems here a breed apart, "the only kangaroo among the beauty."

In *Emily Dickinson and Her Culture* (1984), Barton Levi St. Armand was readier to admit that the Amherst poet made positive uses of her surrounding culture, insisting that Dickinson's art was "an assemblage, a 'quilting' of elite and popular ideas on to a sturdy underlying folk form, frame, or fabric."[4] In his comparison of her grief poems with those of Lydia Sigourney, he found evidence that tied the two poets together through the "gospel of consolation." "Sometimes she accepted its formulas without question; sometimes she subverted them through exaggeration, burlesque, and distortion; sometimes she used them only as pretexts for outright skepticism and satire."[5] Yet St. Armand comes close to reducing the legacy of American women poets entirely to sentimentalism, as though grief were the only subject where Dickinson's interests intersected with theirs.

Even David Reynolds, who followed up St. Armand's lead with his study of the influence of popular culture on America's most significant nineteenth-century writers, found little to appreciate in the popular women poets of Emily Dickinson's day. In *Beneath the American Renaissance: The Subversive Imagination in the Age of Emerson and Melville* (1988), Reynolds found Dickinson's "treatment of highly experimental themes through dense images in rhythmic poetry . . . constituted her greatest departure from other women writers of the day."[6] Having disposed of American women poets as insufficiently "subversive," he then went on to compare Dickinson's strategies of disruption and her sensationalist imagination to those of male (and a few female) novelists and prose writers.

None of these studies was prepared to take seriously the notion that women poets had a special relationship to one another both because of their shared circumstances within Victorian culture and because of the almost universal tendency of nineteenth-century criticism to place gender at the center of all considerations of women's poetry. That argument was put forward primarily by feminist critics. In *Literary Women: The Great Writers* (1976), Ellen Moers made a compelling case that, for any woman writer in a strictly gendered society, the writing of other women is likely to be of special interest, and she drew particular attention to Dickinson's infatuation with Elizabeth Barrett Browning's *Aurora Leigh*, the verse narrative that explores the development of a woman poet in Victorian England.

In the decade after Ellen Moers's highly successful volume, further arguments were made—by Joanne Dobson, Vivian Pollak, and myself, among others—that greater attention to the peculiarities of *women's culture* in the nineteenth century might help us to understand the phenomenon of Dickinson's life as well as the types of poems she wrote. As the gendered oppressiveness of this culture came into clearer focus, feminist critics were eager to unveil an Emily Dickinson in conflict with her family and her times. In *My Life a Loaded Gun: Female Creativity and Feminist Poetics*, Paula Bennett made Dickinson's creative energy inextricable from her rebelliousness; Suzanne Juhasz, in *Naked and Fiery Forms: Modern American Poetry by Women—A New Tradition*, spoke of Dickinson's wholesale rejection of "woman's traditional roles."[7] Of course, these arguments tended to lead one away from comparing Dickinson to other, less rebellious, women poets.

Much of this early feminist criticism was psychological rather than deeply cultural, with the poet's family looming large, in such works as Cynthia Griffin Wolff's monumental biography and Barbara Antonina Clarke Mossberg's *When A Writer Is a Daughter*, as a source of oppression. But there were also those who examined the conditions of women's publishing (Nina Baym and Susan Coultrap-McQuin), the influence of the Cult of True Womanhood on Dickinson's milieu (Joanne Dobson and I), and the anxiety inevitably provoked in a strong woman poet by gender constructs (Vivian Pollak, Sandra Gilbert, and Susan Gubar).

According to these arguments, women poets were largely inhibited by two tenets of bourgeois ideology: one, that women violated the "cult of true womanhood" (piety, purity, domesticity, and submissiveness)[8] by writing for a public audience; and two, that, when they did write, women poets must avoid transgressing the boundaries of their allotted sphere. For us as feminist critics, the example of Rufus Griswold, the premier anthologist of his day, was instructive. Griswold published a popular anthology of women's poetry, *The Female Poets of America* (1849, rev. 1873), comparing women's poems to "dews and flowers" gratefully encountered after the "glaciers and rocks" of male productions. Enormously influential, Griswold had no fondness for women who indulged in "rude or ignoble passion," praising Frances Osgood in her commemorative volume *The Memorial*, because "she had no need to travel beyond the legitimate sphere of women's observation."[9]

Though Dickinson seems strangely unaware of the ubiquitous Rufus Griswold, it is easy to find poems that operate well within the acceptable parameters of Griswold's notion of women's sphere. Like many in *The Female Poets of America*, she wrote a great deal about renunciation and secret sorrow. In a poem such as "I tie my Hat - I crease my Shawl" (Fr 522), Dickinson details the little tasks that make up bourgeois female identity, trivial tasks described as "life's little duties," which she too declares necessary, even to the volcanic spirit, "To hold our Senses - on." A whole host of women poets in Griswold's anthology—Lydia Sigourney, Catherine Warfield, Eleanor Lee, Elizabeth Oakes-Smith, Frances Osgood, Amelia Welby, Julia Ward Howe, and others—confessed to similar frustrations simmering just below the surface of their seemingly conventional lives but reaffirmed their commitment to the structures (and strictures) of domesticity nevertheless. This is the burden of what I called the "free bird" poem.

Many feminist critics noted that Emily Dickinson spoke of the "poetical" tendencies of young women of her day but rejected the role of the "poetess" in order to keep her independence. Nevertheless, she was no political firebrand, and even in her unpublished poems, she was often coy and duplicitous, as Alicia Suskin Ostriker noted in *Stealing the Language: The Emergence of Women's Poetry in America* (1986).

Recognition of this duplicity was the task of 1980s feminist critics, who emphasized Dickinson's decision to "Tell all the truth but tell it slant" (Fr 1263). Like the tapestries of Philomela, the nightingale of myth who was raped and then rendered mute by her brother-in-law, these poems, I argued in *The Nightingale's Burden*, encode messages of rage and longing. For her part, Joanne Dobson studied the "strategies of reticence" in poets such as Dickinson, Frances Osgood, Lydia Sigourney, and Elizabeth Oakes Smith. Insisting that these women were unable to speak freely about such matters as ambition and sexuality, Dobson like Vivian Pollak saw their poems as variously ingenious responses to a shared threat of censure.

Recently, Elizabeth Petrino's *Emily Dickinson and Her Contemporaries: Women's Verse in America, 1820–1885,* has further updated these now historical arguments by looking at specific topoi—the child elegy, the flower poem, the poem of exotic location—that were used extensively by nineteenth-century women poets including Emily Dickinson. Published in 1998, this book provides evidence of continuing interest in placing Dickinson in the context of other nineteenth-century American women poets.

Of course, from the beginning all of us, including those who looked most extensively at nineteenth-century women poets such as Alicia Ostriker and Emily Stipes Watts, were anxious to acknowledge that, despite a shared predicament, Emily Dickinson stood out among her contemporaries as an original voice. Her circumstances might be seen as limiting her poetic subject matter in some respects, but we all agreed that she was adept at transforming the inhibitions she inherited. Petrino makes the most extended case for reading Dickinson in the context of other women poets, and she puts it this way: "Dickinson was steeped in the culture and literature of nineteenth-century America. [Yet] she exploded many of the tropes and popular myths of nineteenth-century poetry, while she made the boldest quest for poetic originality."[10]

Changing the Story

It should be noted, however, that Petrino is not saying quite the same thing we were in the 1980s. Indeed, the past decade has seen a reaction against any suggestion that Dickinson's situation is best understood in a context of inhibition. Camille Paglia launched this counter offensive in 1991 by calling Dickinson Amherst's Madame de Sade. "It is a sentimental error," Paglia wrote in *Sexual Personae*,

> to think that Emily Dickinson was the victim of male obstruc-
> tionism. Without her struggle with God and father, there
> would have been no poetry. . . . Her sadism is not anger,
> the a posteriori response to social injustice. It is *hostility*, an a
> priori Achillean intolerance for the existence of others, the fe-
> male version of Romantic solipsism.[11]

In a more scholarly but no less polemical argument, with implications similar to Paglia's, Betsy Erkkila in *The Wicked Sisters* sought to disabuse her readers of the notion that women necessarily derived mutual inspiration and support from one another's work. Though Erkkila acknowledges the repressiveness of Victorian culture and believes Dickinson constructed a "literary sisterhood" out of her reading of the Brontës and Elizabeth Barrett Browning, she departs from our earlier feminist hypothesis that, *because of shared anxieties,* women's poetry, including Dickinson's, evolved into a special category of literary production, governed by similar themes and tropes; furthermore, she dismisses almost completely the value to Dickinson of other American women

poets. According to Erkkila, even Elizabeth Barrett Browning did
not impress Dickinson as a poet worthy of imitation, and, she
adds, Helen Hunt Jackson "represented precisely the model of the
popular poetess that Dickinson most abhorred."[12] For Betsy
Erkkila, as for Camille Paglia, Dickinson is best understood as a
Romantic genius, towering above her contemporaries, isolated,
disdainful, and pursued by her *own* demons rather than those of
her culture.

One can't help noticing in these critics an almost complete
reversal of the assumptions of the 1980s. In place of anxiety of
authorship, strategies of reticence, and sisterhood, we find self-
empowerment, excess, and ego. Even Paula Bennett, who in
Emily Dickinson: Woman Poet at least took seriously the example
of other women poets, reinforced a view of Dickinson as "a
being who was self-conceived," uninhibited, and, contrary to
Dobson, quite clearly ambitious. Though her later work (for example, on Sarah Piatt) has complicated this view by looking at
other bold individualists, in 1990, Bennett believed that Dickinson was the main exception. In *Woman Poet* she concludes: "Dickinson was able to take the hesitant explorations made by her fellow women poets into nature and into their own female power
and create from them a unique and fundamentally paradoxical
discourse that put into words her own subjectivity as a woman
and the specifics of her situation and desire."[13]

Very few of these arguments have had anything directly to say
about linguistic similarities between Dickinson and her contemporaries, and it was partly to supplement that deficiency that I
wrote my own polemical piece, delivered at the Emily Dickinson
Society International Conference in Washington, D.C. in 1992,
and subsequently published in *The Emily Dickinson Journal*. In
"Teaching Dickinson as a Gen[i]us: Emily among the Women," I
was intent to show that it was misleading to study Dickinson apart
from her contemporaries; I addressed similarities of expression in
Dickinson and other friends and family members (especially
Susan Gilbert) and compared her forms of expression to those of
nineteenth-century American poets such as Rose Terry Cooke, arguing that there were distinct echoes in Dickinson that deserved
further study. I tried to be evenhanded in that piece, but I suspect I

overstated my case in claiming that the "i" in the word
was a lie since Dickinson belonged to a genus, a group
whose shared literary characteristics defined her para

Now, looking back on thirty years of thinking about
Dickinson's relationship to other American women poets of her
day, I think that there is much to be gained from exploring in
some depth both sides of the issue. Gender constructs *did* affect
the way all of them presented themselves. Furthermore, there
are distinct echoes of other women poets in Dickinson's poetry,
and yet she was a thoroughgoing original at the same time. As
many feminist critics have admitted, we need to take account of
both the anxiety (the inhibitions she shared with others) and the
exceptionalism: Dickinson both defied *and* conformed to expectations about the kind of poetry women should write, and one
should acknowledge her immersion in the culture of her day
while, at the same time, measuring her radical divergence.

Hearing the Echoes

Let us consider this double positioning now in more detail as
Dickinson herself invites us to do. In a poem written about 1865,
according to both Thomas Johnson and R. W. Franklin, Dickinson makes one of her typically double-edged comments about
her poetic project.

> I was a Phebe - nothing more-
> A Phebe - nothing less -
> The little note that others dropt
> I fitted into place -
>
> I dwelt too low that any seek -
> Too shy, that any blame -
> A Phebe makes a little print
> Opon the Floors of Fame - (Fr 1009)

Dickinson often presented herself as diminutive, claiming to
make few demands upon her time or locality. Here she identifies

herself with a little bird who echoes the calls of others: "The little note that others dropt / I fitted into place." Of course, she
also often undercuts her own apologetics. Here it is well to remember that Phoebe is also associated with Artemis and Diana,
goddesses of the moon and the hunt. And one should ask oneself, is she making a large claim or a little one when she says "A
Phebe makes a little print / Opon the Floors of Fame"? Perhaps
others (other women poets?) make none. One interpretation of
this poem suggests that she was aware of reworking the themes
and phrases of other poets. But when we hear them in her uncanny cadences, such "notes" often sound very different. One
might think of her fascicles as her "little print" made upon the
"Floors of Fame," and, as we have come to see recently, with the
response to R. W. Franklin's work, they hardly represent an un-
demanding legacy. Indeed, the fascicles now form the basis of a
whole scholarly industry. Dickinson has certainly made her
mark, her "little print," a lasting source of interest to the literary
world.[15]

To see the benefit of placing Dickinson's poetry beside that of
other American women poets, one can hardly do better, I still believe, than to look at the work of Rose Terry (Cooke).[16] Her 1861
volume, *Poems*, shows Terry writing against the grain of most
women poets; a true Romantic, she is quite as wild in her way as
Dickinson was in hers. We do know that Rose Terry was a regular contributor to the *Atlantic Monthly* and worked with T. W.
Higginson, though the records of this connection have apparently been lost. We also know that Samuel Bowles gave his wife a
copy of Rose Terry's poem in the early 1860s.[17] Though we have
no proof that Dickinson read these poems,[18] the echoes of
Terry's "Daisies" in Dickinson's "Further in Summer than the
Birds" still seem to me startling.

Terry writes:

> Fair and peaceful daisies,
>   Smiling in the grass,
> Who hath sung your praises?
>   Poets by you pass,
> And I alone am left to celebrate your mass.[19]

Dickinson echoes:

> Further in Summer than the Birds -
> Pathetic from the Grass -
> A Minor Nation celebrates
> It's unobtrusive Mass - (Fr 895a)

According to both Franklin and Johnson, this poem was composed in the mid-1860s, well after the publication of Terry's book. Though Dickinson is speaking of crickets and Terry of daisies, it is also tantalizing to remember that Dickinson often associated herself with daisies (for example, in the Master letters where she calls herself Daisy) and that she described her project, in "The Robin's my criterion for tune," as being about as New England/American as the daisy.

One might easily compare Terry's "Bluebeard's Closet" with its gothic refrain "The chamber is there!" with Dickinson's equally gothic and equally psychological "One need not be a Chamber to be Haunted," composed about 1862. Both poems make the point that the ghosts we fear most are those that cannot be defended against because they inhabit ourselves. In Terry's poem: "Flying or staying, / *The chamber* [of horrors] *is there!*";[20] it is there (as Bluebeard is) within as well as without. In Dickinson's poem, the interior spectre is most to be feared: "Ourself behind ourself, concealed - / Should startle most - / Assassin hid in our Apartment / Be Horror's least -" (Fr 407).

One might also consider Terry's "Wood Worship" with its Sabbath observed in Nature and its "sermons from a flower" as an incentive for Dickinson's "Some keep the Sabbath going to church" (Fr 236), probably composed a year or so after Terry's volume of poems appeared. Terry is more reverent:

> Here the thick leaves that scent the tremulous air
>   Let the bright sunshine pass with softened light,
> And lips unwonted breathe instinctive prayer,
>   In these cool arches filled with verdurous night.
>
> There needs no bending knee, no costly shrine,
>   No fluctuant crowd to hail divinity;

> Here the heart kneels, and owns the love divine,
>> That made for man the earth so fair and free.[21]

Dickinson's poem is wittier—"With a bobolink - for a Chorister - / And an Orchard - for a Dome -"—but it resembles Terry's in terms of the desire to dispense with the formal trappings of religion.

Though David Reynolds assumes that only Dickinson "treated highly experimental themes through dense images in rhythmic poetry," some of Rose Terry's poems might also be described in these very same terms. Like the popular prose sensationalists Reynolds explores as sources for Dickinson's work, Rose Terry's poetry sometimes verges on melodrama. In "Basile Renaud," her speaker Clara murders her unfaithful lover and, like Julia Kristeva's Medusa-figure, laughs about it. In "After the Camanches," which was published anonymously in *Putnam's* in August 1856,[22] the poet relishes the image of Indian scalps taken in revenge for the kidnapping of a white woman.

> Saddle, saddle, saddle!
>> Redden spur and thong;
> Ride like the mad tornado,
>> The track is lonely and long.
> Spare not horse nor rider;
>> Fly for the stolen bride;
> Bring her home on the crupper,
>> A scalp on either side! (AWP 273)

St. Armand notwithstanding, not all women poets were sentimentalists. Rose Terry (Cooke) violates the code of True Womanhood when, in "Captive," she insists upon being let out of the cage of gender inhibitions.

> I beat my wings against the wire,
>> I pant my trammelled heart away;
> The fever of one mad desire
>> Burns and consumes me all the day.

> What care I for your tedious love,
> For tender word or fond caress?
> I die for one free flight above,
> One rapture of the wilderness! (AWP 272)

Though Terry's commitment to freedom over romance gives "Captive" a special edge, this poem might make a fit companion to Dickinson's feverishly romantic "Wild nights - Wild nights."

Terry, who took the name Cooke when she married, is better known as an early Realist writer of local-color stories, yet her poetry can be as feverishly Romantic as Dickinson's. In "Semele" she, like a female Ahab, solicits the erotic spirit of fire: "Come Power! Love calls thee,—come, with all the god endowed!" (AWP 267). And in "Monotropa," where she explores the construction of the Indian Pipe flower (one of Dickinson's favorites), Terry condemns the self-protective flower of chastity in words that sometimes remind one of the Amherst poet.

> Sweetest souls of beauty-lovers,
> Above your cups the gold bee hovers,
> In sequestered maze and awe,
> Repelled by instinct's sacred law;
> Knowing well no sweetness lies
> In your frosted chalices.
> Never bird, nor bee, nor moth,
> Inebriate with sunny sloth,
> Dare intrude on hallowed ground,
> Cease thyself, vain rhythmic sound! (AWP 264)

The fascinating thing about this floral tribute is that the beauty of the Indian Pipe comes to seem entirely selfish (monotropic) in its self-reflexive teleology. The Greek word, monotropa, means living alone or solitary, but the as-yet unmarried Rose Terry is less than complimentary to this "utterly intact and calm" symbol of virginity. Thus, the last line (directed, it seems, to some wayward bird, bee, or moth) sounds almost bitter as it reproves the hungry heart in similarly self-reflexive terms ("Cease thyself"). The indict-

ment of the vanity of the "rhythmic sound," then, disengages itself from bird, bee, and moth and becomes attached to its
metonymic other, the heart of chastity, which, it is suggested, is
more culpable because it brings no creature pleasure but itself.
Those who are "inebriate with sunny sloth" seem by contrast
preferable because at least they are not "cold to Summer's rapturous balm." They are the true pagan spirits of Nature.

It is also worth noting that in the same year as the publication
of Terry's *Poems*, Emily Dickinson's "I taste a liquor never
brewed" appeared in the *Springfield Republican* with its tribute to
the hummingbird, an "Inebriate of Air" and "debauchee of dew"
(Fr 207). At times Dickinson was also critical of the virginal life
and found herself driven to imagine poetic alternatives.

As I have suggested elsewhere,[23] Rose Terry Cooke is one of
those subversive nineteenth-century women poets whom we did
not take account of in our early assessments of Dickinson's exceptionalism. There are others, too, such as Maria White Lowell,
who, though more conventional in some ways than either Terry
or Dickinson, also invites comparison with the Amherst poet.
Lowell, who was James Russell Lowell's first wife, had a brief
vogue during which her poems were published in contemporary
journals, but she suffered from tuberculosis and died at an early
age. After her death, her husband had privately printed an edition of her poems, but Emily Dickinson wrote to T. W. Higginson in 1870, expressing ignorance of her work: "You told me of
Mrs. Lowell's Poems. Would you tell me where I could find them
or are they not for sight?" (L 352). Of course, this does not prove
that she hadn't ever read Lowell's poetry, especially since she was
often less than forthright with Higginson.

Strangely enough, some poems by Maria Lowell sound surprisingly Dickinsonian. For example, "The Sick Room" uses the
word "punctual" as no other nineteenth-century poet to my
knowledge did except for Emily herself. Lowell's poem contrasts
the burgeoning springtime outside the window with the omi-
nous shadows inside the sick room, beginning:

> A spirit is treading the earth,
>   As wind treads the vibrating string;

I know thy feet so beautiful,
   Thy punctual feet, O Spring! (AWP 195)

In "New feet within my garden go," Dickinson similarly writes:

> New Children play opon the green -
> New Weary sleep below -
> And still the pensive Spring returns -
> And still the punctual snow! (Fr 79)

Both poems use the word "punctual" to drive home the timely un-timeliness of illness and death.

Franklin dates this poem about 1859. Lowell died in 1853, but not before composing her poignant appreciation of the beauties of Nature that those in "the sick room" can only regard with typically Dickinsonian baffled longing:

> Thou flushest the sunken orchard
>   With the lift of thy rosy wing;
> The peach will not part with her sunrise
>   Though great noon-bells should ring. (AWP 195)

In "great noon-bells" perhaps we can hear a precursor of Dickinson's image in "It was not Death, for I stood up" (Fr 355): "It was not Night, for all the Bells / Put out their Tongues, for Noon."

An even more unusual moment of convergence occurs in a poem entitled "An Opium Fantasy," where Lowell recounts a dream or at least a vision. Many critically ill patients used opium in the nineteenth century, so one does not wonder that Maria White Lowell knew something of its effects. Other women poets wrote about drug experiences too, but Lowell's account is the most Dickinsonian, especially where she says:

> What wakes me from my heavy dream?
>   Or am I still asleep?
> Those long and soft vibrations seem
>   A slumberous charm to keep.

> The graceful play, a moment stopped,
>   Distance again unrolls,
> Like silver balls, that, softly dropped,
>   Ring into golden bowls. (AWP 196–97)

The second of these stanzas is the one that, to my ear, sounds most like Emily. I think particularly of "I felt a Cleaving in my Mind," which is also about an experience of mental disjunction. In one of Dickinson's versions, she puts it this way:

> I felt a Cleaving in my Mind -
> As if my Brain had split -
> I tried to match it - Seam by Seam -
> But could not make them fit -
>
> The thought behind, I strove to join
> Unto the thought before -
> But Sequence ravelled out of Sound -
> Like Balls - upon a Floor - (Fr 867B)

Unlike the echoes of "The Sick Room," there is no exact match here, and yet Lowell's silver balls and golden bowls stanza and this poem sound as though they might have been written by the same poet. To the question, what is the value of placing them side by side if one is not arguing influence, I would answer that it provides a fuller, more accurate, literary history.

On the issue of intellectual range (often invoked as an argument *against* comparing Dickinson to other, less demanding, nineteenth-century women poets), it is well to take note of the space-time conflation in Lowell's line "Distance again unrolls."[24] It is, in fact, reminiscent of similar surprises in Dickinson's work, where she too assigns materiality to abstractions such as space and time (see "Behind Me - dips Eternity") or conflates the one with the other.

As Lowell attempts here to reproduce the strange sensations evoked by the opium, she approaches the disorienting space-time conflation of Dickinson's "Midnight to the North of Her - / And Midnight to the South of Her - / And Maelstrom - in the Sky" (Fr

743). Though speaking of distance, Lowell, like Dickinson, is also talking about time here. The hooting of the owl, described as "graceful play," stops for a moment but then resumes. However, sound—and the temporal dimension it implies—are converted into space as the renewing of the call is marked by distance rather than by timbre. And the use of the abstraction "Distance" with the kinesthetic "unrolls" is very Dickinsonian. There is a parallel, though not an echo, in the line from "I felt a Cleaving in my Mind" where Dickinson says: "Sequence ravelled out of Sound." One feels that something similar is going on in the strategies employed by the two poets to suggest forms of disorientation, and this similarity helps us to see that Dickinson was not the only woman poet to push against the intellectual envelope that confined many of her peers.

Acknowledging Dissonance

One can find silver balls in Emily Dickinson's work: "The Spider holds a Silver Ball," for instance. And there is golden music in the wind in "Of all the Sounds." But if we examine the rest of Maria White Lowell's "An Opium Fantasy" against Dickinson's poems, one can also see how different Dickinson seems when compared with less quirky woman poets. This is the reverse effect of what we have seen before when juxtaposing Dickinson's work with that of other nineteenth-century women. One needs to take account of both the similarities and the differences to measure Dickinson's relationship to published women poets of her day.

In "An Opium Fantasy," Lowell sets the scene in the first stanza with the words:

> Soft hangs the opiate in the brain,
> And lulling soothes the edge of pain,
> Till harshest sound, far off or near,
> Sings floating in its mellow sphere.

After the intervention of the two stanzas quoted above, the speaker goes on to describe a dream in which she, as a weed, speaks to the poppies with their "scarlet-kerchiefed heads" and they respond. The poet inquires about the new minstrel "who can lap / Sleep in his melody." And they answer by saying:

> "Oh, he is but a little owl,
>   The smallest of his kin,
> Who sits beneath the midnight's cowl,
>   And makes this airy din."

The speaker then pounces on the poppy fairies and reveals that she knows more than they think.

> "Deceitful tongues, of fiery tints,
>   Far more than this you know, —
> That he is your enchanted prince,
>   Doomed as an owl to go;
>
> "Nor his fond play for years hath stopped,
>   But nightly he unrolls
> His silver balls, that, softly dropped,
>   Ring into golden bowls." (AWP 197)

However, by the time we get to this last stanza, all similarity to Dickinson seems to have vanished.

Through the example of "An Opium Fantasy," we can see that other women poets were also capable of creating striking images and ingenious phrasing. There *are* interesting poetic effects in both "The Sick Room" and "An Opium Fantasy." In addition to the stanza where "Distance again unrolls," the "long and soft vibrations" of the owl's hooting, the idea that he "can lap / Sleep in his melody," the image of the "midnight's cowl" all inspire admiration. Even the notion that the owl is somehow the prince of opiates is interesting. But it isn't Dickinsonian. As Maria Lowell sets out to examine the nature and causes of her mental distraction (the effects of opium and its metonymy, the owl's call), she parts company with Emily Dickinson who typically leaves us less certain about the features of her mental landscape at the end than we were at the beginning.

This is certainly the case in "I felt a Cleaving in my Mind," where we start out with a visceral metaphor in which parts of the brain are severed one from another. There is a certain logic to the notion of fitting the pieces back together "Seam by Seam." And when this becomes "The thought behind, I strove to join / Unto the thought before," we might think the poet is helping us to see how the metaphor is working. The literal splitting of the brain is a metaphor for a radical disjunction between thoughts. However, the final two lines are seriously disorienting: "But sequence ravelled out of Sound- / Like Balls - opon a Floor." A new element is added (sound, perhaps a reference to poetry) along with a new metaphor about the mind coming apart like balls of yarn unrolling on the floor. These lines are also reminiscent of the ending of "It was not Death, for I stood up," when "everything that ticked - has stopped - / And space stares - all around" (Fr 355), for here, too, sound (time) gives way to distance (space).

The experience of reading the poem is one of controlled disorientation as compared to Lowell's where, after "Distance again unrolls," the poem increasingly attempts to orient the reader. The dream Lowell recounts produces a little story to explain the enchantment of the poppy prince: now as an owl he "unrolls" his special effects to call attention to his altered state. What was initially simply eerie gradually gets explained, and the silver balls and golden bowls seem somehow less interesting at the end than they did in the third stanza.

A different contrast presents itself if we compare Lowell's silver balls to the silver bulbs in Dickinson's "Split the Lark." In this poem, also composed about 1865, Dickinson seems to follow Lowell's model of providing the reader with a greater sense of orientation as the poem unfolds. So the peculiarly Dickinsonian touches here do not have to do with its techniques of destabilization but instead with its unusual degree of linguistic compression and, at the same time, emotional aggression.

With a few exceptions,[25] openly hostile poems are rare among nineteenth-century women poets, reflecting the influence of those like Rufus Griswold, who felt that women poets must compose poems like dews and flowers that comfort their readers. But here we find Dickinson using what Camille Paglia describes as aggressively "cutting remarks."[26] Like "Sang from the Heart, Sire," a poem Paglia addresses, "Split the Lark" brings us a speaker who deals her pretty words like blades, savaging the person addressed and filling the poetic canvas with blood.

> Split the Lark - and you'll find the Music -
> Bulb after Bulb, in Silver rolled -
> Scantily dealt to the Summer Morning
> Saved for your Ear, when Lutes be old -
>
> Loose the Flood - you shall find it patent -
> Gush after Gush, reserved for you -
> Scarlet Experiment! Sceptic Thomas!
> Now, do you doubt that your Bird was true? (Fr 905)

There is, of course, no echo of Lowell in this poem, but by comparing the effect of silver balls in the one poem with silver bulbs in the other, Dickinson's divergence from her nineteenth-century counterparts becomes clearer.

In "An Opium Fantasy," Lowell produces a soporific effect by describing the owl's call as "those long and soft vibrations [that] seem / A slumberous charm to keep." Her conversion of these vibrations into the image of "silver balls that, softly dropped, ring into golden bowls" certainly performs an imaginative leap, and, in my view, the effect produced is quite effective, much more so than the stanzas about the poppy fairies. To understand these lines, we have to think about the convergence of the senses, the way certain sounds might suggest certain colors, in this case gold and silver. But this is a highly lyrical form of synesthesia. It doesn't make us uncomfortable, whereas Dickinson's poem certainly does.

Dickinson addresses these words to a beloved who has, it seems, cast doubt on her fidelity. She seems to be saying that evidence of her loyalty is right there in her body and, by extension, in the body of her art. By beginning her poem with the words, "Split the Lark - and you'll find the Music," she establishes an ironic frame, however, one that contradicts the appeal to common experience. She knows that her reader doesn't believe that splitting open the lark will literally reveal its music so even this first line represents, in some sense, an act of aggression, like flinging down the poetic gauntlet.

The second line, "Bulb after Bulb, in Silver rolled," so wonderful in its way, is partly a retrenchment, however. Lesser in affect than the first line, it nevertheless offers a greater intellectual challenge. What are these bulbs, after all? They could be the lark's lungs (to further the metaphor of song) or they could be the heart if we want to think of the organs that would come into view if you split open a lark's body and revealed its delicate silver membranes. Like the silver balls that represent the owl's call in "An Opium Fantasy," these bulbs also serve as a metonymy for "music," perhaps piano rolls or rolled up poems. They have been scantily dealt to the Summer Morning because the poet/bird has saved them for "your Ear, when Lutes be old." Now we see that the "you" who is asked to find the music by splitting open the lark's body in the first line is not just a generic you, a "one," but a specific you who, as doubting beloved, is the target of the poet's anger.

In the next stanza the emotional ante is raised when the poet suggests opening her blood vessels. She's clearly engaging in masochistic hyperbole as she addresses this doubting Thomas, but she is also very much in control of the effect she is creating. She asks him to cut her open, but she is cutting him open as well, through her use of what she calls in Fr 458, "pretty words like blades."

The word "patent," at the end of the first line—"Loose the Flood - you shall find it patent"—is an example of Dickinsonian word play, since patent can mean both "evident" and "spreading" (as in the gush of blood that would occur if one opened a vein), but it also means "assigned to a particular individual," as in the next line: "Gush after Gush, *reserved for you.*" Three possible meanings are condensed here, a typical Dickinsonian strategy and one rare indeed in other nineteenth-century American women poets.

The emotional crescendo peaks with the last two lines: "Scarlet Experiment! Sceptic Thomas! / Now, do you doubt that your Bird was true?" One can certainly see that the speaker is angry, but at the same time one cannot help registering the ingenious condensation of the four words that make up the next to last line, for in addition to being summary, they are also carefully gauged in terms of consonance and rhythm: two scathing dactyls ("Scarlet Experiment!") castrated into two trochees ("Sceptic Thomas!"). If you make this "scarlet experiment," by cutting me open, she seems to be saying, you, like a doubting Thomas, will find that the evidence of the body is indisputable. Rarely do we find a poem by Dickinson that begins every line with a stressed syllable, but when we do, as we do here, we can certainly see that this poet was not everywhere inhibited by the assumptions about poetic decorum that governed most women's literary productions. These volcanic lines are anything but reticent or ladylike.

Finally, we should not leave this poem without mentioning that, in addition to being a kind of love poem, it is also a poem about poetry, as so many of Dickinson's poems are. In that way, too, it illustrates her dissimilarity to other nineteenth-century American women and her convergence with more modern poets. Most nineteenth-century women poets were not very self-conscious about their craft, as though they believed that the best models (created by men) were good enough to justify imitation. They expressed their "difference" mostly through subject matter.

Dickinson, on the other hand, was the great innovator, looking ahead to twentieth-century experimental poets such as Amy Lowell, H.D., Marianne Moore, and Elizabeth Bishop. If we take this poem as a request that the lover acknowledge her as a poet and a poet writing for a particular person (him or her), the flood of poems that will establish her patent looks forward to Sylvia Plath's lines from "Kindness": "The blood jet is poetry. / There is no stopping it."[27]

Double Positioning

The benefits of examining Emily Dickinson's poems side by side with those of more published women poets of the nineteenth-century are twofold. One can see more clearly what is valuable about these other poets, the ways that they confound stereotypes of the sentimental "poetess" and her mostly banal poetic lines. In their own terms, many of these poems are quite impressive; though, unlike Emily Dickinson's, they rarely suggest Modernist or Postmodernist constructions. Dickinson probably read a great many poems by nineteenth-century American women poets, some without even knowing the names of their authors, since poems in journals such as the *Atlantic Monthly* or *Putnam's* were published anonymously. It would not be at all surprising if an image or a memorable turn of phrase from their verses lodged in her mind and resurfaced in her poetry. She was playfully coy about her use of others' "notes," as we can see from "I was a Phebe."

Of course, Dickinson was by nature a nonconformist. It is certainly the case that her poems in toto sound like no one else's, male or female. Historical context can only provide us with a few clues: philosophical, religious, cultural, aesthetic. Feminist criticism, as a form of historical contextualizing, has done important work in reconstructing the nature of women's lives in the nineteenth century and the challenges faced by extraordinary women like Emily Dickinson. Her strategies of defamiliarization and compression, her playfulness with abstractions, her evocation and revocation of gender constructs—these separate her from *most* of her sisters. But Dickinson herself knew she was not entirely alone, not writing in a vacuum. She was both at home and at sea in her New England female context. The most accurate judgment we can make is that her work remembers others' poems even as it forgets them.

NOTES

Dickinson's poems are quoted from *The Poems of Emily Dickinson: Variorum Edition*, ed. R. W. Franklin, 3 vols. (Cambridge, Mass.: Harvard University Press, 1998). Subsequent references are cited as (Fr) in the text.

Citation from (L) refers to *The Letters of Emily Dickinson*, ed. Thomas H. Johnson and Theodora Ward, 3 vols. (Cambridge, Mass.: Harvard University Press, 1958).

1. Emily Stipes Watts, *The Poetry of American Women from 1632 to 1945* (Austin: University of Texas Press, 1977), 125.

2. Robert E. Spiller et al., eds., *Literary History of the United States*, 3 vols. (New York: Macmillan, 1948), 2:907.

3. Karl Keller, *The Only Kangaroo among the Beauty: Emily Dickinson and America* (Baltimore: Johns Hopkins University Press, 1979), 249.

4. Barton Levi St. Armand, *Emily Dickinson and Her Culture* (Cambridge: Cambridge University Press, 1984), 9.

5. Ibid., 44.

6. David S. Reynolds, *Beneath the American Renaissance: The Subversive Imagination in the Age of Emerson and Melville* (New York: Knopf, 1988), 432.

7. Suzanne Juhasz, *Naked and Fiery Forms: Modern American Poetry by Women—A New Tradition* (New York: Harper & Row, 1976), 20.

8. The Cult of True Womanhood was a term used by Barbara Welter in her path-breaking study "The Cult of True Womanhood," first published by *American Quarterly* in 1966 and later reprinted as part of *Dimity Convictions: The American Woman in the Nineteenth Century* (Athens: Ohio University Press, 1976), 21–41.

9. Rufus Griswold, "Preface" to *The Memorial: Written by Friends of the Late Mrs. Osgood* (New York: George Putnam, 1861), 29.

10. Elizabeth Petrino, *Emily Dickinson and Her Contemporaries: Women's Verse in America, 1820–1885* (Hanover: University Press of New England, 1998), 201.

11. Camille Paglia, *Sexual Personae: Art and Decadence from Nefertiti to Emily Dickinson* (New York: Random House-Vintage, 1991), 653.

12. Betsy Erkkila, *The Wicked Sisters: Women Poets, Literary History, and Discord* (New York: Oxford University Press, 1992), 87.

13. Paula Bennett, *Emily Dickinson: Woman Poet* (Iowa City: University of Iowa Press, 1990), 183.

14. Cheryl Walker, "Teaching Dickinson as a Gen[i]us: Emily among the Women," *The Emily Dickinson Journal* 2, no. 2 (1993): 178–79.

15. Dickinson often uses dimensions ironically, as in "A solemn thing - it was - I said" (Fr 307), where the word "small" (like the "little print" in this poem) comes to seem very large indeed.

16. Rose Terry (1827–1892) married Rollin Cooke at the age of

forty-six. She is best remembered as Rose Terry Cooke because of her later local-color short stories, but she began as a poet, publishing many poems in the 1850s and 1860s.

17. In the two-volume *Years and Hours of Emily Dickinson* (New Haven: Yale University Press, 1960), Jay Leyda mentions two presents given by Samuel Bowles at Christmas in 1860, one (*The Household Book of Poetry*) to Susan Gilbert Dickinson and the other (Terry's poems) to his wife. Both books have publication dates of 1861, however, so one can conclude only that Leyda meant to list them as Christmas presents given the following year.

18. In my essay "Teaching Dickinson as a Gen[i]us: Emily among the Women," I rehearse the evidence for Dickinson's probable exposure to other nineteenth-century American women poets. Lowell, for example, was one of the poets represented in *The Household Book of Poetry* that Samuel Bowles gave to Susan. Emily and Susan often shared such books between the houses.

19. Rose Terry, *Poems* (Boston: Ticknor & Fields, 1861), 116.

20. Cheryl Walker, *American Women Poets of the Nineteenth Century: An Anthology* (New Brunswick: Rutgers University Press, 1992), 269. Subsequent poems from this anthology will be indicated by an AWP, with the page reference following.

21. Terry, *Poems*, 29–30.

22. When considering whether or not Dickinson was influenced by American women poets she does not name, it is well to remember that journals such as the *Atlantic Monthly* and *Putnam's* did not give the names of the poets they published. She could have admired their works without knowing the authors' names.

23. See Walker, "Teaching Dickinson as a Gen(i)us: Emily Among the Women," Walker, "The Whip Signature: Violence, Feminism and Women Poets," in *Women's Poetry, Late Romantic to Late Victorian*, ed. Isobel Armstrong and Virginia Blain (New York: St. Martin's, 1999), 33–49, and Walker, "In Bluebeard's Closet: Women Who Write with the Wolves," *LIT: Literature, Interpretation, Theory* 7 (1996): 13–25.

24. For a different argument, also recognizing Maria White Lowell's intellectual range, see Mary Loeffelholz, "Poetry, Slavery, Personification: Maria Lowell's 'Africa'," *Studies in Romanticism* 38 (Summer, 1999): 171–202.

25. For these see the poems by Rose Terry (Cooke) in note 19, Adah Isaacs Menken's "Judith" (AWP, 315–18), and Sarah Morgan Bryan Piatt's "Giving Back the Flower," in *Palace-Burner: The Selected Poetry of Sarah Piatt,* ed. Paula Bernat Bennett (Urbana: University of Illinois Press, 2001), 7-8.

26. Paglia, *Sexual Personae*, 629.

27. Sylvia Plath, *Ariel* (New York: Harper & Row, 1965), 82.

The Sound of Shifting Paradigms, or Hearing Dickinson in the Twenty-First Century

Cristanne Miller

In 1862, Emily Dickinson wrote a poem about the "Melody" of the wind—a melody so powerful it hides within us "inner than the Bone" for "the Whole of Days." The poem begins:

> Of all the Sounds despatched abroad
> There's not a Charge to me
> Like that old measure in the Boughs -
> That Phraseless Melody -
> The Wind does - working like a Hand -
> Whose fingers comb the Sky -
> Then quiver down, with tufts of tune -
> Permitted Gods - and me -
>
> Inheritance it is to us
> Beyond the Art to Earn - . . .   (Fr 334)[1]

The wind's melody is like a poem: "Inheritance . . . to us / Beyond [our] Art to Earn." The "sounds" of Dickinson's poems that we hear at the turn of the twenty-first century, however, are different from those she heard when she wrote them, because in the twenty-first century, in the United States, very different "sounds" are "despatched abroad" from those dispatched in the

1860s. Twenty-first century readers hear the residues of multiple social and technological revolutions, two world wars, terrorism, and postmodernism, as part of the background framing the texts we read. More specifically, educated literary readers contextualize nineteenth-century sounds differently from Dickinson—for example, to such ears Whitman's poetry provides the primary counterpoint to hers while Dickinson claims never to have read Whitman.[2] In short, we "hear" and read poetry in the context of everything else we hear or experience, as she did. Moreover, twenty-first century ears are generally less acute than were those of Dickinson's generation. Our world is visually oriented. We read silently and spend much of our lives watching screens. We are bombarded with sounds we try not to hear—air conditioning, the hum of computers or other machines, muzak, traffic. And we rarely listen to poetry with any but the inner ear. As Nick Piombino writes, "listening" is "becoming a lost art."[3] In contrast, for Dickinson, hearing was the key artistic response.

I will develop here a two-part argument that is both historical and propositional. Although since the development of the printing press poetry has increasingly been associated with the printed page, I will argue that in the United States, nineteenth-century readers tended to perceive poetry aurally more than visually and poets wrote more for the ear than the eye. This is an argument of degree, not of dichotomies. One can both see and hear a poem now, just as readers did then. The historical aspect of my argument is based both on the limited resources and technologies accessible to the mid-nineteenth-century reader in small-town America and on the formal properties of nineteenth-century verse, as represented primarily by the poetry of Longfellow, the century's most popular and esteemed poet. The formal experiments of nineteenth-century American poetry are overwhelmingly centered on sound play, especially rhythmic (generally metrical) variation, rhyme, and alliteration and assonance. By the early twentieth century, this dominance of sound play and the tendency to perceive poetry as primarily aural was changing. Modernist poets and critics wrote about the increasing visual properties of modern culture—sometimes linking such general observations to poetry. Cultural studies scholars have noted the increasing privatization of Western culture throughout the modern period, a trend related to silent reading. Jerome McGann's *Black Riders: The Visible Language of Modernism* establishes the relation of a new enthusiasm for the craft of printing and book production to the development of modern literature, highlighting visual properties of the book and page.[4] There has, however, been surprisingly little attention to the possibility of a paradigm shift in the perception of American poetry. Hence, the propositional edge to my historical thesis: as the culture of the United States changed, so did critical expectations for and perceptions of poetry, giving increasing attention to visual elements of the poem.

No historical tendency exists in isolation. There has been visual poetry, or a poetry that plays on visual structures, since at least the medieval period in Europe, and all important poetry of any age attends to the sounds it produces, as does twentieth-century verse. One cannot read Pound, Williams, Stevens, or Moore, for example, without hearing their distinctive and extraordinary sounds. There have, similarly, always been readers and critics attentive to sound. Nonetheless, by the early twentieth century, the dominant orientation of American poetry toward the ear was changing or had changed and, by the end of the century, critical paradigms for understanding poetry assumed visual or spatial properties of the poem. Again, this is a matter of degree. Assuming a poem's visual properties does not prohibit attention to its sounds, but it does shift the focus of attention in ways that may have significant implications for understanding a poet's work.

As a test case for this historical argument regarding both nineteenth-century poetry's aurality and twentieth-century criticism's focus on the visual, I want to explore the implications of this critical shift for the study of Emily Dickinson's poetry. Her verse serves the function of test case well because she writes on the cusp of this change and because debate continues over the extent to which visual features of her manuscripts should dominate perceptions of her poetic. Focus on the manuscripts has encouraged new editions of the poems, increased attention to the poet's manuscript books ("fascicles") and correspondence, and led to reconsiderations of her poetic. For some critics, it has also become inseparable from the exploration of Dickinson's multiple life choices—whether to publish, how she regarded the construction of her fascicles, and her relationship to her sister-in-law Susan Dickinson and other correspondents. It is these hypothesized biographical and cultural links between Dickinson's handwritten pages and readings of her life that spur me to question the extent to which such apparently historical interpretation is based on a twentieth-century paradigm.[5]

Four editions of Dickinson's poetry are now readily available. Most familiar is the 1955 Thomas H. Johnson edition, which was the first to reproduce Dickinson's extensive use of dashes, the first reasonably to justify its claim to completeness, and the first to make no word-based "corrections" of the manuscripts.[6] His edition immediately became the standard and remained so for more than forty years; consequently, it is what students of Dickinson for the rest of the century read as definitive. In 1998, Johnson's edition was updated and revised by Ralph W. Franklin, who follows Johnson's lead in printing the vast majority of the poems in metrical lines and stanzas, although he includes Dickinson's misspellings as well as her dashes and provides much greater precision in chronological arrangement of the poems. Franklin also includes as poems lines not considered poems by Johnson and removes from his edition lines Johnson had included. While Franklin's and Johnson's editing philosophies are similar, the details make Franklin's edition significantly different.[7] Almost simultaneously, Ellen Louise Hart and Martha Nell Smith published their edition of the correspondence Dickinson sent to her sister-in-law in *Open Me Carefully: The Intimate Letters of Emily Dickinson to Susan Huntington Dickinson*. This edition of letters and poems lineates all texts written after the late 1850s following the irregularities of Dickinson's handwriting. In particular, they do not distinguish between poetic and epistolary texts and argue that this distinction is moot for Dickinson. Hart and Smith refer to all print renditions of Dickinson's poems as "translations"; hence, they strive to bring the reader as close as possible to the look of individual manuscripts. They include material information about each manuscript artifact (numbers of folds, condition of the page, tears, size of paper), and they distinguish one particularly slanted kind of dash from the poet's midline, more or less straight dashes.[8] The fourth accessible version of Dickinson's poems stems from the earliest editions of her work; poems from these volumes are frequently reprinted in gift books, on calendars, and in other popular formats.[9] Consequently, lay readers are most likely to know these nonscholarly printings, which "correct" metrical and rhythmic regularities, omit stanzas from several poems, and generally clean up Dickinson's verse according to the conventions of the late nineteenth century.

As a consequence of these competing editions, printed over the course of more than a century, one cannot even quote this poet without identifying one's critical position as to what constitutes a Dickinson line or poem. Both the Johnson/Franklin and the Hart and Smith editorial positions have strong proponents— the latter including many of the critics asserting the primacy of manuscript representations of poems, hence implicitly assuming a visual aesthetic for Dickinson. In the context of such debate, it is useful to think about the dominant paradigms for constructing and perceiving poetry both in Dickinson's century and now.

Especially since the advent of feminist criticism in the late 1970s, many critics have argued that Dickinson participated in the modernizing climate of her times by creating a protomodernist lyric, a poetry that rebels against "patriarchal" meters, conventions of punctuation, grammar, rhyme, or even print to construct a new kind of poem.[10] According to this argument, Dickinson constructs a lyric closer in form to William Carlos Williams's or H.D.'s than to Lydia Sigourney's or Henry Wadsworth Longfellow's. She was a poet ahead of her times and presaging (as well as influencing) the development of poetic modernism a half century later. This is an argument that I myself have made and that I still find valid in several respects. The extreme compression of Dickinson's language and its multiple forms of disjunction— grammatical, syntactic, tonal, and logical—strikingly anticipate features of modernist verse. At the same time, however, it seems likely to me that Dickinson conceived of poetry in a nineteenth-century fashion, as part of a culture more attuned to structures of sound than sight in poetry.

This argument may seem counterintuitive to the extent that

"sound" was less powerful a metaphor than "sight" for nine-teenth-century poets and philosophers. Emerson could not have imagined a "transparent eardrum" as providing the gateway to his transcendent experience of nature; and, while Whitman writes of blabs, screeches, and barbaric yawps, his primary images are also visual. For example, in "Crossing Brooklyn Ferry," we are linked with the poet over centuries by the "dumb beautiful ministers" of "appearances," not by sound. Dickinson also frequently uses nouns and verbs of seeing and images of light ("Noon," the sun). The huge range of common idioms linking sight to spiritual vision and insight reveals how long and deeply Western culture has associated seeing with understanding and experiencing the world.[11]

Yet despite her participation in a phenomenology of sight, for Dickinson, sound emphatically grounds the poem. Her poems about poetic spirit and her figure for the poet typically have an aural foundation. As she writes in "Of all the Sounds despatched abroad," the "Melody" of wind in trees marks us so deeply that even our dead dust may "arise" and dance to its tunes. "The spirit is the Conscious Ear - / We actually Hear / When We inspect," she writes (Fr 718). In "The saddest noise, the sweetest noise" the poet concludes, "An ear can break a human heart / As quickly as a spear. / We wish the ear had not a heart / So dangerously near" (Fr 1789). In an 1873 letter, she writes, "The ear is the last face" (L 405) and later writes again of the "ear of the Heart" (L 807, 1883). Other poems imagine the transformations of poetry as aural. In "I think I was enchanted," the effect of reading Elizabeth Barrett Browning's poems is at first "Lunacy of Light," but then the poet fills three stanzas imagining the "Titanic Opera" of all creatures in nature and "Days" stepping to "Mighty Metres" (Fr 627). Similarly, in "I cannot dance opon my Toes," the poet demonstrates "Ballet Knowledge" by parodying that highly visual art and then celebrating her verse as having the vocal fullness of "Opera" (Fr 381). In another poem she defines poetry as the sound of a storm: "To pile like Thunder to it's close / Then crumble grand away . . . would be Poetry" (Fr 1353). In "I would not paint - a picture" she explains that she would not "be a Poet" because "It's finer - Own the Ear"—or, better yet, combine creativity and "Ear" hence, "stun myself / With Bolts - of Melody!" (Fr 348). Poetry electrifies through the "Ear."[12]

Dickinson's association of poetry with the ear takes its most frequent form in poems linking the poet with the songbird, as for example in "I shall keep singing! . . . I - with my Redbreast - / And my Rhymes - " (Fr 270) or "Split the Lark - and you'll find the Music -" (Fr 905). As Judy Jo Small writes in her masterful study of sound patterns, especially rhyme, in Dickinson's poetry, in depicting herself as a songbird, Dickinson aligns herself with contemporary female poets at the same time that she "exploits the songbird convention" of nineteenth-century popular poetry. According to Small, Dickinson's aesthetic is "musical"; she uses multiple "auditory images and aural figures referring to metaphysical conceits," and she writes frequently about the profound effects of sound.[13] For example, in "Further in Summer than the Birds" the poet can hear the changing of the seasons through the crickets' "unobtrusive Mass" before any visible change can be seen: "Remit as yet no Grace - / No furrow on the Glow" but the cricket has already "Enhance[d] Nature" through its "Canticle" or song (Fr 895). Dickinson was also well-known within her family and among her friends for her own musical abilities and interest, especially at the piano. For example, Jay Leyda quotes Kate Scott Anthon recalling that Dickinson played "weird and beautiful melodies, all from her own inspiration."[14] According to her own report, she practiced the piano for two hours a day until entering Mount Holyoke and for an hour a day while there. In addition she studied voice, sang in the Amherst church choir, and at Mount Holyoke participated with the whole student body in thirty minutes of singing a day.[15] School and church singing was primarily of hymns and, while the influence of hymns on Dickinson's prosody has perhaps been exaggerated, there can be no question that hymnody affected the tuning of her ear for rhythms and rhymes.[16] The words of her own poems and her musical experience provide ample pragmatic evidence that Dickinson's aesthetic was strongly if not fundamentally aural. Such an aesthetic was supported by multiple aspects of nineteenth-century American culture.

Patterns of nineteenth-century poetry itself indicate that

poetry was primarily an aural (albeit no longer an oral) art: poetic innovation was based on alliteration, assonance, multiple and elaborate rhyme schemes, varying meters, and other rhythmic structures—that is, on sound. Twentieth-century innovation, in contrast, rejected structures of controlled variation from a clearly heard, metered norm for nonmetrical rhythms, irregular line lengths, visual puns, and varying spatial arrangements of lines or words on the page.[17] What makes so much of nineteenth-century poetry sound "the same," or even "bad," to the twentieth- and twenty-first-century ear is that it valued clearly heard patterning—along with grammatical completeness, narrative sequencing, and elevated diction—elements of verse rejected by many modernists. To get a sense of this period's aesthetics, one need only think of the hypnotic alliteration and rhythms of Poe's extremely popular "The Raven."

> Once upon a midnight dreary, while I pondered, weak and weary,
> Over many a quaint and curious volume of forgotten lore—
> While I nodded, nearly napping, suddenly there came a tapping
> As of some one gently rapping, rapping at my chamber door—
> "'Tis some visitor," I muttered, "tapping at my chamber door—
> Only this and nothing more."[18]

Poe's dense use of alliteration, assonance, repetition, and rhyme is extreme even by nineteenth-century standards but nonetheless representative in the direction of its attention toward complexly ordered rhythms and sounds. In strongly trochaic meter, and not including the multiple line-internal rhymes, Poe uses an abcbbb rhyme scheme, alternating a 16- and a 15-syllable line, with a 7-syllable refrain. This alteration of weak and strong line-endings, or trochaic and catalectic lines, keeps the verse balanced between the initial trochaic beat of each line and the stressed final syllable of lines 2, 4, 5, and 6—a balance repeated internally in the lines in ways that maintain the beat of the verse while syncopating its pulse. Rhyme, sound play, and rhythm all contribute to the suspense and pleasure of the poem's narrative.

While Poe is perhaps the easiest poet on which to demonstrate the nineteenth-century fascination with sound, the contemporary poets more important to Dickinson were Elizabeth Barrett Browning, Robert Browning, Ralph Waldo Emerson, William Cullen Bryant, and Henry Wadsworth Longfellow—all poets of strongly rhymed and metrical verse. The poet she quoted most frequently was Longfellow, a poet now largely discredited despite the fact that during Dickinson's lifetime he was by far the most celebrated American writer and rivaled Tennyson in international fame.[19] Even today, virtually all descriptions of his poetry refer to his extraordinary technical mastery and to the influence of his poetry on his age.[20] Longfellow's verse serves best to exemplify what Dickinson and her contemporaries admired.

Contrary to most current assumptions about nineteenth-century verse, Longfellow—like many of his peers—wrote in multiple, experimental, and irregular verse forms. In particular, Longfellow was a master of metrical variation. Among his more frequent strategies for creating fluidly irregular rhythms within a general metric norm, he alternated two- and three-syllable feet: iambs with anapests or trochees with dactyls. In the ballad-style "The Wreck of the Hesperus," for example, he writes in quatrains with the sequence of 8, 6, 10, and 6-syllable lines, but this is a norm that rarely occurs, as any or all lines in a given stanza may vary by as many as 3 syllables in length from this pattern. The first and penultimate stanzas read:

It was the schooner Hesperus,	8
That sailed the wintry sea;	6
And the skipper had taken his little daughter,	12
To bear him company.	6

* * *

The salt-sea was frozen on her breast,	9
The salt tears in her eyes;	6
And he saw her hair, like the brown sea-weed,	10
On the billows fall and rise.[21]	7

Particularly in the latter stanza, the rhythm is quite varied within the line, even though the basic pattern of a 4- then a 3-stress meter holds.

In "Rain in Summer," Longfellow uses both lines and stanzas of irregular length—from a 3- to a 12-syllable line and a 5- to a 20-line stanza. Moreover, while most lines end with a rhyme word, there is no rhyme scheme. Again, poetic diction and frequent rhyme give the sense of a traditional and regular rhythm, but the sound patterns are striking in their syncopated variation. Stanza four reads:

	Line length	Rhyme scheme
From the neighboring school	6	a
Come the boys,	3	b
With more than their wonted noise	7	b
And commotion;	4	c
And down the wet streets	5	d
Sail their mimic fleets,	5	d
Till the treacherous pool	6	a
Ingulfs them in its whirling	7	e (no rhyme)
And turbulant ocean. [22]	6	c

Because the poem's lines follow no pattern of corresponding lengths (a 3-syllable line may rhyme with a 7-syllable line), it is difficult to determine any metrical norm. At the same time, the end-line rhymes and coincidence of line and syntax stabilize line structure, and the contrast between stressed and unstressed syllables is marked, giving an impression of rhythmic order even where it is not regular. In this stanza, the first line is clearly anapestic, the second trochaic catalectic, the third combines iambs and anapests, and the fourth could be read as anapestic or trochaic. Lines 6 and 7 are indiscriminately headless iambic or catalectic—assuming one elides the final two syllables of "treacherous" to read as one unaccented syllable. Lines 8 and 9 begin as iambic lines but end with the falling word-based stress pattern of trochees (whirling, ocean). In short, this stanza combines duple and triple meter in rising and falling patterns in a complex rhythm.

In a completely different aural tour de force, Longfellow uses dramatic rhythmic variation within a strict metrical norm in

"The Warning." This iambic pentameter description of Samson's tragedy includes caesurae, enjambment, complex syntax, and polysyllabic sequences worthy of Dickinson. The poem begins:

> Beware! The Israelite of old, who tore
>   The lion in his path,—when, poor and blind,
> He saw the blessed light of heaven no more,
>   Shorn of his noble strength and forced to grind
> In prison, and at last led forth to be
>   A pander to Philistine revelry,—
>
> Upon the pillars of the temple laid
>   His desperate hands, and in its overthrow
> Destroyed himself, and with him those who made
>   A cruel mockery of his sightless woe; . . .[23]

The strong falling word-based rhythms of "pander to Philistine revelry" and the later phrase "cruel mockery of his sightless" effectively syncopate the iambic narrative. Simultaneously, the echoing long "o" sounds (old, tore, poor, no more, Shorn, noble, forced, forth, overthrow, those) build to a powerful midstanza cadence with the word "woe." This cadence caps the sequence of alliteration and rhyme and forcefully returns from the falling pattern of "cruel mockery" and Samson's "sightless" state to a strongly stressed line and phrase ending, rhythmically underlining its sympathy with Samson in his "woe" and prefiguring the strength of his doomed heroism.

Dickinson quotes twice from Longfellow's "The Day Is Done," a poem that takes as its theme the speaker's desire for a friend to read poetry aloud to him in the evening. The poem ends:

> Then read from the treasured volume
>   The poem of thy choice,
> And lend to the rhyme of the poet
>   The beauty of thy voice.
>
> And the night shall be filled with music,
>   And the cares, that infest the day,

> Shall fold their tents, like the Arabs,
> And as silently steal away.[24]

While it is the last two or three lines only that Dickinson quotes, it seems likely that she hears in them the context of shared reading: cares depart when you hear the "music" of poetry read aloud. Longfellow's use of a loosened ballad stanza in this poem (alternating tetrameters and trimeters) might also appeal to Dickinson, given her own repeated use of this form.

Several years ago in comparing Dickinson with Longfellow, I wrote that Dickinson's verse does not sound like Longfellow's: his verse "works through extension and repetition, whereas Dickinson's works through compression and juxtaposition."[25] I would make the same argument today: unlike Longfellow, Dickinson is interested neither in narrative nor in speaking accessibly to a broad, popular audience about subjects of common concern. Dickinson also distinctly counters Longfellow's lifelong program of linking the craft of the poet with masculinity and divorcing the poet from all associations with the feminine. Yet Dickinson may have rejected what Matthew Garner calls the "incipient paternalism" of his poetry and the "specifically masculine virtues" of his artisan poet while admiring his craft.[26] I now think that, in my earlier argument, I underestimated the extent to which the structuring norms of her verse were influenced by those of her contemporaries.

For example, the metaphor of the last stanza of Dickinson's "Of all the Sounds despatched abroad" bears marked resemblance to Longfellow's in "The Day Is Done":

> I crave Him Grace of Summer Boughs -
> If such an Outcast be -
> Who never heard that Fleshless Chant -
> Rise solemn on the Tree -
> As if some Caravan of Sound -
> Off Deserts in the Sky -
> Had parted Rank -
> Then knit and swept
> In Seamless Company - (Fr 334, 1862)

Here Dickinson's abstract "Caravan of Sound - / Off Deserts in the Sky" that sweeps away "In Seamless Company" recalls Longfellow's cares that "fold their tents, like the Arabs, / And as silently steal away." Both metaphors are striking—perhaps Longfellow's more than Dickinson's because of its greater clarity. Both orientalize in order to describe the disappearance of something unseen—again Longfellow's more than Dickinson's. While both poems maintain relative metrical regularity, Longfellow's stretches the boundaries of that regularity more than Dickinson's, moving from a stanza of alternating tetramaters and trimeters to lines of more or less equal length, folding trisyllabic feet into the iambic pattern and using two weak or unstressed final syllables in the last stanza. In contrast, Dickinson's splitting of the penultimate metrical line into two rows or visual lines, as Franklin prints the poem, seems tame—as do the other calligraphic line breaks found at various points in her three manuscript versions of this poem that syncopate but do not disrupt its meter. The earliest extant manuscript (Fascicle 12, H 77) includes underlined variant word choices written in above the lines; the other two copies use the fascicle's underlined words and include no variants.[27] All three manuscripts use multiple nonmetrical line breaks but agree on only four: after "old measure" (line 3), "some odd fashion [Pattern]" (line 19), "Winds go round" (line 21), and "Had parted Rank" (line 31)—the only division maintained by both Franklin and Johnson. In the fascicle copy, only this last division occurs in a space where the poet had ample room to include at least one more word—that is, where she indicates a choice to break a metrical line in a particular place. Dickinson's poems, I would argue, sound more modern than Longfellow's because of their compression and syntactic deletion and disjunction, not because they depart more radically from metrical norms. Both poets, I believe, wrote for the ear that expected traditional patterns, an expectation they played with and against in differing ways.

Dickinson lived in an age and a culture utterly bound to print, as did most Anglo-Europeans in New England from the time of the earliest Puritan settlements. In this sense, she is typically a reader of the poem's page, a visual object, as well as a hearer of the poem, whether or not she learns a poem by hearing it. Yet the perception of the page as object would also have been different in the nineteenth century from what it is in the early twenty-first century. Walter Benjamin's "The Work of Art in the Age of Mechanical Reproduction" (1936) perhaps best explains the principle whereby changes in basic social structures are linked to both the perception and the production of art. As Benjamin argues, when technologies of production change, so do basic structures in the ways people live. Such sociological change, in turn, affects human sensory perception, and this affects the production of art which then again alters human perception. To take his example, the technology of film "has enriched our field of perception"; it "introduces us to unconscious optics" or structural formations of being and movement not capable of being perceived before the advent of film: in short, film changed the ways people could see. Benjamin summarizes: "During long periods of history, the mode of human sense perception changes with humanity's entire mode of existence. The manner in which human sense perception is organized, the medium in which it is accomplished, is determined not only by nature but by historical circumstances as well."[28]

Benjamin's focus is more on the capitalistic and "social bases" of this change than it is on the actual changes that have occurred. Yet he sees the two as inseparable. The desire "to bring things 'closer' spatially and humanly" and to "overcom[e] the uniqueness of every reality by accepting its reproduction," on the part of the "masses" (and through the process of capitalist commodification) creates a demand for new technologies of production, which in turn affect the function and structures of art: "To an ever greater degree the work of art reproduced becomes the work of art designed for reproducability."[29] Benjamin pays little attention to aural aspects of perception. While auditory technologies contribute to the general shift toward "mechanical reproduction," in his views photography and film—the technologies of visual reproduction—constitute the exemplary modern art and media.

Benjamin's essay is typical of commentary on cultural paradigms of the early twentieth century: the visual is associated so powerfully with modern aspects of civilization that one apparently need not heed either parallel innovations in aural technologies or the more aurally based paradigms or structures that presumably preceded the modern era, except as belonging to some very distant, medieval, or even primitive past. Benjamin, for example, contrasts the visual orientation of technological commodification with undated, presumably premodern concepts of "cult" and "ritual": his "two polar types" of works of art have, on the one hand, an "accent . . . on the cult value" and, on the other, "on the exhibition value of the work":

> With the emancipation of the various art practices from ritual go increasing opportunities for the exhibition of their products. . . . With the different methods of technical reproduction of a work of art, its fitness for exhibition increased to such an extent that the quantitative shift between its two poles turned into a qualitative transformation of its nature. . . . the work of art becomes a creation with entirely new functions.[30]

According to Benjamin, in the twentieth century, art becomes an icon for display, not joined with communal behavior or action in ceremonies that themselves confer at least, in part, the value of the work. This distinction seems to me crucial and I will return to it in speculation about reading practices of the nineteenth century.

In 1914, in defining "Vorticism," Ezra Pound claims to "wish to give people new eyes, not to make them see some new particular thing."[31] Pound's fellow Vorticist Wyndham Lewis takes more than 450 pages in *Time and Western Man* to "contradict, and if possible defeat" what he calls "time-notions," claiming instead the increasing importance of a "spatializing" process of mind.[32] In *The Medium is the Message* (1951), Marshall McLuhan specifically contrasts the visual to the aural, or the logic of visually oriented "modern man" to the prehistoric "magic world of the ear": "The rational man in our Western culture is a visual man."[33] Among literary critics, while individuals have attended to visual elements in particular poetic styles, the theoretical debate has predominantly attended to the temporal and spatial distinction. Joseph Frank's 1945 "Spatial Form in Modern Literature" argues for spatial form as a "particular phenomenon of modern avant-garde writing," implying that the temporal is more dominant in earlier periods.[34] Arguing on the basis of epistemological, not typographical, structure, W. J. T. Mitchell attempts to break down the binary opposition of the temporal with the spatial, contending that all literature manipulates "spatial form"— a claim assuming although not specifying some aspect of visual production.[35] Max Nänny slants this debate on spatial form toward the pragmatically visual: "Considering that the entire tendency of western civilization and art has been towards visualization and spatialization, . . . it is no wonder that especially since Imagism and Vorticism there have been demands that poetry ought to be remodeled in order to become iconic of visible reality."[36] As he writes in a later essay, the high modernists "spatialize temporal succession" through a method that is "only possible in print on paper and unthinkable in oral form." Analyzing poems by Pound, Williams, Cummings, and others, Nänny contrasts the age when "poetry was still seen in oral-aural terms and its printed text as a mere notation of speech" with modernism's exploitation of the "visual resources of typography."[37] Eniko Bollobás has written extensively on this topic, and identifies modernist poets as initiating "a new prosodic principle": "Already in the middle of the eighteenth century," she writes, "the distinction between the audible and the graphically metrical was taken for granted. . . . With the disappearance of the metrical superstructure [in the twentieth century], the roles of these visual contextual pressures became only more important. Imagist poetry introduced a new prosodic principle, shape: 'A rhythm is shape,' Pound declared."[38] To the extent that twentieth-century innovative poetry is associated with "free verse," Derek Attridge's definition is also telling. Although Attridge argues that all verse is speech-based, he writes that "in free verse, the line *on the page* has an integrity and function of its own. This has important consequences for the movement and hence the meaning of the words" (emphasis mine).[39] Susan Howe is similarly page-oriented in her description of "Poetry": "In the precinct of Poetry, a word, the space around a word, each letter, every mark, silence, or sound volatizes an inner law of form—moves on a rigorous line."[40]

Most persuasive in demonstrating the completeness of the paradigmatic shift in thinking about the properties of poetry is *Close Listening*, an extremely interesting collection of essays edited by Charles Bernstein in 1998. Bernstein's introduction takes for granted that "sound" has become secondary in responses to poetry. These collected essays, he claims will "fundamentally transform" the subject of hearing poetry: they "work with sound as material, where sound is neither arbitrary nor secondary but constitutive"—an idea nineteenth-century poets would have taken for granted but that seems revolutionary in the context of late twentieth-century experimental poetry.[41] Indeed, one of Bernstein's stated goals for the book "is to overthrow the common presumption that the text of a poem—that is, the written document—is primary and that the recitation or performance of a poem by the poet is secondary and fundamentally inconsequential to the 'poem' itself"; "when a poem," he continues, "has an auditory rather than a visual source . . . our perspective on, or of, the work shifts." Later in the collection, Bruce Andrews writes that "sound has become functional" and calls for "the emancipation of sound" now "held back by the great weight of heritage."[42] Bernstein's focus is on poets' reading their own poems and the phenomenon of public poetry readings; this is a different matter from others reading a poem aloud (whether as public performance or privately). Nonetheless, his emphatic contrast of the "primary" "written document" with the "secondary" heard poem reveals the pervasiveness of this twentieth-century conception.[43]

As stated earlier, Dickinson has been claimed as a poet writing within the concerns of the twentieth-century, primarily visual paradigm. Jerome McGann has made this argument most specifically.[44] *Black Riders: The Visible Language of Modernism* follows a Benjaminian argument about technological production and related changes in artistic forms, focusing on the renaissance of printing fostered by the Arts and Crafts movement, with its attention to fine printing in small press runs rather than on the commodification of popular arts. According to McGann, the concern of this "Renaissance" with visible features of craft in printing "brought important constructivist and reflexive elements" to textual language "that in turn generated linguistic innovations." Dickinson, McGann argues, turns to similar innovations in crafting her handwritten manuscript books; her "openings to alternative sense arrangements emerge principally because of [her] text's visual structure." "It does no good to argue," he asserts, "that these odd lineations are unintentional"—or even more emphatically, "Dickinson's scripts *cannot* be read as if . . . they were composed with an eye toward some state beyond their handcrafted textual condition" (emphasis mine).[45] Dickinson writes, McGann tells us, according to what Charles Olson called "composition by field"; she deploys writing in the given space of a page; she constructs her texts visually and spatially. Marta Werner and Susan Howe make similar claims: Dickinson's "compositions" resemble "leaves of a sketchbook"; "each *copy* of a draft may be fully realized only outside the modes of mechanical reproduction and mass production" (Werner); "these manuscripts should be understood as visual productions. . . . The author paid attention to the smallest physical detail of the page" (Howe).[46]

Yet I find persuasive historical and textual evidence that Dickinson's art does not consist primarily or substantively in the visual irregularities of her handwritten texts and that, as a mid-nineteenth-century poet, she is unlikely to have constructed poetry along these lines. Not only her own musical aesthetic and patterns of innovation in the work of other nineteenth-century poets but also early and mid-nineteenth-century cultural patterns support this hypothesis. In an age before the radio, TV, tape recorders, or movies, entertainment was largely self-produced and familial or communal. Families listened to someone recite or read aloud—giving rise to the sobriquet "fireside poets" for those authors most popular for such readings. In a recent case study of "Women's Reading in Late-Victorian America," Barbara Sicherman reports that even near the end of the century, when scholars suppose reading behavior to have changed from public to private, the women in the family she studied read aloud on a regular basis—often while their listeners sewed or did other domestic work. Reading aloud was a duty often associated with women, who were most often the ones to read to children and to invalids.[47]

The Dickinsons and their Amherst friends read aloud together at least occasionally: the poet refers frequently, for example, to reading aloud in her letters, particularly in her more social, younger years. In 1851, at the age of eighteen, Dickinson refers to a "Reading Club" that she attended for some months, commenting in a letter to her brother Austin, "*Stebbins* comes in to read now, and *Spencer* . . . the Tutors come after us, and walk home with us" (L 44). In 1859, she enquires whether Fanny and Loo Norcross still attend Fanny Kemble's public readings of Shakespeare, commenting "I have heard many notedly *bad* readers, and a fine one would be almost a fairy surprise" (L 199). In 1853, she reports reading the news aloud while Vinnie sewed (L 133), and she repeatedly read Austin's or others' letters aloud to the family—suggesting that family consensus held her to be the best, or most dramatic, reader among them (L 31, 53, 57, 108, 116). Similarly, Dickinson often read letters with or to Sue, or Sue read them to her (L 18, 114, 115, 128). Edward Dickinson read aloud during family prayers—as Emily mentions in 1863 and 1875, long after she had presumably ceased to attend this ritual (L 285, 432). And the poet read to her mother when she was ill (L 666, 667, 721, 727). Dickinson's own poems received some oral performance within the family and community circles as well. As Hart and Smith document, Sue at least occasionally read Dickinson's poems to friends.[48] More significantly, Martha Ackmann has found evidence that Dickinson herself at least occasionally "said" her poems to the family: cousin Anna Norcross Swett referred to hearing Dickinson "talk poetry," and Louisa Norcross reports that Dickinson read her poems to her while she worked in the pantry.[49]

In the early part of the nineteenth century, reading was necessarily a communal activity. The expense of corrective eyewear made it difficult for many to read with ease—especially among the elderly. Expensive and poor lighting also determined that one person monopolize the lamplight to read to others rather than each family member enjoying private light. As Domhnall Mitchell points out, it is a sign of Dickinson's class and family privilege that as an adult she burned a lamp in her bedroom at night.[50] The expense of books also encouraged families to enjoy their cherished volumes repeatedly: they returned to known texts rather than acquiring "new" ones. During Dickinson's lifetime, as Mitchell notes, "economic instability was a feature of everyday life" in Amherst; "instances of failure and bankruptcy were most spectacularly illustrated during the financial panics of 1837, 1847, 1857, and 1873, but the cycle of fluctuation was endemic before, between, and after these years." The poet was well aware of her family's economic instability and of the relation of market fluctuations to its economic stability. In 1830, Edward Dickinson bought half of the house built by his father on Main Street, but in 1833 he was forced to sell. It was not until 1855, when the poet was twenty-four, that he had accrued the wealth to buy back the house the Dickinsons always thought of as "the Homestead." The Dickinson family could afford to buy books and did so, but the rate of buying undoubtedly increased as technological innovation in the printing industry and transportation of books by railroad lowered their cost and as the Dickinson family itself recovered economic stability.[51] Similarly, while Dickinson's primary reading was probably individual and silent throughout her lifetime, reading aloud seems to have been an ordinary aspect of her world.

Here Benjamin's distinction between cult or ritual on the one hand and technologies of iconic reproducibility on the other is suggestive. As Sicherman suggests, reading aloud occurs regularly (for example, in the evening) and with strong associations of personal bonding, especially among those who read to lessen the tedium of work or as an aspect of caretaking for the young, sick, and old. In this sense, reading aloud might be regarded as secularly ritualistic or as partaking in some of the affects of ritual. Perhaps more powerful as a pattern of nineteenth-century behavior is the similarly secular ritual of memorization, a practice stressed pedagogically in all levels of schooling and in religious catechism. As is clear from her frequent practice of quotation in letters and poems, Dickinson was fully a part of the nineteenth-century culture of memorization.[52] Poetry, like other subjects, was taught by memorization: one "learned by heart" one's fa-

vorite verses just as one memorized scientific data or long passages from the Bible. Moreover, memorization was encouraged
"by ear" as well as from a text. From Homer and Sappho on,
rhythm and rhyme have functioned to make verse not only
memorable but memorizable, repeatable, and such repetitions
within a community suggest both shared sources and shared values. Quoting memorized texts is not in itself ritualistic because
of its spontaneity and because the texts themselves may take any
stance or tone, including irreverence, but like reading aloud it
may gain resonance from its similarity to ritual—especially inso-
far as seasons, religious holidays, or memories might dictate that
certain texts be quoted at certain times.

Could Dickinson have conceived of poetry in a way radically
different from her contemporaries—for example, as significantly
visual in its forms? Certainly! Walt Whitman, for instance, provides clear evidence of valuing visual aspects of presentation—
with his experimental typeface, formatting, and photograph in
the 1855 edition of *Leaves of Grass*, then use of widely differing
fonts, formatting, and photographs in later editions of the poem.
That is not, however, for me, the most persuasive historical or
aesthetic reading of Dickinson. Yet why not privilege the manuscripts? One might, for example, argue that, in any era, every
aspect of a printed or manuscript page influences a poem's
sound, hence, that we can only learn more about a poem from
reading it in manuscript. As Howe says, "Letters are sounds."[53]
Certainly, spatial organization of words or punctuation or use of
different-sized letters or fonts may influence the timing, stresses,
or breathing of an oral performance of a poem; how a poem
sounds is not divorced from how it looks on the page, especially
if a poem is composed for a page. All this seems persuasive to
me. Nonetheless, there are degrees of emphasis and attention assumed in attending to different kinds of poetic texts and texts
from different eras. One does not, for example, conceive of a
Shakespeare sonnet differently when it is printed with the closing
couplet indented or in multiple font sizes; one's immediate reaction to that particular printing will register such features, but
they will not be confused with the "poem" because the poem's
form is determined by metrical and stanzaic structures. One

does, however, take distinct and explicit pleasure in the sight of an e.e. cummings or Williams poem, or other poem composed by the line, and these poems would indeed lose major elements of form if printed differently. Cummings's "SNO" begins:

> a white idea(Listen
>
> drenches:earth's ugly)mind.
> ,Rinsing with exact death
>
> the annual brain
> > clotted with loosely voices
> look
> look.[54]

This kind of typographical play may be marked vocally by pitch, variations in speed, or syncopation, but no listener can associate such aural cues with the "look" of the page. For example, there is no sound for the extraneous comma at the beginning of the third line. A sense of these poems is enriched by hearing them read aloud, but one cannot transfer what one sees on these pages precisely into sound as one can with a Shakespeare poem. Shakespeare did not write poetry for the page in the same sense that cummings did. Nor, I believe, did Dickinson.

Dickinson's manuscripts document the way a brilliant mind may respond to the peculiarity of immediate material circumstances of writing—an oddly shaped page, a slip of the pen, or not quite room for an entire metrical line, hence, the need to decide where to break it. How could a mind so lively not notice the correspondence of features of a page, or torn envelope, to her own words? Dickinson was also quite possibly playful in aspects of her iconography, as are many letter writers today who have not yet given up handwriting for the electronic page. Susan Howe, among others, has repeatedly and marvelously demonstrated the pleasures of reading Dickinson's words in relation to their manuscript contexts, using every aspect of the material page as potentially informative.[55] Indeed such readings suggest the expanded pleasure of critical readings we may anticipate from the Dickinson Electronic Archives project of making all

Dickinson's manuscripts visually available to large numbers of readers.[56] I object only to (implicit or explicit) claims that reading Dickinson accurately *demands* such attention to the material forms of her orthography and manuscripts, or that any print transcription ignoring the visual elements of a manuscript page misrepresents Dickinson's poems.

In addition to the historical and paradigmatic reasons suggested above, Dickinson's own manuscript practices persuade me that she regards a poem as separable from any single manifestation of its material appearance. In copying the poems, Dickinson usually did not repeat nonmetrical or otherwise unconventional visual features, such as the arrangement of variant words on a page or a slant of handwriting on a particular kind of torn page. Franklin's introduction to his variorum edition and Mitchell's painstaking measurements and comparisons, indicating that Dickinson's manuscripts as iconic documents are not "the most reliable guide to her meaning(s)," provide the most persuasive evidence of the poet's calligraphic inconsistency.[57] Mitchell notes, for example, that even when a manuscript contains nonmetrical calligraphic rows (nonmetrical line breaks), other features of the page typically distinguish metrical lines, or that Dickinson, in fact, typically distinguished prose from poetry through paragraph structure and other aspects of lineation or chirography.[58] Such pragmatic evidence supports my understanding of both nineteenth-century poetic culture and Dickinson's own poetic: for her, as for Poe or Longfellow or even the more visually oriented Whitman, the "poem" does not depend fundamentally or primarily on the calligraphic, iconic manuscript for its meaning, despite the fact that her manuscripts may enhance our appreciation of individual poems by providing us with historical, aesthetic, or biographical information or pleasures—as do the manuscripts of any poet, in any period.

Descriptions of Dickinson's manuscripts have led to aesthetic and critical claims based on those descriptions. For me, the most important of these arises from Susan Howe's argument that printed editions of Dickinson's poems have "domesticated and occluded" the poet, and a return to the manuscripts in effect liberates her and her work from the constricting fetters of a century of patriarchal editing.⁵⁹ This reading has been influential and moving to a wide variety of readers and helped to generate the recent enormous upswing of attention among innovative and feminist poets to Dickinson's verse. Howe's argument implies that Dickinson was too radical a poet for her time, or even for most of the twentieth century, to have understood accurately. Yet one can see Dickinson as a radical poet without claiming that she constructed a distinctly visual poetic. For example, one can hear the unarguably innovative compression, syntactic deletion, metaphor, slant-rhyme, and disruptive rhythms of her poems by listening, or from Johnson's or Franklin's printed versions, as well as by looking at a manuscript page. My preference of the Johnson or Franklin editions over the Todd and Higginson texts acknowledges the importance of seeing Dickinson's general use of dashes and irregular capitalization, but these are irregularities fully within the print capacity of her own as well as our times and do not demand attention to the singularity of any particular manuscript's conditions. The details of a manuscript page suggest even more disruptive rhythms in some poems, but I find the differences slight, given the shortness of Dickinson's metrical line and its obvious disruptions through syntactic deletion, multiple disjunctions, and features easily represented in standard typography. Similarly, the perception of Dickinson's increasing inclusion of variants on a handwritten page may alter one's sense of her conception of the poem without demanding the primacy of the visual. Dickinson may well conceive of a fluid text—or of multiple possibilities for finishing a text—without conceiving of a particular spatial arrangement of variants on a page as constituting an essential part of the poem. In his attempt to shift the attention of contemporary innovative poetics away from exclusive focus on the page, for example, Charles Bernstein argues that understanding a poem as a heard event both divorces it from an iconic page and makes of it necessarily a "plural event": "the work is not identical to any one graphical or performative realization of it, nor can it be equated with a totalized unity of those versions or manifestations"; "to speak of the poem in performance is, then, to overthrow the idea of the poem as a fixed, stable, finite linguistic object."⁶⁰ Perhaps by taking a clue from

Dickinson's own "performances" of her poems to her family and attending to the aural tensions, movement, and play of the poems, we will hear a far more revolutionary destabilization of poetic form than she could have achieved by iconicizing the poem as a visual act on a particular page. Here, anachronistically, I come full circle, using late-twentieth-century poetics to suggest the radical resonance that a nineteenth-century perception of the poem as a primarily aural event may continue to have for twenty-first-century readers.

A corollary to Howe's argument suggests that a return to Dickinson's manuscript art reveals Dickinson as a more feminist poet, with the handwritten page as the mark of both her resistance to patronizing male editors and her association with feminine production.[61] Yet decades of critical work have demonstrated feminist elements of Dickinson's writing—thematic, structural, and cultural—that are independent of the manuscript page. Furthermore, as Joanne Dobson and Betsy Erkkila, among others, have argued, Dickinson's feminism was as complex and contradictory as other aspects of her art: while the poet's life and poetry are feminist in some respects, she was in other ways more conservative socially and politically than many of her female contemporaries, who chose to publish poems of explicit cultural and political critique—albeit in less interesting verse forms.[62] To understand both Dickinson's textual experimentation and her feminism within the complicated and contradictory expanded context of what Pierre Bourdieu has called the "field of cultural production" is not to diminish either aspect of her greatness or interest for the twenty-first century.[63]

Although she did not publish, Dickinson did care about a contemporary audience and wrote, I believe, so as both to communicate with and elude it. In "Good to hide, and hear 'em hunt!" she implies that it is good to be heard without being altogether caught:

Good to hide, and hear 'em hunt!	7
Better, to be found,	5
If one care to, that is,	6
The Fox fits the Hound -	5

Good to know, and not tell -	6
Best, to know and tell,	5
Can one find the rare Ear	6
Not too dull - (Fr 945)	3

In the trochaic meter of this poem, 5 lines are catalectic: they drop the expected final unstressed syllable and so have an odd number of syllables and end on a stress. The other three lines end with a spondee, and the poem concludes with a sequence of 5 relatively stressed syllables ("rare Ear / Not too dull -"). For trochaic meter the ends of the lines of this poem are heavily stressed, and because the lines are so short these line-end stresses disrupt the falling beat of the initial trochees almost as soon as the line has begun. Moreover, the most significant line of the poem, line 4, begins with an iamb—a rhythmic inversion unusual in trochaic verse. What complicates the rhythm of this poem most, however, is that semantic stress is so important to its meaning. Does one stress "not" or "tell" more emphatically in line 5? Line 6 would seem to demand greater semantic stress on the conjunction "and" than on either of the grammatically more significant verbs "know" or "tell." This poem is on the one hand utterly simple—like Longfellow's "Rain in Summer." On the other hand, it flaunts its cleverness, playing "fox" to an audience sophisticated in rhythmic nuance. The meter is more or less trochaic, but this may be like saying that the fox runs in a more or less straight line to its den. It is the "more or less" that saves the fox's skin and makes the poem.

"The Fox fits the Hound," states the poem. This suggests that the apparently wild fox is no more independent than the domesticated hound. The prey adapts to suit its predator. A fox learns its feints and dodges by what it knows the dogs do not understand or cannot do. Once the hounds learn a new trick or discover one of the fox's, the fox must also increase its cleverness. In Dickinson's parable, there is pleasure in the chase for both fox and hound if they are well matched—if each can push the other to become increasingly adept, agile, alert. Regardless of whom among her own acquaintances might have "fit" the bill of adequate "Hound," I propose that Dickinson's fox-like irregularities of rhyme, rhythm, punctuation, and grammar were trained by her own "Hound" behavior: her acute attention to the rhythmic and sound-patterning poems of her contemporaries.

The more I read Dickinson, the more I see her as a fox who indeed "fit" the hounds of her century. She was not, like Whitman, a radical who rebelled openly: where he rejected all meter and rhyme for forms he described as organic, growing like melons in the sun, she wrote largely in ballad form or using other fundamentally regular rhythmic and rhyming patterns, which she disrupted continuously, in sly ways. She "could not drop the Bells whose jingling cooled [her] tramp" (L 265). While she wrote some free verse poems, for the most part, Dickinson bent given structures of meter, syntax, and rhyme—poetic structures based on patterns of sound. Fox-like, she appeared to conform while rebelling indirectly, through omission, dissonant or slant-rhymes, irony, and wit. Unlike Longfellow, Poe, Sigourney, Bryant, she did not experiment with multiple verse forms; in this sense, one might say she was less adventurous than many of her contemporaries in the forms of her verse—although not in other aspects of her aesthetic or, frequently, in what she said. She preferred simple stanzaic and metrical forms, varying their rhythm through syntax, compacted metaphor, grammatical neologism, and extreme compression. To my mind, the boundaries of traditional, aurally based forms, like the walls of her parents' house, enabled the freedoms Dickinson constructed and prized. For her, freedom arose from such constraint: "Captivity is Consciousness - / So's Liberty -" (Fr 649).

NOTES

1. I use Ralph W. Franklin's three-volume *The Poems of Emily Dickinson, Variorum Edition* (Cambridge, Mass.: Harvard University Press, 1998) in quoting Dickinson's poems, subsequently referenced as (Fr) in the text, and Thomas H. Johnson and Theodora Ward's *The Letters of Emily Dickinson*, 3 vols. (Cambridge, Mass.: Harvard University Press, 1958) for her letters, subsequently referenced as (L) in the text.

2. On April 25, 1862, Dickinson wrote Higginson that she had heard he was "disgraceful" (L 261).

3. Piombino, "The Aural Ellipsis and the Nature of Listening in Contemporary Poetry," in *Close Listening: Poetry and the Performed Word*, ed. Charles Bernstein (New York: Oxford University Press, 1998), 53–72, 70.

4. McGann, *Black Riders: The Visible Language of Modernism* (Princeton: Princeton University Press, 1993).

5. I am not the first to address this question. In a 1998 essay, Domhnall Mitchell states that "the contemporary preoccupation with Dickinson's manuscripts may be seen as an attempt to lift her texts out of history, to say here was a poet who made eminently modern collages using visual forms and using form visually" ("Revising the Script: Emily Dickinson's Manuscripts," *American Literature* 70, no. 4 [December 1998]: 705–37, 731). Mitchell then examines the manuscripts themselves to question the "positivistic" assumptions of Dickinson scholars calling for a return to the manuscripts. Marjorie Perloff has repeatedly addressed the question of the historicity of verse forms and how we understand them; see, for example, her claim that "verse, like the materials used in any art medium, . . . is subject to historical change as well as cultural and political constraint" in "After Free Verse: The New Nonlinear Poetries," in *Close Listening*, 86–110, 87.

6. *The Poems of Emily Dickinson*, 3 vols. (Cambridge, Mass.: Harvard University Press, 1955). Disputes within the Dickinson family and between the family and editor Mabel Loomis Todd prevented any previous editor from obtaining access to all extant manuscripts. For a concise history of these disputes, see Martha Nell Smith, "Dickinson's Manuscripts," in *The Emily Dickinson Handbook* (Amherst: University of Massachuetts Press, 1998), 113–37, or the introduction to Franklin's variorum edition (1999).

7. Franklin also edited *The Manuscript Books of Emily Dickinson*, 2 vols. (Cambridge, Mass.: Harvard University Press, 1981), printing photographic facsimiles of all the poems Dickinson compiled as fascicles or sets; this constitutes about two-thirds of her poems. Because *The Manuscript Books* does not make the choices demanded by representing the poems in print, I do not include it in the list above.

8. Hart and Smith, eds., *Open Me Carefully: The Intimate Letters of Emily Dickinson to Susan Huntington Dickinson* (Ashfield, Mass.: Paris Press, 1999), xxii. An important predecessor to Hart and Smith's editing choices appears in Marta Werner, *Emily Dickinson's Open Folios:*

Scenes of Reading, Surfaces of Writing (Ann Arbor: University of Michigan Press, 1995), a study of forty late fragments of Dickinson's writing, including photographic facsimiles.

9. The earliest editions are *Poems by Emily Dickinson*, ed. Mabel Loomis Todd and T. W. Higginson (Boston: Roberts Brothers, 1890), and *Poems by Emily Dickinson: Second Series*, ed. T. W. Higginson and Mabel Loomis Todd (Boston: Roberts Brothers, 1891). Todd alone edits a third volume of the poems in 1896.

10. See, for example, Susan Howe, *My Emily Dickinson* (Berkeley: North Atlantic Books, 1985), Cristanne Miller, *Emily Dickinson: A Poet's Grammar* (Cambridge, Mass.: Harvard University Press, 1987), A. R. C. Finch, "Dickinson and Patriarchal Meter," *PMLA* 162, no. 2 (March 1987): 166–76, Martha Nell Smith, *Rowing in Eden: Rereading Emily Dickinson* (Austin: University of Texas Press, 1992), and Werner, *Emily Dickinson's Open Folios*.

11. In 1980, W. J. T. Mitchell comments on "the ubiquity of the word 'vision' in the vocabularies of critics of all persuasions in the last twenty years" ("Spatial Form in Literature: Toward a General Theory," *Critical Inquiry* 6 [Spring 1980]: 539–67, 547). In 1993, Martin Jay asserts the pervasiveness of the visual in Western thought since the ancient Greeks, arguing that this emphasis has changed in the last two decades, especially in France (*With Downcast Eyes: The Denigration of Vision in Twentieth-Century French Thought* [Berkeley: University of California Press, 1993]). In contrast, Elisa New begins *The Line's Eye: Poetic Experience, American Sight* (Cambridge, Mass.: Harvard University Press, 1998) with a list of recent critical works on American culture, using vision as their primary metaphor: Angela Miller's *The Empire of the Eye* (1994), Donald Pease's *Visionary Compacts* (1987), Myra Jehlen's *American Incarnation* (1986), and Carolyn Porter's *Seeing and Being* (1981). She then remarks, "Such studies as these have rendered the equation of American originality and expansionist vision *the* critical axiom of our day" (2; emphasis mine).

12. Dickinson does occasionally associate the poet with sight, for example, in "This was a Poet," where "He" is "Of Pictures, the Discloser." I argue, however, that this is also a kind of "Poet" Dickinson does not admire or aspire to become (*A Poet's Grammar*, 120–22).

13. Cheryl Walker is the first to link Dickinson with the songbird convention in *The Nightingale's Burden: Women Poets and American Culture before 1900* (Bloomington: Indiana University Press, 1982).

Among others, Small mentions Fr 270, 268, 240, 281, 1009, 955, 766, 462, 1516, 928, 810, 268, as poems in which Dickinson represents the poet as songbird (*Positive as Sound: Emily Dickinson's Rhyme* [Athens: University of Georgia Press, 1990], 31, 36, 30). Even more poems link birds' song or flight with transcendence, for example, "At Half past Three, a single Bird" (Fr 1099) and "A Bird, came down the Walk" (Fr 359). Small also writes at length of the general nineteenth-century interest in the music of poetry, with reference to Poe, Whitman (who claimed the influence of opera on his free verse), Emerson, Lanier, Verlaine, Carlyle, and Pater (36–37).

14. Leyda, *The Years and Hours of Emily Dickinson*, 2 vols. (New Haven: Yale University Press, 1960), 1: 367. Richard Sewall also summarizes Dickinson's musical abilities by speculating that her "particular talent . . . was for improvising"; *The Life of Emily Dickinson*, 2 vols. (New York: Farrar, Straus and Giroux, 1974), 2:407.

15. See Small, *Positive as Sound*, 48–52 for documentation in letters from the poet and from various of her friends referring to her musical abilities, practice time, and interests.

16. On this subject, see Christine Ross, "Uncommon Measures: Textbook Instruction and Emily Dickinson's Subversive Prosody," *The Emily Dickinson Journal* 10, no. 1 (Fall 2001): 70–98.

17. There are, of course, exceptions. In "After Free Verse," Perloff points out that much free verse poetry of the twentieth century is "remarkable in its lack of visual interest," but it also "depends upon the unobtrusiveness of sound structure" in its uses of language (95). This is, as it were, poetry of internal meditation, *as if* spoken but not highlighting structures of sound. There has also been a late twentieth-century renewed interest in metered verse, as articulated most vocally in the "New Formalism" (see, for example, a whole line of books published by Story Line Press, including Annie Finch's edited *After New Formalism: Poets on Form, Narrative, and Tradition*, 1999). My concern, however, is with innovative poetry and with what generally constitutes innovative form.

18. *The Complete Poetry and Selected Criticism of Edgar Allan Poe.* Ed. Allen Tate (1968; New York: New American Library, 1981), 113. "The Raven" was first published in the *New York Evening Mirror*, Jan. 29, 1845.

19. The two works of Longfellow's from which Dickinson quotes most frequently are "The Rainy Day" and the novel *Ka-*

vanaugh. See Jack L. Capps, *Emily Dickinson's Reading, 1836–1886* (Cambridge, Mass.: Harvard University Press, 1966), 119, 178–79.

20. Among the more enthusiastic accounts, in *Poetry of the American Renaissance: A Diverse Anthology from the Romantic Period* (New York: George Braziller, 1995), Paul Kane describes Longfellow as "a major American poet whose narrative gifts and mastery of poetic technique place him at the junction between the popular forms of fiction and poetry. His readership was immense and his influence on nineteenth-century American culture virtually incalculable" (85).

21. "The Wreck of the Hesperus" (1840), in *The Complete Poetical Works of Henry Wadsworth Longfellow* (Boston: Houghton, Mifflin, and Co., The Riverside Press, 1902), 15, 17. All Longfellow poems are cited from this edition, abbreviated below as CPL.

22. "Rain in Summer" (1845), CPL, 74–75.

23. "The Warning" (1842), CPL, 27.

24. "The Day Is Done" (1845), CPL, 82.

25. Miller, *A Poet's Grammar*, 141.

26. On this topic, see Matthew Garner, "Becoming Longfellow: Work, Manhood, and Poetry," *American Literature* 72, no. 1 (March 2000): 59–86, 61, 65.

27. From *The Manuscript Books of Emily Dickinson* 1:253–55. For description of the other extant manuscripts, see Franklin's variorum edition, 356–60.

28. Quoted from pages 235, 237, 222 in *Illuminations: Walter Benjamin, Essays and Reflections*, ed. with an introduction by Hannah Arendt, trans. Harry Zohn (New York: Schocken Books, 1969).

29. Ibid., 223, 224.

30. Ibid., 224–25.

31. Pound, "Vorticism," *Fortnightly Review* 571 (September 1, 1914): 464.

32. Lewis, *Time and Western Man* (London: Chatto and Windus, 1927), 3.

33. McLuhan, *The Medium is the Message* (Seattle, Wash.: Vanguard Press, 1951), n.p.

34. Frank, "Spatial Form in Modern Literature," *Sewanee Review* 53 (1945). See also Frank's "Spatial Form: An Answer to Critics," *Critical Inquiry* 4 (Winter 1977): 231–52.

35. W. J. T. Mitchell, "Spatial Form in Literature," 560–61.

36. Nänny, "Iconic Dimensions in Poetry," *Swiss Papers in English*

Language and Literature, vol. 2, special issue "On Poetry and Poetics," ed. Richard Waswo (1985): 111–36, 113.

37. Nänny, "Imitative Form: The Modernist Poem on the Page," in *International Poetry Symposium,* ed. Roland Hagenbüchle and Laura Skandera-Trombley (Regensburg, Germany: F. Pustet, 1986), 213–31, 215, 213. Here Nänny also writes of "Modernist efforts towards mimetic or representational typography" as "an offshoot of a pervasive tendency towards visualization in early twentieth century culture" (213).

38. Bollobás quotes Pound's "Antheil and the Treatise on Harmony," p. 134, in "New Prosodies in 20th Century American Free Verse," [sic] *Acta Litteraria Academiae Scientiarum Hungaricae* 20, no. 1–2 (1978): 99–121, 113. See also her essays "On the Role of Visuality in Free Verse: A Study of English and American Modernist Poetry," *Studies in English and American Poetry* 4 (1978): 157–79, and "Visuality and Concretism: Enactments of the Real: On the Poetics of the American Avant-Garde," *Acta Litteraria Academiae Scientiarum Hungaricae* 30, no. 3–4 (1988): 229–41.

39. Attridge, *Poetic Rhythm: An Introduction* (Cambridge: Cambridge University Press, 1995), 172.

40. Howe, *The Birth-Mark: Unsettling the Wilderness in American Literary History* (Hanover, N.H.: University Press of New England, 1993), 145.

41. Bernstein, "Introduction," *Close Listening,* 4. Subsequent quotes are from pp. 8 and 11.

42. Andrews, "Praxis: A Political Economy of Noise and Information," in *Close Listening,* 73–85, 74.

43. This paradigm may again be shifting, as Bernstein's volume also indicates. There are now increasing numbers of projects attentive to the poem as aural event—most spectacularly Robert Pinsky's "Favorite Poem Project: Americans Saying the Poems They Love" (see www.favoritepoem.org).

44. D. Mitchell in "Revising the Script" also suggests that McGann's "perspective derives from modernist experiments with the medium of print, which he then inscribes onto a premodernist body of writing" (730).

45. McGann, *Black Riders,* 21, 31, 28, 38.

46. Werner, *Emily Dickinson's Open Folios,* 36–37, 27 (emphasis hers); Howe, *The Birth-Mark,* 141, 142.

47. Sicherman, "Sense and Sensibility: A Case Study of Women's Reading in Late-Victorian America," in *Reading in America: Literature & Social History*, ed. Cathy N. Davidson (Baltimore: Johns Hopkins University Press, 1989), 201–25, 302. Sicherman also points out that women have been disproportionately responsible for institutions of public reading: "one source estimates that women founded 75 percent of all American public libraries," and in the Hamilton family she studied, the men neither read aloud nor supported public libraries while the women did both (201). The men instead accumulated huge private libraries.

48. See *Open Me Carefully*, 226, 272, 275. Twice the editors note that Susan wrote a note either about reading or not reading one of Dickinson's "letter-poems" to others; once they quote from Mabel Loomis Todd's 1882 diary that Susan read poems out loud to her.

49. Ackmann, "'I'm Glad I Finally Surfaced': A Norcross Descendant Remembers Emily Dickinson," *The Emily Dickinson Journal* 5, no. 2 (1996): 120–26, 123.

50. Electrical service was not available in Amherst until 1893, although residential gas lighting was adopted in some Amherst homes as early as 1877, when Dickinson was forty-seven years old. Gas lighting was not adopted in her house during her lifetime.

51. For general information on the revolution in printing and other social factors affecting people's reading patterns, see Ronald J. Zboray, "Antebellum Reading and the Ironies of Technological Innovation," in *Reading in America*, 180–200. On the early economic instability of Dickinson's family see Domhnall Mitchell, *Emily Dickinson: Monarch of Perception* (Amherst: University of Massachusetts Press, 2000), 64–77.

52. See Marietta Messmer, *"A vice for voices": Reading Emily Dickinson's Correspondence* (Amherst: University of Massachusetts Press, 2001), which contains a chapter on Dickinson's use of quotation. Capps in *Emily Dickinson's Reading* also refers to Dickinson as subject to an "educational philosophy that placed great emphasis on repeated readings and the memorizing of vast quantities of detail" (104).

53. Howe, *The Birth-Mark*, 141.

54. E. E. Cummings, *Complete Poems 1913–1962* (New York: Harcourt Brace Jovanovich, 1972), 99.

55. I was pleased to witness such reading most recently at the

Emily Dickinson International Society conference, "Zero at the Bone: New Climates for Dickinson Study," August 3–8, 2001, in Trondheim, Norway, where Howe presented the paper "Graphicer for Grace." Others engaged in similar readings of Dickinson's manuscripts include Smith, *Rowing in Eden*, McGann, *Black Riders*, McGann, "Emily Dickinson's Visible Language," *The Emily Dickinson Journal* 2, no. 2 (1993), and Melanie Hubbard, "Dickinson's Advertising Flyers: Theorizing Materiality and the Work of Reading," *The Emily Dickinson Journal* 7, no. 1 (1998).

56. Dickinson Editing Collective, Martha Nell Smith, Ellen Louise Hart, and Marta Werner, general editors. See http://jefferson.village.virginia.edu/dickinson/.

57. D. Mitchell, "Revising the Script," 706.

58. D. Mitchell, "The Grammar of Ornament: Emily Dickinson's Manuscripts and Their Meanings," *Nineteenth-Century Literature* 55, no. 4 (March 2001): 479–514. The work mentioned in the first part of this sentence appears in D. Mitchell's 1998 essay, "Revising the Script."

59. Howe, *The Birth-Mark*, 131.

60. Bernstein, "Introduction," *Close Listening*, 9.

61. These arguments are implied or made by Elizabeth Petrino, *Emily Dickinson and Her Contemporaries: Women's Verse in America, 1820–1885* (Hanover, N.H.: University Press of New England, 1998), Smith, *Rowing in Eden*, and Hart and Smith, *Open Me Carefully*, as well as implied by the Dickinson Electronic Archives site, which initially presented as factual Dickinson's participation in a poetry "workshop" with Susan Huntington Dickinson (http://jefferson.village.virginia.edu/dickinson/).

62. Dobson, *Dickinson and the Strategies of Reticence: The Woman Writer in Nineteenth-Century America* (Bloomington: Indiana University Press, 1989), and Erkkila, *The Wicked Sisters: Women Poets, Literary History, and Discord* (New York: Oxford University Press, 1992). See also Petrino, *Emily Dickinson*.

63. See, for example, *The Field of Cultural Production: Essays on Art and Literature*, ed. and with an introduction by Randal Johnson (New York: Columbia University Press, 1999).

ILLUSTRATED
CHRONOLOGY

1830: In the fall, Edward and Emily Norcross Dickinson and small son William Austin move into The Homestead, which they share with Edward's father and other family members. Birth of Emily Elizabeth Dickinson (December 10).

1830: Birth of poet, novelist, and Indian Rights activist Helen Maria Fiske (Helen Hunt Jackson) in Amherst. Massachusetts residents no longer required to pay taxes to support churches. Abraham Lincoln moves with his father's family from Indiana to Illinois. There are thirteen million Americans.

1831: In Virginia, Nat Turner leads an unsuccessful slave rebellion.

1832: Andrew Jackson reelected president on the Democratic ticket.

1834: Abraham Lincoln elected to a first term in the Illinois legislature. Burning of Charlestown convent by anti-Catholic nativists.

The poet's father, Edward Dickinson, painted by O. A. Bullard in 1840. By permission, Houghton Library, Harvard University.

The poet's mother, Emily Norcross Dickinson, painted by O. A. Bullard in 1840. By permission, Houghton Library, Harvard University.

Poet and novelist Helen Hunt Jackson, Dickinson's schoolmate and friend in her later years. "H. H." prided herself on her work as an Indian Rights activist. By permission, Jones Library, Inc., Amherst, Massachusetts

1831: The poet's maternal grandfather Joel Norcross remarries. The poet's mother is admitted to church membership.

1833: Birth of the poet's sister Lavinia Norcross Dickinson. Never married for fear of displeasing her father, she becomes Emily's indispensable friend and advocate in later years. "She has no Father and Mother but me and I have no Parents but her" (1873 letter to Elizabeth Holland).

Poor and broken-spirited, Edward's father Samuel Fowler Dickinson moves to Cincinnati, Ohio, where he supervises building construction at Lane Theological Seminary. His wife and several remaining children follow shortly thereafter.

1834: Lavinia Norcross, the poet's aunt, marries her first cousin, Loring Norcross.

1835: Edward Dickinson appointed treasurer of Amherst College, a post he holds for thirty-seven years. Emily begins attending school.

1838: Edward Dickinson begins a two-year term in the Massachusetts legislature. Death of his father Samuel Fowler Dickinson, his financial affairs in a "sorry mess."

1836: Battle of the Alamo, San Antonio, Texas. Ralph Waldo Emerson publishes *Nature*.

1837: Victoria becomes queen of England. Mary Lyon establishes Mount Holyoke Female Seminary. Birth of Mark Twain. Financial panic, economic depression cause widespread unemployment.

1838: Edgar Allan Poe publishes his only novel, *The Narrative of Arthur Gordon Pym, of Nantucket*. Melville's future father-in-law Lemuel Shaw becomes the last chief justice of Massachusetts to send a man to prison for blasphemy. Abner Kneeland, the victim of his decision, later founds a utopian community in Iowa. Trail of Tears, as the Cherokee nation is displaced beyond the boundary of the Mississippi River.

1839: First photo-daguerreotypes taken in the United States.

1840: William Henry Harrison elected president on the Whig ticket after a hard fought campaign ("Tippecanoe and Tyler too"). Orestes A. Brownson's "The Laboring Classes" contributes to Martin Van Buren's defeat. Margaret Fuller edits *The Dial*.

1841: Utopian community Brook Farm founded in West Roxbury, Massachusetts, near Boston. Later satirized by Hawthorne, one of the residents, in *The Blithedale Romance*.

Amherst Academy. By permission of the Jones Library, Inc., Amherst, Massachusetts.

Lithograph of Phoenix Row and Main Street, Amherst, 1840. By permission of the Jones Library, Inc., Amherst, Massachusetts.

The house on North Pleasant Street where the Dickinsons lived from 1840 to 1855. Photographed ca. 1870. Courtesy of the Todd-Bingham Picture Collection, Yale University Library.

1840: The Dickinsons move into a spacious wooden house on Pleasant Street. Emily enters Amherst Academy, in "the English course," as does her sister Lavinia.

1842: In January, Edward Dickinson begins another term in the Massachusetts legislature; Austin's schoolfriend Joseph Lyman boards with the Dickinsons during Edward's absence. Emily enters "The Classical Department" at Amherst Academy.

1844: Depressed by the death of her schoolmate Sophia Holland, Emily Dickinson is sent to stay with her mother's sister Lavinia Norcross Norcross in Boston. The trip does her good.

The Dickinson children, Emily, Austin, and Lavinia, painted by O. A. Bullard in 1840. By permission, Houghton Library, Harvard University.

1842: Abraham Lincoln marries Mary Todd in Illinois. Nathaniel Hawthorne marries Sophia Peabody in Massachusetts. Harriet Jacobs escapes North, from her garret in Edenton, North Carolina. P. T. Barnum's American Museum opens in New York City.

1843: Birth of Henry James, Jr., in New York City; Whitman's temperance novel *Franklin Evans or The Inebriate: A Tale of the Times.*

1844: Nativist anti-Catholic riots in Philadelphia. Mormon leader Joseph Smith killed by mob in Carthage, Illinois. Elizabeth Barrett Browning publishes "A Vision of Poets." Emerson, *Essays: Second Series.*

1845: Irish potato famine accelerates immigration to America. Elizabeth Barrett elopes with Robert Browning; they take up residence on the Continent. Margaret Fuller publishes *Woman in the Nineteenth Century.* Frederick Douglass, *Narrative of the Life of Frederick Douglass, an American Slave, Written by Himself.*

1846: United States declares war on Mexico; Lincoln elected to Congress, his only term. Thoreau at Walden Pond; arrested for not paying taxes.

1847: Beginning in September, Emily Dickinson attends Mount Holyoke Female Seminary, where she finds herself all engrossed in the study of sulphuric acid.

1848: Emily Dickinson completes her year at Mount Holyoke and returns to Amherst, her parents having decided that no further formal education is necessary.

1849: Writes satiric valentine letter to William Cowper Dickinson, valedictorian of Amherst College, class of 1848.

Emily Norcross Dickinson, daguerreotype, ca. 1847. The only known photograph of the poet's mother. After her death in 1882, the poet wrote to her friend Elizabeth Holland, "When she became our Child, the Affection came." By permission, Monson Free Library, Monson, Massachusetts.

1847: Publication of Charlotte Brontë's *Jane Eyre* and Emily Brontë's *Wuthering Heights.*

1848: Women's Rights convention in Seneca Falls, New York. Gold discovered in California. In Europe, revolutions in France, Germany, and Italy that influence democratic thinking in the United States. Herman Melville publishes *Typee*; Walt Whitman edits the *Brooklyn Daily Eagle* and travels to New Orleans, where he edits *The Crescent.* Death of Emily Brontë, in Yorkshire, England, of consumption.

Emily Dickinson, daguerreotype. The only known photograph of the poet, probably taken in the winter of 1847 when she was sixteen. Courtesy of the Todd-Bingham Picture Collection, Yale University Library.

1850: In January, Benjamin Franklin Newton, her father's former law clerk, gives her Emerson's *Poems*. In February, Dickinson's first known publication, a comic valentine letter, appears in *The Indicator*, a new publication edited by Amherst College students. In March, Dickinson sends a comic valentine to her father's law partner, Elbridge Gerry Bowdoin. This is her first known poem (Fr 1).

1852: Dickinson sends a love letter to Susan Huntington Gilbert, who is teaching in Baltimore. Austin Dickinson teaching Irish immigrants in Boston. Edward Dickinson elected to the U.S. House of Representatives on the Whig ticket.

Lavinia Norcross Dickinson (Vinnie), the poet's sister, in 1852. By permission of the Jones Library, Inc., Amherst, Massachusetts.

1849: Death of Edgar Allan Poe under tragic circumstances, in Baltimore. Hawthorne writing *The Scarlet Letter,* after losing his job in the Salem Custom-House.

1850: Compromise bill enacted that restricts slavery in the territories. The Fugitive Slave Law is passed following Daniel Webster's speech. Death of Margaret Fuller, now the Marchese Ossoli, returning from Italy with her (perhaps) husband and small son, off Fire Island, in a storm. Elizabeth Barrett Browning publishes her politically radical poem "The Runaway Slave at Pilgrim's Point."

1851: Amelia Bloomer suggests in her feminist publication that women wear a kind of short skirt and pants, to free themselves from the encumbrances of traditional dress. *Moby Dick* and *The House of the Seven Gables* are published.

1852: Harriet Beecher Stowe's *Uncle Tom's Cabin;* first edition of five thousand copies gone in two days.

1854: The nativist Know-Nothing Party is organized. Thomas Wentworth Higginson a war correspondent in "bleeding Kansas." Thoreau publishes *Walden.*

1853: Austin Dickinson attends Harvard Law School; he becomes engaged to Susan Gilbert, who is Emily's best friend. Death of Benjamin Franklin Newton, who wanted to live until Emily was a poet. Railroad comes to Amherst.

1854: A meeting to organize the antislavery Republican Party held in Washington, D.C., in rooms shared by Edward Dickinson and Thomas D. Eliot of New Bedford, granduncle of another American poet. Edward, however, remains a Whig and supports the Kansas-Nebraska bill. Quarrel between Emily and Sue; Sue leaves town for seven months.

1855: Edward Dickinson unsuccessful in his bid for reelection to Congress. Emily and Lavinia visit Mount Vernon and spend several weeks in Washington, D.C., where Emily attends fashionable dinner parties and impresses the company with her wit. On the way home, they stop to visit in Philadelphia and Emily meets the Rev. Charles Wadsworth, pastor of the Arch Street Presbyterian Church. He becomes her "Shepherd from Little Girl'hood" and probably the recipient of her "Master" letters. In November, the Dickinsons move back to The Homestead on Main Street in Amherst. Emily's mother suffers a depression that continues for years after the move.

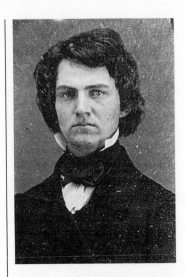

Austin Dickinson in 1850, photographed at the time of his graduation from Amherst College. By permission of the Jones Library, Inc., Amherst, Massachusetts.

The poet's close friend and sister-in-law, Susan Gilbert Dickinson, ca. 1855, shortly before her marriage to Austin. Courtesy of the Todd-Bingham Picture Collection, Yale University Library.

Washington's Tomb, visited by Dickinson in February 1855 during her visit to Washington, D.C., while her father was a member of Congress. Vivian Pollak Collection.

Charles Wadsworth, minister of the Arch Street Presbyterian Church in Philadelphia, undated photograph. By permission of the Jones Library, Inc., Amherst, Massachusetts.

1855: "Fanny Fern" (Sara Payson Willis) publishes a sensational roman à clef, *Ruth Hall*. *Leaves of Grass* published, containing twelve untitled poems in free verse. Longfellow publishes *Hiawatha*.

1856: Second edition of *Leaves of Grass* published, as is Elizabeth Barrett Browning's feminist novel in verse, *Aurora Leigh*.

1857: Economic depression grips the nation.

1858: Lincoln-Douglas debates. Douglas wins reelection to U.S. Senate from Illinois.

The Homestead on Main Street, built by Samuel Fowler Dickinson in 1813 and photographed at a later time. The bedroom where the poet did most of her work is to the upper left. Courtesy of the Todd-Bingham Picture Collection, Yale University Library.

The Evergreens, the elegant home of Austin and Susan Dickinson, which was located next door to The Homestead, was built by Edward Dickinson for the young couple as a wedding present in 1856. Photographed by Charles Prouty at some later time. By permission, Jones Library, Inc., Amherst, Massachusetts.

1856: Austin and Sue marry on July 1 in Geneva, New York. They move into The Evergreens, which becomes a center of Amherst social life. Emily wins second prize for her rye and Indian bread at the autumn Cattle Show.

1857: Virtually undocumented, a transformative year in the life of the poet. A strategic retreat. Emerson lectures on "The Beautiful in Rural Life" and stays overnight with Austin and Sue, but Dickinson does not meet him.

1858: Dickinson begins organizing her poems into booklets, or fascicles, a practice she continues into 1864, eventually compiling some forty of these handsewn gatherings and a smaller number of unbound "sets." Drafts the first of three letters to someone she calls "Master" and experiences an intensifying crisis of self-definition.

1860: In August, Charles Wadsworth visits Emily: "There came a day at summer's full." Massachusetts Governor Nathaniel Banks attends the Dickinsons' annual Commencement Tea and stays overnight in The Homestead. Emily impatiently compares him to the pope, whom she wishes to Rome. Edward Dickinson declines the nomination of the Bell and Everett Party for lieutenant governor. Dickinson and Lavinia visit their friend Eliza Coleman and her husband in Middletown, Connecticut, Emily's last social visit away from Amherst.

1859: Unsuccessful antislavery raid at Harpers Ferry, Virginia, led by John Brown, who is captured and executed. Higginson is one of his financial backers.

1860: Abraham Lincoln elected on the Republican ticket. Third edition of *Leaves of Grass* published, containing "Calamus" poems of male-homoerotic love, together with controversial heterosexual poems, "Children of Adam." In England, George Eliot publishes *The Mill on the Floss.*

Drawing of a dark-skinned pearl-diver from an article by J. W. Watson, "Pearls and Gems," Harper's Monthly *21 (November 1860). A possible source for Dickinson's "The Malay - took the Pearl," the image suggests the importance of regional and national newspapers and magazines as a daily social and cultural context for her writing. Vivian Pollak Collection.*

Manuscript version of "I taste a liquor never brewed," a poem composed ca. 1861. By permission, Houghton Library, Harvard University.

1861: Birth of Austin and Sue's first child, Ned, in June. In September, Dickinson experiences a mysterious "terror" which has been variously attributed to a range of psychosocial and physical problems.

1862: Dickinson responds to Higginson's essay in the April *Atlantic Monthly*, encouraging young writers to submit their manuscripts for publication. She sends him four poems: "Safe in their Alabaster Chambers," "The nearest Dream recedes - unrealized," "We play at Paste," and "I'll tell you how the Sun rose." Samuel Bowles, friend and journalist, in Europe for his health. Rev. Charles Wadsworth is in San Francisco. Higginson departs for South Carolina, as Colonel of a black regiment.

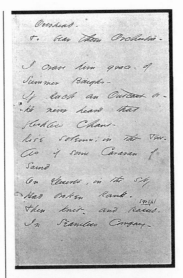

Manuscript version of "Of all the Sounds despatched abroad," a poem composed ca. 1862. By permission, Houghton Library, Harvard University.

Samuel Bowles, the nationally prominent editor of the Springfield Republican. *Emily wrote him that he had "the most triumphant face out of paradise." By permission, Houghton Library, Harvard University.*

Thomas Wentworth Higginson, New England reformer and man of letters, in uniform as the colonel of a black regiment. Dickinson initiated a correspondence with him in April 1862 that turned into one of the mainstays of her writing life. Frontispiece, 1898, Outlook. Vivian Pollak Collection.

1863: Dickinson's most productive year. She writes or transcribes almost 300 poems.

1864: In February, accompanied by her sister Lavinia, Dickinson returns from Boston, where she has consulted a distinguished opthamologist about her eye problems. In March, two of her poems appear in *Drum Beat*, a Brooklyn newspaper designed to raise funds for the Union cause. In April, Emily moves into a Cambridge boarding house where her cousins Louisa and Frances Norcross are also living. She is depressed, suffers from intermittent eye pain, and fears that she is losing her sight. Works in her "prison" and makes "guests" for herself, that is, she continues to write poetry. Austin Dickinson drafted, but he buys his way out with a substitute. In November, Dickinson returns to Amherst. The sunlight still hurts her eyes, but she is able to take up some of her household tasks, although she still suffers from low spirits and her family cannot understand why she does not get well. Begins reading eagerly.

1865: In April, Dickinson returns to Cambridge for another seven-month stay and for further eye treatments. Again, she lives in Mrs. Bangs's boarding house on Austin Street, near present day Central Square.

1861: Harriet Jacobs publishes *Incidents in the Life of a Slave Girl, by Herself.* Civil War begins in April, after American troops are fired on by Confederate forces at Fort Sumter. Whitman's youngest brother George enlists in the New York State Militia. Mark Twain enlists in the Marion Rangers, a Confederate militia unit in Missouri, but resigns after two weeks. Rebecca Harding Davis publishes *Life in the Iron-Mills* in the *Atlantic Monthly.* Death of Elizabeth Barrett Browning, Dickinson's favorite contemporary poet and the subject of several poems. Battle of Bull Run.

1862: Birth of Edith Wharton, later a powerful critic of Old New York. Battles of Second Bull Run, Antietam, and Fredericksburg. Homestead Act gives public lands to settlers; Morrill Act creates land grant colleges.

Adjutant Frazar Stearns, son of the Amherst College president, died in the battle of Newbern, North Carolina, in 1862. Vivian Pollak Collection.

In November, Dickinson returns to Amherst in better spirits and no longer complaining of eye pain/strain. She is able to return to tasks such as sewing that require visual concentration.

1866: The *Springfield Republican* features "The Snake" on its front page, February 14. Dickinson continues her clandestine correspondence with the Rev. Charles Wadsworth, enlisting friends such as Elizabeth Holland to address the letters and to mail them from out of town. Birth of Martha, second child of Austin and Sue.

1868: Dickinson goes out at night with her brother to see the new church on Main Street, which could be viewed from the edge of the Dickinson property.

1869: Higginson invites Dickinson to a literary salon in Boston; she refuses, stating, "I do not cross my Father's ground to any House or town."

1870: Higginson visits Dickinson in August.

1873: At her father's request, the pastor Jonathan Jenkins examines Emily and pronounces her sound, despite her failure to attend church services. Higginson pays a second visit.

1863: Lincoln issues Emancipation Proclamation. Whitman in Washington, D.C., visiting wounded in Civil War hospitals. Battles of Chancellorsville and Gettysburg. Draft riots in New York City. Henry James drafted and is exempted by reason of physical disability. Death of abolitionist hero Robert Gould Shaw at Fort Wagner, South Carolina, leading a regiment of black soldiers.

1864: Death of Hawthorne, in a hotel room, accompanied by his friend, former president Franklin Pierce. Lincoln reelected. Sherman's march through Georgia.

1865: In April, Lincoln assassinated while attending a performance of *Our American Cousin* at Ford's Theater with his wife; shortly thereafter, Whitman begins to draft the elegy, "When Lilacs Last in the Dooryard Bloom'd." Civil War ends.

1868: Whitman publishes "Personalism," the second installment of *Democratic Vistas*.

1869: War hero Ulysses S. Grant inaugurated as president. Transcontinental Railroad completed at Promontory Summit, Utah.

1870: Higginson publishes *Army Life in a Black Regiment*.

1871: George Eliot begins publishing *Middlemarch: A Study of Provincial Life*, one of Dickinson's favorite novels.

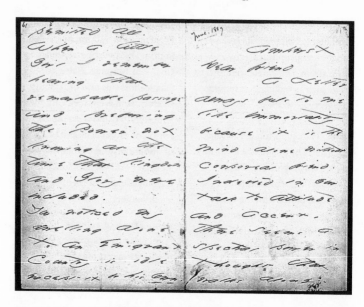

A letter to Thomas Wentworth Higginson in 1869 refusing his invitation to visit him in Boston and again inviting him to visit her in Amherst, which he did the following year. Higginson's account of their 1870 meeting is an important source for the poet's biography. By permission, Boston Public Library/Rare Books Department—Courtesy of the Trustees.

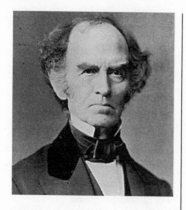

The poet's emininently respectable father Edward Dickinson, ca. 1874, the year of his death. By permission, Houghton Library, Harvard University.

1872: Victoria Woodhull runs for president, advocates free love, and scandalizes the nation by publicizing the adultery of the Rev. Henry Ward Beecher (with Elizabeth Tilton, the wife of a parishioner).

1873: Economic depression. Whitman suffers paralytic stroke and moves from Washington, D.C., to Camden, New Jersey.

1874: Edward Dickinson again serving in the Massachusetts legislature; he dies in June in a Boston hotel room after an injection of morphine; the Dickinsons believe that he was the victim of medical malpractice.

1875: Dickinson's mother has a stroke on the anniversary of her husband's death. Emily Dickinson signs her own will, saying nothing explicit about her manuscripts.

1877: Death of Higginson's first wife, Mary Elizabeth Channing.

1878: Helen Hunt Jackson visits, with her husband. "Success" published anonymously in *A Masque of Poets.* Dickinson's romance with Judge Otis Phillips Lord, whom she describes as her father's best friend.

Judge Otis Phillips Lord, who proposed marriage to Dickinson in the late 1870s. He was a friend of her father's and a staunch political conservative. Courtesy of the Todd-Bingham Picture Collection, Yale University Library.

1874: Birth of Gertrude Stein, daughter of Jewish immigrants, in Allegheny, Pennsylvania.

1875: Smith College (for women) opens in Northampton, Massachusetts.

1876: George Eliot begins publishing *Daniel Deronda,* "That wise and tender Book."

1879: Henry James publishes *Daisy Miller.*

1880: George Eliot marries John Walter Cross and dies seven months later. "The Life of Marian Evans had much I did not know."

1881: Helen Hunt Jackson publishes *A Century of Dishonor* and sends a copy of this treatise to every member of Congress at her own expense. President Garfield assassinated; Chester A. Arthur inaugurated. Henry James publishes *The Portrait of a Lady.*

1884: Helen Hunt Jackson publishes her novel *Ramona,* urging justice for Indians in California; Twain publishes *The Adventures of Huckleberry Finn.*

1879: In February, Higginson marries Mary Potter Thacher of Newton, Massachusetts.

1881: Mabel Loomis Todd, a young and ambitious faculty wife, begins recording her impressions of the Dickinsons, including Emily, whom she calls "the myth."

1882: Death of the poet's bedridden mother.

1883: Sudden death of the poet's eight-year-old nephew Gilbert, from typhoid fever. Dickinson goes to The Evergreens and suffers from "revenge of the nerves." That fall, Austin and Mabel Loomis Todd consummate their romance, in The Homestead dining room.

1884: Death of Otis Phillips Lord, following a long period of ill health.

1885: Helen Hunt Jackson, who had asked to be Dickinson's literary executor, predeceases her; Dickinson "unspeakably shocked."

1886: On May 15, Emily Dickinson dies at around six o'clock in the evening. The official diagnosis is "Bright's Disease," a kidney disorder, but hypertension is more likely to have been the primary cause. Higginson attends her funeral and reads Emily Brontë's poem, "No coward soul is mine." Susan Gilbert Dickinson writes the obituary that appears in the *Springfield Republican*.

The charming and duplicitous Mabel Loomis Todd, coeditor with Thomas Wentworth Higginson of the 1890 Poems, ca. 1882. Courtesy of the Todd-Bingham Picture Collection, Yale University Library.

The poet's nephew Gilbert, the gifted and charming child whose sudden death in 1883 devastated the entire family. Courtesy of the Todd-Bingham Picture Collection, Yale University Library.

The poet's beloved sister Lavinia with one of her many cats in 1896. By permission, Jones Library, Inc., Amherst, Massachusetts.

1886: Henry James publishes *The Bostonians*, a novel of homosocial and homoerotic female friendship. James calls it "a study of one of those friendships between women which are so common in New England."

1888: Amherst resident Mabel Loomis Todd is transcribing the poems; she is assisted by her husband and several others. This activity is kept secret from Sue.

1890: *Poems*, edited by Higginson and Mabel Loomis Todd, published by Roberts Brothers. It contains 115 poems.

Bibliographical Essay

Jonathan Morse

On November 12, 1890, Roberts Brothers of Boston published *Poems by Emily Dickinson,* a posthumous selection containing 115 poems. Except for the ten poems and one short prose piece that her friends had published during her lifetime, this little book was Emily Dickinson's first appearance in print.

On January 1, 1955, Harvard University Press published *The Poems of Emily Dickinson, Including Variant Readings Critically Compared with All Known Manuscripts*: three volumes containing 1,775 poems and a scholarly apparatus. This was the first comprehensive edition of Dickinson's poetry.

During the years between those two events, literature in English was undergoing a profound change. In 1890, Walt Whitman was still alive and still a figure of scandal; in 1955, Vladimir Nabokov published *Lolita.* In between came the era of T. S. Eliot, James Joyce, Ernest Hemingway, and the historical catastrophes that made their new ways of writing seem necessary. So the textual history of Emily Dickinson's poetry isn't just a matter of dates and formats and editorial decisions; it is also one of the histories of reading in the twentieth century. As of the beginning of the twenty-first century, this history can be divided into four chapters.

From Dickinson's Lifetime through 1913

"I smile when you suggest that I delay 'to publish,' " wrote Dickinson to Thomas Wentworth Higginson at the beginning of their long correspondence, "—that being foreign to my thought, as Firmament to Fin" (L 265, June 7, 1862). To the end of her life, she remained firm in this fastidious reticence. When her friend Helen Hunt Jackson, a well-known poet and novelist, repeatedly urged her to give her poetry to the world, she was noncommittal. When a publisher, Thomas Niles of Roberts Brothers, asked her point-blank for a manuscript (L 813b, March 1883), she ignored his letter. To the day of her death, May 15, 1886, Dickinson kept a tight control over her readership, dispatching her poems a few at a time in letters and allowing them to be published only at rare intervals and for specific reasons.

After the funeral, however, her sister Lavinia began sorting through her papers and made an amazing discovery: for decades, Emily had been hoarding the poems she used to send in letters and recite to the family—hoarding them by the hundreds. Some of the manuscripts were rough jottings on telegraph blanks and the backs of labels; others were fair copies, written out in a special script on sheets of gilt-edged ladies' stationery and sewn into little books. An unattested legend tells us that Emily had asked her sister to destroy them, and it certainly is true that some other members of Dickinson's extended family felt obliged to destroy their letters from her. But these poems were too precious to burn. What was to be done?

Emily had been a recluse, unfitted for ordinary life. Lavinia was an eccentric, prematurely old woman with thirteen cats and a volatile temper. Because the task of preparing the manuscripts for publication was clearly beyond her, she turned for help to Susan Dickinson, the sophisticated and ambitious sister-in-law who had been Emily's confidante since the early 1850s. Susan immediately set herself and her two grown children to work recopying the manuscripts and querying editors of newspapers and magazines, but she seems to have been at cross-purposes with herself. She may have been overambitious when she dreamed of what she came to call "The Book of Emily": a volume intended to combine Emily's poetry with "many bits of her prose—passages from early letters . . . quaint bits to my children &c &c."[1] On the other hand, her concentration may also have been affected by what Richard Sewall calls "personal hostility and indifference to the poems."[2]

In any case, Susan accomplished almost nothing. Her only significant contribution to Emily Dickinson's memory remains the long, thoughtful obituary she wrote for the *Springfield Republican:* the world's first piece of Dickinson scholarship.[3] After a while, Lavinia retrieved her manuscripts from Susan and turned them over to Emily's talented young friend Mabel Loomis Todd, an aspiring novelist who had moved to Amherst in 1881. Late in 1887, a year and a half after Emily's death, Mabel began transcribing the poems on her typewriter. Late in 1889, she persuaded Emily's friend Thomas Wentworth Higginson, an influential man of letters, to help her see them into print.[4]

Under the best of circumstances, Susan could have been forgiven for hard feelings. In this worst of cases, however, the relationship between Susan and Mabel was poisoned from the start. Susan's marriage to Dickinson's brother Austin had been bitterly unhappy for years, and Mabel was a pretty young mother with an unfaithful husband. Only a year after Austin and Mabel met, they confessed their love to each other. In 1883, Mabel became Austin's mistress. Appearances were kept up until Austin's death in 1895, but after that it was impossible for Lavinia to mediate between Mabel and Susan. In 1898, a lawsuit over a bequest from Austin completed Mabel's estrangement from the Dickinson family, and from that moment she closed her camphorwood box of Emily's manuscripts. But in 1890 and 1891, she and Higginson had published their editions of Dickinson's *Poems* and *Poems, Second Series.*[5] Working alone, Todd then published two volumes of Dickinson's letters in 1894 and *Poems, Third Series,* in 1896. The debacle of 1898 could not erase that accomplishment. Mabel Loomis Todd and Thomas Wentworth Higginson had brought Emily Dickinson to the attention of the world.

Because the Todd-Higginson texts are now in the public domain and can be reprinted without permission, they still exert their influence. Specialists know that Todd and Higginson made changes in the poems they published: adding titles, conventional-izing rhyme and grammar and vocabulary. Specialists know, too, that Todd and Higginson had a bias toward the themes and points of view established half a century earlier by Emerson, Longfellow, and the respectable figures known as the Fireside Poets. Todd and Higginson's Fireside Emily is occasionally pro-found but mostly sentimental or (in Susan Dickinson's word) quaint. Today, this is the Dickinson of the Web and the greeting card store: the author of "Have you got a brook in your little heart" and "If I can stop one heart from breaking," two favorites from the 1890 collection. In that little book, bound in virginal white with Mabel's painting of white flowers on the cover, origi-nates the perennial image of the poet as fey vestal and cute little girl. The Emily Dickinson who wrote funny, sexy love letters to an elderly admirer would have to be read later.

The Daughters' Era, 1914–1945

"Poor old Susan died last night," sneered Mabel Loomis Todd to her diary on May 13, 1913.[6] Another eighteen years went by, and then Mabel reopened the camphorwood box. The Age of Hitler lay just months ahead, and *Ulysses* and *The Waste Land* had been in print for nine years.

The modernist poet Conrad Aiken had published his own se-lection from the Todd-Higginson texts in 1924, with an introduc-tory essay, and the modernist poet Hart Crane had published his sonnet "To Emily Dickinson" in 1927. As Klaus Lubbers has demonstrated, readers after World War I required a new Emily Dickinson: a poet whose language could fit into a canon that now included Ezra Pound and T. S. Eliot.[7] For those modernist readers, new texts became available in installments between the beginning of World War I and the end of World War II.

The first of these was *The Single Hound: Poems of a Lifetime*, published in 1914 by Susan's daughter, the poet and novelist Martha Dickinson Bianchi. Its 142 poems from Susan's trove of manuscripts showed the world a different Dickinson: a Dickin-son to whom *The New Republic's* reviewer Elizabeth Shepley

Sergeant could refer as an early Imagist.[8] Bibliographically, it was also an important dispatch from the war between Susan and Mabel. Mabel's camphorwood box, for example, contained a copy of "One Sister have I in our house" (Fr 5)—inked completely over by Austin to obliterate its reference to his hated wife. But Susan had kept the original of this love poem to her, and now Susan's daughter presented it to the world.

There were now four collections of primary texts on the market, plus the 1894 *Letters*. In 1924, an attempt at consolidation began with Bianchi's *Complete Poems*. This collection consisted simply of the three Todd-Higginson volumes (appropriated without acknowledgment, now that their copyrights had lapsed), plus *The Single Hound*, plus five previously unpublished poems. That is (as readers know now and guessed then), it wasn't complete. But it made 597 of Dickinson's poems available within a single cover, and, as Jean Carwile Masteller says, this "encouraged the 'discovery' of Dickinson in the 1920s as part of the American literary canon."[9]

A companion volume, also published in 1924, was Bianchi's *Life and Letters of Emily Dickinson*. Bianchi has a bad reputation among scholars, and this book is the main reason. Was Emily Dickinson's relationship with Susan Dickinson, Mme. Bianchi's mother, passionate at the beginning, sympathetic at the end, but indifferent or worse for at least fifteen years in between? No problem; Mme. Bianchi just postdated some of Aunt Emily's early letters to make the record more uniformly smiley. From book to book she got no better, either at reading her aunt's handwriting or remembering the existence of Mabel Loomis Todd. When Todd and Higginson published "Because I could not stop for death," they added a title, deleted one stanza, and altered four additional lines. When Martha Dickinson Bianchi republished the poem, she incorporated all of Todd and Higginson's changes without acknowledgment and made one more of her own—a genuinely ridiculous one.[10] Surely this was unprofessional. But the influence of the Bianchi texts is important nevertheless.

The reason is this: in 1929, Bianchi resumed her series of publications with *Further Poems of Emily Dickinson, Withheld from Publication by Her Sister Lavinia,* and in that volume she began at-

tempting to print the poems in the lineation of the original manuscripts. Todd and Higginson had regularized Dickinson's lines
into the quatrains of a New England hymnal, but in the facsimile
of "There came a Day - at Summer's full" that they printed in
Poems, Second Series, readers could see that Dickinson wrote not

> The sun, as common, went abroad;
> The flowers, accustomed, blew,

but

> The Sun - as Common - went
> abroad -
> The Flowers - accustomed -
> blew -

With many errors of omission and commission, Bianchi attempted to transcribe lines like those as Dickinson wrote them.
At the time, critics generally failed to appreciate what she was
doing. In 1929, for example, the anthologist Louis Untermeyer
complained, in an otherwise favorable review of the *Further
Poems:*

> Such an arrangement shows either a lack of courage or a too
> literal editing. A Cummings might enjoy this typography, not
> Emily. The quatrain is implicit here as in most of her work. I
> suspect that had Emily supervised her own manuscript she
> would have printed such poems as orthodox four-line stanzas,
> and that they were written thus only because Emily's paper
> was not long enough to give the quatrain its customary
> shape.[11]

But a claim can be made for the Bianchi transcriptions—an important claim. As we shall see, Bianchi's work anticipated poststruc-
turalist textual studies like Jerome McGann's and Marta Werner's
by three quarters of a century. When she called readers' attention
to the visual expressiveness of Dickinson's manuscripts, Martha
Dickinson Bianchi was ahead of her time. But she never articulated what she was trying to do, and she didn't do it well.[12]

After *Further Poems,* Bianchi produced three more volumes of her aunt's work: *Emily Dickinson Face to Face: Unpublished Letters with Notes and Reminiscences* (1932), *Unpublished Poems of Emily Dickinson* (1935), and a second attempt at a collected edition, *Poems by Emily Dickinson* (1937). In that year, R. P. Blackmur opened his essay "Emily Dickinson: Notes on Prejudice and Fact" by complaining, "The disarray of Emily Dickinson's poems is the great obvious fact about them as they multiply from volume to volume—I will not say from edition to edition, for they have never been edited."[13] However, another daughter was also at work on the Dickinson manuscripts, and this daughter, unlike Martha Dickinson Bianchi, was a professional scholar: a Harvard Ph.D. who had taught French at Vassar and Wellesley.

This was Millicent Todd Bingham, the daughter of Mabel Loomis Todd and an eager volunteer in her war against Martha Dickinson Bianchi. In 1924, the year of the *Complete Poems* and *Life and Letters,* Millicent had written to her friend Amy Lowell, "When mamma came from Boston, I met her in Amherst, and we extracted the Emily things from the barn, and today we have been looking them over. They are simply superb! . . . What an orgy we shall have when the said *MDB* steps out one day!"[14] In 1929, Conrad Aiken wrote of the *Further Poems,* of Martha Dickinson Bianchi, "They have been edited with a clumsiness and unperceptiveness which one is tempted simply to term unintelligence"—and Mme. Bianchi wrote the president of Mount Holyoke College a letter calling Mabel "a cheat and a fraud."[15] Finally, in 1931, Mabel broke her long silence with an expanded version of her 1894 *Letters,* compiled with Millicent's help. Just one year later, she was dead. Mining her mother's papers and the contents of the camphorwood box, Millicent would go on to write *Ancestors' Brocades* and *Emily Dickinson's Home,* two important literary histories of Dickinson's milieu.[16] More: as an editor, she gave the world *Bolts of Melody: New Poems of Emily Dickinson.*

But until the mid-1940s, undertakers were in charge of the timetable. Because the two mothers had each claimed control of the Dickinson copyright, Millicent's publisher prudently held off printing *Bolts of Melody* during Martha's lifetime.[17] In the event,

Martha died in 1943, but *Bolts of Melody* did not go on sale until 1945. Emily Dickinson and her world must have seemed inconceivably ancient in the year of Hiroshima, and few of the poems in *Bolts of Melody* could be called major. In fact, about half of them had been laid aside by Mabel Loomis Todd or Thomas Wentworth Higginson, usually with good reason. But there were 668 of them—and all 668 had been withheld from readers since the nineteenth century![18]

The effect was devastating. George Frisbie Whicher's jacket copy called *Bolts of Melody* "the most stunning surprise in the history of American literature,"[19] but one of the emotions generated by that surprise was indignation. By now, after all, Emily Dickinson was solidly a part of the academic canon of American literature—a canon that had long since been redirected away from the values of Longfellow and Whittier and Todd and Higginson and Mme. Bianchi. Yet readers still were not permitted to think about her poems canonically, with confidence that the words on the page were a good approximation of what she had written. There had been too many scattered collections of the poetry, controlled by too many editorial agendas. Clearly, what American literature required by the middle of the twentieth century was *one* edition of Emily Dickinson—a real, professionally produced one.

The Age of Johnson

By 1950, most of Dickinson's surviving manuscripts had been centralized in three Massachusetts collections: those of the Boston Public Library, Amherst College Library, and Harvard University's Houghton Library. In that year, Harvard University Press entrusted the task of editing them to Thomas H. Johnson, the prep-school teacher whose archival research had been responsible for the discovery of Edward Taylor's verse manuscripts.[20] The result was magisterial: the three-volume *Poems of Emily Dickinson* in 1955, followed by the three-volume *Letters of Emily Dickinson* in 1958. In these massive books Johnson attempted to publish Dickinson's manuscripts as she wrote them:

in chronological order, with idiosyncrasies of spelling and punctuation intact, and (in the case of the *Poems*) with variant readings as well. Readers opened the *Poems* and found revelation. Every previous editor had arranged Dickinson's poems thematically, and every one likewise had imposed more or less drastic editorial strictures on Dickinson's verbal originalities. But to follow a word now from Johnson's subject index to the astonishing depths of the book was, it seemed, to be admitted at last to the penetralia of Emily Dickinson's mind. This, we thought, was Emily Dickinson herself, no longer clad in her stepsisters' rags. And the *Letters*, with their extensive notes, proved to be (among much else) something very like an autobiography. Half a century ago, it must have been an amazing experience to open a volume of the *Letters* next to a volume of that great compendium of raw historical fact, Jay Leyda's *Years and Hours of Emily Dickinson*.[21]

In 1960, Johnson supplemented the bulky, expensive variorum with his *Complete Poems*: a reading edition in one volume, containing a single unannotated text of each poem. In 1961 and 1971 came Johnson's selected editions of Dickinson's verse and prose, *Final Harvest* and *Selected Letters,* and the academic monument was complete.[22] Johnson's editions were the first on which reliable scholarship could be based, and for more than forty years they stood alone.

Dickinson's Texts Today

But as early as 1956, Jay Leyda had called attention to two "flaws in principle" in Johnson's work: inconsistency in deciding which texts should be called verse and which should be called prose, and an attempt to key the chronology of some poems to events in the life of Charles Wadsworth. "The tendency to read the poems as autobiography," complained Leyda, "should be combatted not reinforced by the editor."[23]

In 1967 R. W. Franklin pointed out a disconcerting connection between those two flaws. "The principle of editing that a text exactly represent the author's final intention is inadequate, since finality cannot be established," says Franklin at the end of *The*

Editing of Emily Dickinson, the book that opens the modern era of Dickinson textual scholarship. "[But] if one attempts, with a biographical concern, to approach the poet through her works, one must have those works exactly as she left them. . . . [The editor of Emily Dickinson], in trying to avoid the twin pitfalls of arbitrariness and relativism, . . . will have to struggle with editorial and critical principles even to the limits of ontology and epistemology."[24] In Baltimore a year before that, Jacques Derrida had read his paper "Structure, Sign, and Play in the Discourse of the Human Sciences," with its throwaway line, "Here or there I have used the word *déconstruction*."[25] The time had come to rethink Johnson's methods.

The first major result of this rethinking was Franklin's facsimile edition of *The Manuscript Books of Emily Dickinson* (1981), with its poems arranged in the order in which Dickinson transcribed them into the little sewn books that Mabel Loomis Todd had called "fascicles."[26] Franklin's rationale was straightforward:

> A facsimile edition is of particular importance to Dickinson studies, for the manuscripts of this poet resist translation into the conventions of print. Formal features like her unusual punctuation and capitalization, line and stanza divisions, and display of alternate readings are a source of continuing critical concern. Because she saw no poem through the press and left her manuscripts unprepared for print, judgments must be informed by the manuscript conventions themselves. Perhaps no less important, interest has developed in the fascicles as artistic gatherings. . . . [Johnson's edition] translated the mechanics of the poems into conventional type and, in presenting them chronologically, obscured the fascicle structure. Such an edition, though essential, does not serve the same purpose as a facsimile of the fascicles.[27]

This was an invitation to find new purposes—in fact, new ways of reading. Readers eagerly accepted the invitation. By the 1990s, possibilities for reseeing the manuscripts had been suggested by such analyses as Sharon Cameron's *Choosing Not Choosing: Dickinson's Fascicles* (1992), Jerome J. McGann's *Black Riders:*

The Visible Language of Modernism (1993), and Marta Werner's *Emily Dickinson's Open Folios: Scenes of Reading, Surfaces of Writing* (1995).[28] As studies like these demonstrated, Dickinson can be read deconstructively in many ways. Mapped by Cameron, a Dickinson fascicle is an unstable semantic borderland, an "'illocality' half-positioned, as it were, outside the poem understood as conventional poem."[29] Displayed in facsimile by Werner, a letter written by Dickinson to Otis P. Lord morphs into an aesthetic construction whose significance seems to compete against the words it is made of—including such words as the editorial contributions "letter" and "to." And Jerome McGann has listened to Dickinson's manuscripts and reported back that "[they] urge us to take them at face value, to treat all her scriptural forms as potentially significant *at the aesthetic or expressive level.*"[30]

Perhaps this way of looking at words on a page was new. At the least, it asked readers to extend Dickinson's aesthetic genealogy forward from Blake and the Renaissance emblem poets to the Dadaists, and perhaps too to madmen like Adolf Wölfli or Henry Darger: obsessives unable to stop hearing words in the sound of crayon going onto paper. By attributing aesthetic value to Dickinson's expressive gestures, McGann seemed to be proclaiming her an artist in a new medium—a medium made of words whose meanings derive from interaction on the page with their physical form.[31] Clearly, the 1990s were an era when the words "edit," "print," and "read" were expanding into new definitions.

By the 1990s, too, the personal computer had made possible an idea that went by the no longer oxymoronic name of "desktop publishing." Thinking of that newly meaningful phrase and taking the first word of Dickinson's line "This is my letter to the world" literally, the Language poet Susan Howe and the textual scholars Ellen Louise Hart and Martha Nell Smith began making claims for the manuscripts as publications in themselves: intimate, feminine publications, publications in which every detail of penmanship and placement on the page must be responded to.[32] Not coincidentally, the work of Smith and her associates at the Dickinson Electronic Archives (discussed at length in Smith's suggestively titled "The Screen and the Book")[33] began making the case for a revaluation of the achievement of Susan Dickinson and her daughter. If we relent from masculine assumptions about what literature is and what kinds of literature are important, Mme. Bianchi's fluttery pages about the exquisiteness of Aunt Emily's communication in the language of flowers ("perhaps three tiny frosted, heart-shaped cakes, or some of her chocolate caramels—with a flower on top, heliotrope, a red lily, or cape jasmine—and underneath always a note or poem for our mother")[34] may tell us something valuable about the semiotics of the nineteenth century.

But conventional bibliographers have a dismissive word for Hart and Smith's readings of the folds of the manuscripts and Howe's fascination with the swoosh of Dickinson's letter S. "Accidentals," the bibliographers call such things. In laying claim to the readability of what may be ineffable, are Howe, Hart, Smith, and McGann merely performing an uncontrolled experiment, impossible to falsify and therefore impossible to confirm? In *Emily Dickinson: Monarch of Perception*,[35] Domhnall Mitchell asks us to consider this skeptical alternative. And half a century after Leyda and a third of a century after Derrida, R. W. Franklin's new variorum edition of *The Poems of Emily Dickinson* (1998) still looks very much like Johnson 2.

Franklin had better access than Johnson to the manuscripts, and several of his appendices display the result: tables of poems added to or deleted from the canon, single poems separated into multiple poems and vice versa, letters redated. Franklin's notes record Dickinson's line breaks in deference to McGann and Smith, too, but in his main text the poems are still arranged in regular quatrains. Howe and McGann lay major claim to the significance of Dickinson's handwriting, but Franklin gives us only seven photographic examples to Johnson's twenty. The old variorum has been superseded by a new one which seems mostly to tinker in the margins. How important is Franklin's observation that Dickinson customarily wrote "opon," not—as conventional-minded Johnson has it—"upon"? As stimuli to poetic experience mediated by a print technology fundamentally unchanged since the fifteenth century, the Johnson and Franklin editions are almost identical.

But in the margins there are premonitory signs of changes to come. Consider, for instance, Johnson's and Franklin's annotations for "I had some things that I called mine" (Fr 101 / J 116). In this poem, Dickinson's little-girl persona takes God to task for sending an unseasonable frost to kill her garden. The poem concludes:

> I'll institute an "Action" -
> I'll vindicate the law -
> Jove! Choose your counsel -
> I retain "Shaw"!

Both Johnson and Franklin append a note by Mabel Loomis Todd identifying Shaw as "a man who used to dig for her—a day laborer." Johnson, characteristically more willing than Franklin to venture into the *hors-texte*, adds a directory reference to let us know that Shaw's first name was Henry.[36] But none of this helps much with the poem. We seem to be eavesdropping on somebody else's family in-joke.

In 1999, however, James Guthrie, reestablishing a connection made earlier by Jane Donahue Eberwein and Owen Thomas, taught a small conference audience how to read the word "Shaw" as it would have been read by a conservative Massachusetts politician in 1859—namely, as the primary referent of Lemuel Shaw, chief justice of the Massachusetts Supreme Court from 1830 to 1860 and one of nineteenth-century America's most influential jurists.[37] In the home of Edward Dickinson, the word "Shaw" commanded reverence. Now that we know this, we can get the joke. Father's law office is upheld from season to season by Father's Shaw, says this poem, but in my garden I have a Shaw of my own—and *my* Shaw can plead before a court ultimately Supreme.[38]

Thanks to Professor Guthrie, we can now start thinking of Dickinson's hard little word "I" in a slightly new way. But how is the text of the poem to keep up with us? Johnson's necessarily unsatisfactory presentation of the poem was superseded in 1998 by Franklin's, but Franklin's has turned out to be just as unsatisfactory. Johnson couldn't incorporate Thomas's annotation; Franklin couldn't incorporate Guthrie's annotation and didn't incorporate Thomas's or Eberwein's. At the exact moment when the *Encyclopaedia Britannica* had transformed itself from thirty-two volumes of paper and leather and matching wooden bookcase to an infinitely updatable idea on the Web, Harvard University Press was dragging Emily Dickinson—Emily Dickinson!—off to the bindery. The Dickinson of the variorum, old or new, is a poet of eternity who has been locked into time. It seems all but certain that twenty-first-century publishing technologies are massing now to liberate her. At the 2001 Conference of the Emily Dickinson International Society, for example, Geoffrey Schramm discussed the Classroom Electric project, a Whitman-and-Dickinson Web page that almost naturally leads students to think of Dickinson's words as hyperlinked to other words.[39]

At the same conference, Martha Ackmann displayed a series of computer-generated images that aged the face of sixteen-year-old Emily in the one authenticated photograph all the way to threescore and ten.[40] The result was startling. Interpreting the 1847 daguerreotype as creatively as a poem, the computer had made a virtual addition to the historical record—and the result on Professor Ackmann's computer monitor was a newly realized picture of the poet of immortality, freed as she must have known she would be from her merely actual death at the age of fifty-five. That event occurred in the nineteenth century, in a New England factory town, just as the whistles were blowing for the end of the workday at 6 P.M. In a different age, with time and space and social relations organized differently, Dickinson is not just read but seen in ways that are ever renewing.

But, as she once wrote,

> What is to be is best descried
> When it has also been - (Fr 1212)

A historical guide works to keep communication open between those two objects of discovery, the past and what is to be. Knowing how much our sense of this poet has changed in the past, we can happily expect it never to stop changing in the future. There will always be new ways to read her words.

NOTES

1. Millicent Todd Bingham, *Ancestors' Brocades: The Literary Debut of Emily Dickinson* (New York: Harper, 1945), 86; quoted in Martha Nell Smith, "Dickinson, Susan Huntington Gilbert,"*An Emily Dickinson Encyclopedia*, ed. Jane Donahue Eberwein (Westport, Conn.: Greenwood, 1998), 81.

2. Richard B. Sewall, *The Life of Emily Dickinson* (1974; rpt. Cambridge, Mass.: Harvard University Press, 1980), 221.

3. "Miss Emily Dickinson of Amherst," *Springfield Republican,* 18 May 1886, in *Emily Dickinson's Reception in the 1890s: A Documentary History,* ed. Willis J. Buckingham (Pittsburgh: University of Pittsburgh Press, 1989), appendix A.

4. Sewall, *The Life of Emily Dickinson*, 218–21; Polly Longsworth, *Austin and Mabel: The Amherst Affair and Love Letters of Austin Dickinson and Mabel Loomis Todd* (New York: Farrar, Straus and Giroux 1984), 294–97.

5. With Boston's Roberts Brothers, the predecessor to Little, Brown, publisher of the later volumes edited by Martha Dickinson Bianchi.

6. Sewall, *The Life of Emily Dickinson,* 194.

7. Klaus Lubbers, *Emily Dickinson: The Critical Revolution* (Ann Arbor: University of Michigan Press, 1968).

8. Elizabeth Shepley Sergeant, "An Early Imagist," *New Republic*, Aug. 14, 1915; rpt. *The Recognition of Emily Dickinson: Selected Criticism since 1890*, ed. Caesar R. Blake and Carlton F. Wells (Ann Arbor: University of Michigan Press, 1964), 88–93.

9. Jean Carwile Masteller, "*The Complete Poems of Emily Dickinson* (1924)," *Dickinson Encyclopedia*, 51.

10. Interrupting the poem's narrative flow with a distracting visual detail, Bianchi changed Dickinson's "We passed the School, where Children strove / At recess - in the Ring -" to "We passed the school, where children strove / At wrestling in a ring." Todd and Higginson had also altered the line; to regularize the rhyme with "We passed the Setting Sun," they changed "At recess - in the Ring" to "Their lessons scarcely done." But at least this preserves the emphasis on passing time that is conveyed by the word "recess."

11. "Colossal Substance" (review of *Further Poems*), *Saturday Review of Literature* (March 16, 1929): 771.

12. Reviewing *Further Poems,* Rolfe Humphries complained:

With readers educated, by the previous three [Todd-Higginson] volumes as well as by "The Single Hound," to a different format, the present arrangement was sure to be something of a shock. It might have been sensible to anticipate the controversy excited, or at least compose it with prefatory explanation. One resorts to "Poems, Second Series" for a clue. ("Too Difficult a Grace," *New Republic* [May 22, 1929]: 39)

Humphries concluded, "This [attempt at reproduction of the manuscripts' lineation] looked like a good idea; but noble experiments that must be worked out constructively are not always foreordained to success."

13. *Southern Review* 3 (1937): 323–47; rpt. Blake and Wells, *Recognition,* 201.

14. Elizabeth Horan, "To Market: The Dickinson Copyright Wars," *The Emily Dickinson Journal* 4 (1996): 98.

15. Aiken, *New York Evening Post,* March 16, 1929, 11; Horan, "To Market," 100.

16. *Ancestors' Brocades: The Literary Debut of Emily Dickinson* (New York: Harper, 1945); *Emily Dickinson's Home: Letters of Edward Dickinson and His Family, with Documentation and Comment* (New York: Harper & Row, 1955).

17. Polly Longsworth, "Bingham, Millicent Todd," *Dickinson Encyclopedia,* 20.

18. Or almost all. Both Johnson and Franklin credit *Bolts of Melody* with the first publication of "I tried to think a lonelier thing" (Fr 570 / J 532), but it appeared earlier in Martha Dickinson Bianchi's *Further Poems,* and V. Sackville-West quoted it in her review of the book, "New Poetry," *Nation and Athenaeum* 46 (November 2, 1929): 178. It's typical of Mme. Bianchi's scholarship that she slipped the poem into the middle of a paragraph in her introduction (xvi) and didn't include it in the book's index of first lines. More such surprises may await, of course. Martha Nell Smith and her students are now trying to disentangle the Bianchi bibliography.

19. Jane Donahue Eberwein, "*Bolts of Melody: New Poems of Emily Dickinson* (1945)," *Dickinson Encyclopedia,* 26.

20. "Publisher's Preface," *Poems* (1955), xi-xii; Johnson, *Letters,* xii.

21. Jay Leyda, *The Years and Hours of Emily Dickinson,* 2 vols. (New Haven: Yale University Press, 1960).

22. *Complete Poems* and *Final Harvest* were published by Little, Brown, and the *Selected Letters* by Harvard University Press.

23. "The Poems of Emily Dickinson," *New England Quarterly* 29 (1956): 245.

24. R. W. Franklin, *The Editing of Emily Dickinson: A Reconsideration* (Madison: University of Wisconsin Press, 1967), 142–43.

25. *The Structuralist Controversy: The Languages of Criticism and the Sciences of Man,* ed. Richard Macksey and Eugenio Donato (1970; Baltimore: Johns Hopkins University Press, 1972), 271.

26. Of the Franklin edition's 1,789 poems, approximately 1,116 were composed between 1858 and 1865—that is, about two-thirds of the total, if we exclude the 104 poems that cannot be dated (*Poems,* appendix 2). Between 1858 and 1864, Dickinson sewed fair copies of most of her poems into the forty fascicles. As she continued writing between 1863 and 1875 (that is, with some overlap with the fascicle period), she gathered her fair copies into fifteen unbound groups that Mabel Loomis Todd called sets (*Poems,* appendix 4). Most of the last poems exist only in letters or as drafts on scraps of paper.

In 1968, Ruth Miller suggested that Dickinson might have regarded her fascicles as unified compositions, each consisting of a thematically related group of lyrics (*The Poetry of Emily Dickinson* [Middletown, Conn.: Wesleyan University Press]). Miller's book was generally ignored by specialists, but after the publication of Franklin's *Manuscript Books* her thesis was taken up again—notably by M. L. Rosenthal and Sally M. Gall in "Emily Dickinson's Fascicles," *The Modern Poetic Sequence: The Genius of Modern Poetry* (New York: Oxford University Press, 1983), 45–73. Franklin himself, however, saw no order in the fascicles except the order of composition and a desire to fit texts into the spaces available on the page. Twenty years later, the ongoing discussion is still inconclusive. For a current overview, see Eleanor Elson Heginbotham, "Fascicles," *Dickinson Encyclopedia,* 108–10.

27. Franklin, *Manuscript Books,* ix.

28. Sharon Cameron, *Choosing Not Choosing: Dickinson's Fascicles* (Chicago: University of Chicago Press, 1992); Jerome McGann, *Black*

Riders: The Visible Language of Modernism (Princeton: Princeton University Press, 1993); Marta Werner, *Emily Dickinson's Open Folios: Scenes of Reading, Surfaces of Writing* (Ann Arbor: University of Michigan Press, 1995).

29. Cameron, *Choosing Not Choosing*, 29.

30. McGann, *Black Riders*, 38.

31. Another textual experiment of the 1990s is *New Poems of Emily Dickinson*, ed. William H. Shurr with Anna Dunlap and Emily Grey Shurr (Chapel Hill: University of North Carolina Press, 1993). These consist of passages from the *Letters*, printed as verse to call attention to their iambic regularities. Like the biographical fantasies of John Evangelist Walsh, who claimed in *The Hidden Life of Emily Dickinson* (New York: Simon and Schuster, 1971) that Dickinson became a recluse out of ladylike embarrassment at having plagiarized Elizabeth Barrett Browning, Shurr's efforts manage to make Dickinson's uniqueness seem conventional.

32. Susan Howe, "These Flames and Generosities of the Heart: Emily Dickinson and the Illogic of Sumptuary Values," *The Birth-Mark: Unsettling the Wilderness in American Literary History* (Hanover, N.H.: University Press of New England, 1993), 2–26; Martha Nell Smith, "Dickinson's Manuscripts," in *The Emily Dickinson Handbook*, ed. Gudrun Grabher, Roland Hagenbüchle, and Cristanne Miller (Amherst: University of Massachusetts Press, 1998), 113–37; Ellen Louise Hart and Martha Nell Smith, eds., *Open Me Carefully: Emily Dickinson's Intimate Letters to Susan Huntington Dickinson* (Ashfield, Mass.: Paris Press, 1998).

33. Smith, "Dickinson's Manuscripts," 130–34.

34. Martha Dickinson Bianchi, *Emily Dickinson Face to Face: Unpublished Letters with Notes and Reminiscences* (Boston: Houghton Mifflin, 1932), 9.

35. Domhnall Mitchell, *Emily Dickinson: Monarch of Perception* (Amherst: University of Massachusetts Press, 2000).

36. Compare Johnson's and Franklin's notes to "If those I loved were lost" (Fr 20 / J 29), a poem whose key words "Ghent" and "Philip" refer to a now forgotten play that the Dickinson family enjoyed. Johnson tells us this and adds enough about the play to make the poem understandable. Franklin writes not a word about the play or anything else relating to paraphrasable content, but his textual analysis of Dickinson's eight-line poem takes up a full page. Like-

wise, only the Johnson edition offers its readers the aid of a subject index. In the purity and rigor of the Franklin edition, text is nothing but text.

37. James R. Guthrie, "'I had some things that I called mine': Dickinson and the Perils of Property Ownership," read at the 1999 conference of the Emily Dickinson International Society. Earlier discussions of the reference to Lemuel Shaw are Jane Donahue Eberwein, "Dickinson's I HAD SOME THINGS THAT I CALLED MINE," *Explicator* 42, no. 3 (1984): 31–33, and Owen Thomas, "Father and Daughter: Edward and Emily Dickinson," *American Literature* 40 (1969): 510–23 (cited by Eberwein).

38. It is unlikely that Dickinson knew this, but Justice Shaw was the father-in-law of Herman Melville and the model for the pompous narrator of "Bartleby the Scrivener." Bartleby is at least partially Melville's self-portrait: the portrait of a dweller in the world who, like Emily Dickinson, told the world, "I would prefer not to."

39. See the collection of essays "Reflections on the Classroom Electric: Dickinson, Whitman, and American Literature," at http://www.mith.umd.edu/mithologies/fipse.html. But Dickinson's absorption by the machinery of reading began long before the Internet. Early in the computer age, S. P. Rosenbaum used the facilities of the Cornell Aeronautical Laboratory to generate his *Concordance to the Poems of Emily Dickinson* (Ithaca: Cornell University Press, 1964), xxii, and, as R. W. Franklin points out in *The Editing of Emily Dickinson,* some of what we think of as Emily Dickinson's poetry is an effect of one or the other of Mabel Loomis Todd's two typewriters.

Unfortunately, the second, newer half of the comprehensive Dickinson concordance, Cynthia J. Mackenzie's *Concordance to the Letters of Emily Dickinson* (Boulder: University Press of Colorado, 2000), has been published only in book form. Forty years after Rosenbaum, publication on CD-ROM with a search engine would seem to answer Emily Dickinson's wish:

> Oh for a Disc to the Distance
> Between Ourselves and the Dead! (Fr 1068)

40. Martha Ackmann, "Morphing Emily Dickinson," Conference of the Emily Dickinson International Society, Trondheim, Norway, August 3, 2001. As I viewed the computer-modified images, it

seemed to me that Dickinson in middle age would have resembled her heavy-featured mother more than the sharp-featured woman whose photograph is reproduced in Alfred Habegger's *My Wars Are Laid Away in Books: The Life of Emily Dickinson* (New York: Random House, 2001) and discussed in appendix 1, "A Second Photograph of Emily Dickinson?"

The list below is meant to be representative rather than comprehensive. It contains a selection of works cited in this volume, together with some additional entries.

BIBLIOGRAPHIES

American Literary Scholarship, 1963–present. Durham, N.C.: Duke University Press, 1965–.

Boswell, Jeanetta. *Emily Dickinson: A Bibliography of Secondary Sources, with Selective Annotations 1890–1987*. Jefferson, N.C.: McFarland, 1989.

Buckingham, Willis J., ed. *Emily Dickinson: An Annotated Bibliography*. Bloomington: Indiana University Press, 1970.

———, ed. *Emily Dickinson's Reception in the 1890s: A Documentary History*. Pittsburgh: University of Pittsburgh Press, 1989.

Clendinning, Sheila T. *Emily Dickinson: A Bibliography 1850–1966*. Kent, Ohio: Kent State University Press, 1968.

Dandurand, Karen. *Dickinson Scholarship: An Annotated Bibliography 1969–1985*. New York: Garland, 1988.

Duchac, Joseph. *The Poems of Emily Dickinson: An Annotated Guide to Commentary Published in English 1890–1977*. Boston: G. K. Hall, 1979.

———. *The Poems of Emily Dickinson: An Annotated Guide to Commentary Published in English 1978–1989*. New York: G. K. Hall, 1993.

Myerson, Joel. *Emily Dickinson: A Descriptive Bibliography*. Pittsburgh: University of Pittsburgh Press, 1984.

EDITIONS OF DICKINSON'S POEMS AND LETTERS

Aiken, Conrad, ed. *Selected Poems of Emily Dickinson*. London: Jonathan Cape, 1924.

Dickinson Editing Collective. *Dickinson Electronic Archives*. Available
    http://jefferson.village.virginia.edu/dickinson

Dickinson, Emily. *Bolts of Melody: New Poems of Emily Dickinson*.
    Ed. Mabel Loomis Todd and Millicent Todd Bingham. New
    York: Harper & Brothers, 1945.

————. *The Complete Poems of Emily Dickinson*. Ed. Martha Dickin-
    son Bianchi. Boston: Little, Brown, 1924.

————. *The Complete Poems of Emily Dickinson*. Ed. Thomas H. John-
    son. Boston: Little, Brown, 1960.

————. *Emily Dickinson Face to Face: Unpublished Letters with Notes
    and Reminiscences by Her Niece, Martha Dickinson Bianchi*.
    Boston: Houghton Mifflin, 1932.

————. *Emily Dickinson: Selected Letters*. Ed. Thomas H. Johnson.
    Cambridge, Mass.: Harvard University Press, 1971.

————. *Final Harvest: Emily Dickinson's Poems*. Ed. Thomas H. John-
    son. Boston: Little, Brown, 1961.

————. *Further Poems of Emily Dickinson: Withheld from Publication by
    Her Sister Lavinia*. Ed. Martha Dickinson Bianchi and Alfred
    Leete Hampson. Boston: Little, Brown, 1929.

————. *Letters of Emily Dickinson*. Ed. Mabel Loomis Todd. 2 vols.
    Boston: Roberts Brothers, 1894.

————. *Letters of Emily Dickinson*. Ed. Mabel Loomis Todd. New
    York: Harper & Brothers, 1931.

————. *The Letters of Emily Dickinson*. Ed. Thomas H. Johnson and
    Theodora Ward. 3 vols. Cambridge, Mass.: Harvard Univer-
    sity Press, 1958.

————. *The Manuscript Books of Emily Dickinson*. Ed. R. W. Franklin.
    2 vols. Cambridge, Mass.: Harvard University Press, 1981.

————. *The Master Letters of Emily Dickinson*. Ed. R. W. Franklin.
    Amherst: Amherst College Press, 1986.

————. *New Poems of Emily Dickinson*. Ed. William H. Shurr with
    Anna Dunlap and Emily Grey Shurr. Chapel Hill: University
    of North Carolina Press, 1993.

————. *Poems by Emily Dickinson*. Ed. Martha Dickinson Bianchi and
    Alfred Leete Hampson. Boston: Little, Brown, 1937.

————. *Poems of Emily Dickinson*. Ed. Mabel Loomis Todd and T. W.
    Higginson. Boston: Roberts Brothers, 1890.

————. *Poems by Emily Dickinson: Second Series*. Ed. T. W. Higginson
    and Mabel Loomis Todd. Boston: Roberts Brothers, 1891.

———. *Poems by Emily Dickinson: Third Series.* Ed. Mabel Loomis Todd. Boston: Roberts Brothers, 1896.

———. *The Poems of Emily Dickinson: Including Variant Readings Critically Compared with All Known Manuscripts.* Ed. Thomas H. Johnson. Cambridge, Mass.: Harvard University Press, 1955.

———. *The Poems of Emily Dickinson: Variorum Edition.* Ed. R. W. Franklin. 3 vols. Cambridge, Mass.: Harvard University Press, 1998.

———. *The Single Hound: Poems of a Lifetime.* Ed. Martha Dickinson Bianchi. Boston: Little, Brown, 1914.

———. *Unpublished Poems of Emily Dickinson.* Ed. Martha Dickinson Bianchi and Alfred Leete Hampson. Boston: Little, Brown, 1935.

Hart, Ellen Louise, and Martha Nell Smith, eds. *Open Me Carefully: Emily Dickinson's Intimate Letters to Susan Huntington Dickinson.* Ashfield, Mass.: Paris Press, 1998.

Werner, Marta L. *Emily Dickinson's Open Folios: Scenes of Reading, Surfaces of Writing.* Ann Arbor: University of Michigan Press, 1995.

CONCORDANCES

Mackenzie, Cynthia J., with Penny Gilbert. *Concordance to the Letters of Emily Dickinson.* Boulder: University of Colorado Press, 2000.

Rosenbaum, S. P. *A Concordance to the Poems of Emily Dickinson.* Ithaca: Cornell University Press, 1964.

BIOGRAPHIES AND BIOGRAPHICAL MATERIALS

Ackmann, Martha. "Morphing Emily Dickinson." Paper presented at the Conference of the Emily Dickinson International Society, Trondheim, Norway, August 2001.

Bianchi, Martha Dickinson, ed. *The Life and Letters of Emily Dickinson.* Boston: Houghton Mifflin, 1924.

Bingham, Millicent Todd. *Ancestors' Brocades: The Literary Debut of Emily Dickinson: The Editing and Publication of Her Letters and Poems.* New York: Harper & Brothers, 1945.

————. *Emily Dickinson's Home: Letters of Edward Dickinson and His Family, with Documentation and Comment.* New York: Harper & Row, 1955.

Cody, John. *After Great Pain: The Inner Life of Emily Dickinson.* Cambridge, Mass.: Harvard University Press, 1971.

Faderman, Lillian. "Emily Dickinson's Letters to Sue Gilbert." *Massachusetts Review* 28 (Summer 1977): 197–225.

Habegger, Alfred. *My Wars Are Laid Away in Books: The Life of Emily Dickinson.* New York: Random House, 2001.

Hirschhorn, Norbert, and Polly Longsworth. "'Medicine Posthumous': A New Look at Emily Dickinson's Medical Conditions." *New England Quarterly* 69 (June 1996): 299–316.

Jenkins, MacGregor. *Emily Dickinson: Friend and Neighbor.* Boston: Little, Brown, 1930.

Leyda, Jay. *The Years and Hours of Emily Dickinson.* 2 vols. New Haven: Yale University Press, 1960.

Liebling, Jerome. *The Dickinsons of Amherst.* Photographs by Jerome Liebling. Essays by Christopher Benfey, Polly Longsworth, and Barton Levi St. Armand. Hanover, N.H.: University Press of New England, 2001.

Longsworth, Polly. *Austin and Mabel: The Amherst Affair and Love Letters of Austin Dickinson and Mabel Loomis Todd.* New York: Farrar, Straus and Giroux, 1984.

————. "The 'Latitude of Home': Life in the Homestead and the Evergreens." In *The Dickinsons of Amherst.* Hanover, N.H.: University Press of New England, 2001: 31–36.

Murray, Aife. "Miss Margaret's Emily Dickinson." *Signs* 24 (1999): 696–732.

Pollak, Vivian R., ed. *A Poet's Parents: The Courtship Letters of Emily Norcross and Edward Dickinson.* Chapel Hill: University of North Carolina Press, 1988.

Sewall, Richard B. *The Life of Emily Dickinson.* 2 vols. New York: Farrar, Straus and Giroux, 1974.

————, ed. *The Lyman Letters: New Light on Emily Dickinson and Her Family.* Amherst: University of Massachusetts Press, 1965.

Walsh, John Evangelist. *The Hidden Life of Emily Dickinson.* New York: Simon and Schuster, 1971.

Wolff, Cynthia Griffin. *Emily Dickinson.* New York: Alfred A. Knopf, 1986.

CRITICISM

Bennett, Paula. *Emily Dickinson: Woman Poet.* Iowa City: University of Iowa Press, 1990.

————. *My Life a Loaded Gun: Female Creativity and Feminist Poetics.* Boston: Beacon Press, 1986.

————. "'The Negro never knew': Emily Dickinson and Racial Typology in the Post-Bellum Period." *Legacy: A Journal of American Women Writers* 19, no. 1 (2002): 53–61.

Blake, Caesar R., and Carlton F. Wells, eds. *The Recognition of Emily Dickinson: Selected Criticism since 1890.* Ann Arbor: University of Michigan Press, 1964.

Cameron, Sharon. *Choosing Not Choosing: Dickinson's Fascicles.* Chicago: University of Chicago Press, 1992.

————. *Lyric Time: Dickinson and the Limits of Genre.* Baltimore: Johns Hopkins University Press, 1979.

Capps, Jack L. *Emily Dickinson's Reading, 1836–1886.* Cambridge, Mass.: Harvard University Press, 1966.

Crumbley, Paul. *Inflections of the Pen: Dash and Voice in Emily Dickinson.* Lexington: University of Kentucky Press, 1997.

Dandurand, Karen. "New Dickinson Civil War Publications." *American Literature* 56 (March 1984): 17–27.

Dobson, Joanne. *Dickinson and the Strategies of Reticence: The Woman Writer in Nineteenth-Century America.* Bloomington: Indiana University Press, 1989.

Eberwein, Jane Donahue. *Dickinson: Strategies of Limitation.* Amherst: University of Massachusetts Press, 1985.

————, ed. *An Emily Dickinson Encyclopedia.* Westport, Conn.: Greenwood, 1998.

Erkkila, Betsy. "Emily Dickinson and Class." *American Literary History* 4 (1992): 1–27.

————. *The Wicked Sisters: Women Poets, Literary History, and Discord.* New York: Oxford University Press, 1992.

Farr, Judith. *The Passion of Emily Dickinson.* Cambridge, Mass.: Harvard University Press, 1992.

————, ed. *Emily Dickinson: A Collection of Critical Essays.* Englewood Cliffs, N.J.: Prentice-Hall, 1996.

Ford, Thomas W. "Emily Dickinson and the Civil War." *University Review of Kansas City* 31 (Spring 1965): 199–203.

Gilbert, Sandra M., and Susan Gubar. *The Madwoman in the Attic: The Woman Writer and the Nineteenth-Century Literary Imagination.* New Haven: Yale University Press, 1979.

Grabher, Gudrun, Roland Hagenbüchle, and Cristanne Miller, eds. *The Emily Dickinson Handbook.* Amherst: University of Massachusetts Press, 1998.

Howe, Susan. *The Birth-Mark: Unsettling the Wilderness in American Literary History.* Hanover, N.H.: University Press of New England, 1993.

———. *My Emily Dickinson.* Berkeley, Calif.: North Atlantic Books, 1985.

Juhasz, Suzanne. *The Undiscovered Continent: Emily Dickinson and the Space of the Mind.* Bloomington: Indiana University Press, 1983.

Keller, Karl. *The Only Kangaroo among the Beauty: Emily Dickinson and America.* Baltimore: Johns Hopkins University Press, 1979.

Lease, Benjamin. *Emily Dickinson's Readings of Men and Books: Sacred Soundings.* New York: St. Martin's Press, 1990.

Loving, Jerome. *Emily Dickinson: The Poet on the Second Story.* Cambridge: Cambridge University Press, 1986.

Lowenberg, Carlton. *Emily Dickinson's Textbooks.* Lafayette, Calif.: Lowenberg, 1986.

Lubbers, Klaus. *Emily Dickinson: The Critical Revolution.* Ann Arbor: University of Michigan Press, 1968.

McGann, Jerome J. *Black Riders: The Visible Language of Modernism.* Princeton, N.J.: Princeton University Press, 1993.

McIntosh, James. *Nimble Believing: Dickinson and the Unknown.* Ann Arbor: University of Michigan Press, 2000.

Messmer, Marietta. *"A vice for voices": Reading Emily Dickinson's Correspondence.* Amherst: University of Massachusetts Press, 2001.

Miller, Cristanne. *Emily Dickinson: A Poet's Grammar.* Cambridge, Mass.: Harvard University Press, 1987.

Mitchell, Domhnall. *Emily Dickinson: Monarch of Perception.* Amherst: University of Massachusetts Press, 2000.

———. "Northern Lights: Class, Color, Culture, and Emily Dickinson." *The Emily Dickinson Journal* 9, no. 2 (2000): 75–84.

———. "Revising the Script: Emily Dickinson's Manuscripts." *American Literature* 70, no. 4 (December 1998): 705–37.

Mossberg, Barbara Antonina Clarke. *Emily Dickinson: When a*

Writer Is a Daughter. Bloomington: Indiana University Press, 1982.

Noble, Marianne. *The Masochistic Pleasures of Sentimental Literature*. Princeton, N.J.: Princeton University Press, 2000.

Oberhaus, Dorothy Huff. *Emily Dickinson's Fascicles: Method and Meaning*. University Park: Pennsylvania State University Press, 1995.

Paglia, Camille. *Sexual Personae: Art and Decadence from Nefertiti to Emily Dickinson*. New Haven: Yale University Press, 1990.

Patterson, Rebecca. *Emily Dickinson's Imagery*. Ed. Margaret H. Freeman. Amherst: University of Massachusetts Press, 1979.

Petrino, Elizabeth. *Emily Dickinson and Her Contemporaries: Women's Verse in America, 1820–1885*. Hanover, N.H.: University Press of New England, 1998.

Pollak, Vivian R. "American Women Poets Reading Dickinson: The Example of Helen Hunt Jackson." In *The Emily Dickinson Handbook*, ed. Gudrun Grabher, Roland Hagenbüchle, and Cristanne Miller, pp. 323–41. Amherst: University of Massachusetts Press, 1998.

———. "Dickinson and the Poetics of Whiteness." *The Emily Dickinson Journal* 9, no. 2 (2000): 84–95.

———. *Dickinson: The Anxiety of Gender*. Ithaca: Cornell University Press, 1984.

Orzeck, Martin, and Robert Weisbuch, eds. *Dickinson and Audience*. Ann Arbor: University of Michigan Press, 1996.

Rich, Adrienne. "'Vesuvius at Home': The Power of Emily Dickinson." *Parnassus* 5 (1976): 49–74.

Sánchez-Eppler, Karen. *Touching Liberty: Abolition, Feminism, and the Politics of the Body*. Berkeley: University of California Press, 1993.

Sewall, Richard B., ed. *Emily Dickinson: A Collection of Critical Essays*. Englewood Cliffs, N.J.: Prentice Hall, 1963.

Sherwood, William R. *Circumference and Circumstance: Stages in the Mind and Art of Emily Dickinson*. New York: Columbia University Press, 1968.

Small, Judy Jo. *Positive as Sound: Emily Dickinson's Rhyme*. Athens: University of Georgia Press, 1990.

Smith, Martha Nell. "Dickinson's Manuscripts." In *The Emily Dickinson Handbook*, ed. Gudrun Grabher, Roland Hagenbüchle, and Cristanne Miller, pp. 113–37. Amherst: University of Massachusetts Press, 1998.

————. *Rowing in Eden: Rereading Emily Dickinson*. Austin: University of Texas Press, 1992.

St. Armand, Barton Levi. *Emily Dickinson and Her Culture: The Soul's Society*. Cambridge: Cambridge University Press, 1984.

Stonum, Gary Lee. *The Dickinson Sublime*. Madison: University of Wisconsin Press, 1990.

Wardrop, Daneen. *Emily Dickinson's Gothic: Goblin with a Gauge*. Iowa City: University of Iowa Press, 1996.

Weisbuch, Robert. *Emily Dickinson's Poetry*. Chicago: University of Chicago Press, 1975.

Wolosky, Shira. *Emily Dickinson: A Voice of War*. New Haven: Yale University Press, 1984.

CULTURAL CONTEXT

Ahlstrom, Sydney E. *A Religious History of the American People*. New Haven: Yale University Press, 1972.

Bercovitch, Sacvan. *The Puritan Origins of the American Self*. New Haven: Yale University Press, 1975.

Buell, Lawrence. *New England Literary Culture from Revolution through Renaissance*. Cambridge: Cambridge University Press, 1986.

Douglas, Ann. *The Feminization of American Culture*. New York: Alfred A. Knopf, 1977.

Edelstein, Tilden G. *Strange Enthusiasm: A Life of Thomas Wentworth Higginson*. New Haven: Yale University Press, 1968.

Erkkila, Betsy. *Whitman the Political Poet*. New York: Oxford University Press, 1989.

Fredrickson, George. *The Inner Civil War: Northern Intellectuals and the Crisis of the Union*. New York: Harper & Row, 1968.

Garner, Matthew. "Becoming Longfellow: Work, Manhood, and Poetry," *American Literature* 72, no. 1 (March 2000): 59–86.

Griswold, Rufus, ed. *The Female Poets of America*. Rev. ed. Rpt., New York: Garrett Press, [1873]. 1969.

Hatch, Nathan O. *The Democratization of American Christianity*. New Haven: Yale University Press, 1989.

[Higginson, Thomas Wentworth]. "A Plea for Culture." *Atlantic Monthly* (Jan. 1867): 29–37.

————. "Letter to a Young Contributor." *Atlantic Monthly* 9 (April 1862): 401–11.

Holt, Michael F. *The Rise and Fall of the American Whig Party: Jacksonian Politics and the Onset of the Civil War.* New York: Oxford University Press, 1999.

Juhasz, Suzanne. *Naked and Fiery Forms: Modern American Poetry by Women: A New Tradition.* New York: Harper & Row, 1976.

Kerber, Linda. "Separate Spheres, Female Worlds, Woman's Place: The Rhetoric of Women's History," *Journal of American History* 75, no. 1 (June 1988): 9–39.

Kilcup, Karen L., ed. *Nineteenth-Century American Women Writers: An Anthology.* Oxford, England: Blackwell's, 1997.

Lincoln, Abraham. *The Collected Works of Abraham Lincoln.* Ed. Roy P. Basler. 9 vols. New Brunswick, N.J.: Rutgers University Press, 1953–55.

McPherson, James M. *Battle Cry of Freedom: The Civil War Era.* New York: Oxford University Press, 1988.

Moers, Ellen. *Literary Women: The Great Writers.* Garden City, N.Y.: Doubleday, 1976.

Ostriker, Alicia Suskin. *Stealing the Language: The Emergence of Women's Poetry in America.* Boston: Beacon Press, 1986.

Piatt, Sarah. *Palace-Burner: The Selected Poetry.* Ed. Paula Bernat Bennett. Urbana: University of Illinois Press, 2001.

Pollak, Vivian R. *The Erotic Whitman.* Berkeley: University of California Press, 2000.

Reynolds, David S. *Beneath the American Renaissance: The Subversive Imagination in the Age of Emerson and Melville.* New York: Alfred A. Knopf, 1988.

————. *Faith in Fiction: The Emergence of Religious Literature in America.* Cambridge, Mass.: Harvard University Press, 1981.

Ryan, Mary P. "Gender and Public Access: Women's Politics in Nineteenth-Century America." In *Habermas and the Public Sphere,* ed. Craig Calhoun, pp. 259–88. Cambridge, Mass.: MIT Press, 1992.

Smith-Rosenberg, Carroll. *Disorderly Conduct: Visions of Gender in Victorian America.* New York: Alfred A. Knopf, 1985.

Terry, Rose. *Poems.* Boston: Ticknor & Fields, 1861.

Walker, Cheryl. *American Women Poets of the Nineteenth Century: An*

Anthology. New Brunswick, N.J.: Rutgers University Press, 1992.

———. *The Nightingale's Burden: Women Poets and American Culture before 1900*. Bloomington: Indiana University Press, 1982.

———. "Teaching Dickinson as a Gen[i]us; Emily Among the Women." *The Emily Dickinson Journal* 2, no. 2 (1993): 172–80.

Watts, Emily Stipes. *The Poetry of American Women from 1632 to 1945*. Austin: University of Texas Press, 1977.

Welter, Barbara. *Dimity Convictions: The American Woman in the Nineteenth Century*. Athens: Ohio University Press, 1976.

Wolosky, Shira. *Poetry and Public Discourse*. Vol. 4 of *The Cambridge History of American Literature*. Ed. Sacvan Bercovitch. Forthcoming.

———. "Public Women, Private Men." *Signs* 28, no. 2 (2003): 665–94.

Contributors

JANE DONAHUE EBERWEIN is Distinguished Professor of English at Oakland University. Her scholarly interests focus on American writers from Anne Bradstreet to Emily Dickinson and are associated with an imaginative tradition rooted in New England Puritanism. She is the author of *Dickinson: Strategies of Limitation* and editor of *An Emily Dickinson Encyclopedia*.

BETSY ERKKILA is Henry Sanborn Noyes Professor of Literature at Northwestern University. Her teaching and research are in the field of American literary and cultural studies, with a particular interest in American poetry, comparative American cultures, race and gender studies, and cultural and political theory. She is the author of *Walt Whitman among the French, Whitman the Political Poet, The Wicked Sisters: Women Poets, Literary History, and Discord,* and *Mixed Bloods and Other Crosses: Rethinking American Literature from the Revolution to the Culture Wars* (forthcoming). She is currently working on a study of ghosts, spooks, and American revolutionary writing.

CRISTANNE MILLER is W. M. Keck Distinguished Service Professor and professor of English at Pomona College. She is the author of *Emily Dickinson: A Poet's Grammar* and *Marianne Moore: Questions of Authority.* She is coauthor of *Comic Power in Emily Dickinson,* and coeditor of *The Emily Dickinson Handbook.* Additionally, she has written on several other U.S. poets, coedited Marianne Moore's *Selected Letters,* and is currently finishing a book manuscript called *New York/Berlin: Modernity and the Poetry of Women.*

JONATHAN MORSE, professor of English at the University of Hawaii at Manoa, is the author of *Word by Word: The Language of Memory* and shorter studies in the representation of history through language, in print and on the Internet. In addition to his work with Dickinson, he has written about twentieth-century authors of the Modernist period.

MARIANNE NOBLE is associate professor of literature at American University, where she teaches nineteenth-century American literature and introductory courses in literary theory and creative writing. She has published widely in numerous journals and is the author of *The Masochistic Pleasures of Sentimental Literature.*

VIVIAN POLLAK is professor of English and women and gender studies at Washington University in St. Louis. She is the author of *Dickinson: The Anxiety of Gender* and *The Erotic Whitman.* She has edited *A Poet's Parents: The Courtship Letters of Emily Norcross and Edward Dickinson* and *New Critical Essays on James's "Daisy Miller" and "The Turn of the Screw."* Her current projects include a study of twentieth-century American women poets "reading" Dickinson.

CHERYL WALKER is Richard Armour Professor of Modern Languages at Scripps College. She is the author of *The Nightingale's Burden: Women Poets and American Culture before 1900,* and *Masks Outrageous and Austere: Culture, Psyche, and Persona in Modern Women Poets.* She has also edited *American Women Poets of the Nineteenth Century: An Anthology.*

SHIRA WOLOSKY received her Ph.D. from Princeton University in comparative literature, and was an associate professor at Yale University before moving to the Hebrew University of Jerusalem, where she is a professor of English and American literature. Her publications include *Emily Dickinson: A Voice of War*; *Language Mysticism*; *The Art of Poetry*; *Poetry and Public Discourse*, *The Cambridge History of American Literature*, Vol. 4 (forthcoming); as well as articles on poetics, literary theory, and feminism. She was a Guggenheim fellow in 2000.

Credits

Index

Page numbers in *italics* indicate illustrations.
Individual poems are listed under "Dickinson, Emily, Works."

Ackmann, Martha, 219, 268
Adams, Abigail and John, 137
Adams, Henry, 153
Adorno, Theodor W., 127
"After the Camanches" (Terry), 186
afterlife. *See* immortality
Ahlstrom, Sydney, 100n.24
Aiken, Conrad, 258, 261
Alcott, Louisa May, 24
Altschuler, Glenn C., 168n.13
American Bible Society, 68
Amherst Academy, 20, 27, *238*, 239
Amherst and Belchertown Railroad,
    28, 142
Amherst College, 20, 27, 73, 76, 83,
    237
Amherst (Mass.), 27, 28, 81, 142,
    157–58, *238*
Ancestors' Brocades (Bingham), 261
Andrews, Bruce, 217
Anthon, Kate Scott, 207
anti-Catholicism, 93, 134
Arminianism, 85–86
art, 164–66, 214–15

Atlantic Monthly, 164, 184
Attridge, Derek, 216
Aurora Leigh (Browning), 178, 243

Banks, Nathaniel, 245
"Battle Hymn of the Republic"
    (Howe), 113
Baym, Nina, 179
Beecher, Henry Ward, 95
Beecher, Lyman, 80, 81, 86
Bell, John, 155, 171n.28
Ben-Hur (Wallace), 96, 102n.38
Beneath the American Renaissance
    (Reynolds), 178
Benjamin, Walter, 214–15, 170n.24,
    220
Bennett, Paula, 40, 171n.25 178, 182
Bercovitch, Sacvan, 118
Bernstein, Charles, 217, 224
Bianchi, Martha Dickinson (niece),
    144, 167n.5, 258–61, 262, 266,
    270n.18
Bible, 68, 74, 82–83, 90–91, 92
Bingham, Millicent Todd, 261

Black Riders: The Visible Language of Modernism (McGann), 203, 217, 264–65

Blackmur, R.P., 261

Blauvelt, Martha Tomhave, 98n.12

Bliss, Abby Wood, 73, 77

Bloom, Harold, 104, 128n.3

"Bluebeard's Closet" (Terry), 185

Blumin, Stuart, 168n.13

Bollobás, Eniko, 216

Bolts of Melody: New Poems of Emily Dickinson (Bingham), 261–62, 270n.18

Bostonians, The (James), 253

Bourdieu, Pierre, 225

Bowdoin, Elbridge Gerry, 37, 241

Bowles, Samuel, 43–44, 47, 48, 53, 92, 105, 146, 148, 157, 159, 184, 247, 247

Briggs, George N., 138, 139

Browning, Elizabeth Barrett, 74, 148, 164, 177, 178, 182, 206, 209, 239, 241, 243, 248

Browning, Robert, 107, 159, 209, 239

Bryant, William Cullen, 209

Bullard, O. A., 239

Bushman, Richard L., 168n.13

Bushnell, Horace, 101n.28

Calvinism, 68, 72, 75, 81, 82, 85, 89

Cameron, Sharon, 264–65

Capps, Jack, 233n.52

"Captive" (Terry), 186

Carlyle, Thomas, 164

Catholicism, 93–94

Celan, Paul, 127

Channing, William Ellery, 24

children, 89

Choate, Rufus, 164

Choosing Not Choosing: Dickinson's Fascicles (Cameron), 264

circumference symbol, 88

Civil War, 69, 90, 103–31, 134, 156, 157–61, 248–49

Clark, James D., 48

Clay, Henry, 140

Cleveland, Grover, 136

Close Listening (Bernstein), 217

Cody, John, 61n.48

Coleman, Eliza, 245

Coleman, Maria, 48

Coleman, Olivia, 48

Coleridge, Samuel Taylor, 87

Colton, Aaron, 71, 80, 85

Concord Saturday Club, 24

Congregationalism, 68, 72, 75, 81–82, 85, 88, 92

Conkey, Ithamar Francis, 137

Constitutional Union Party, 155, 171n.28

Cooke, Rose Terry, 182, 184–88, 198n.16, 199n.17

Coultrap-McQuin, Susan, 179

Crane, Hart, 258

creation, 83, 90–91

Cult of True Womanhood, 179, 186, 198n.8

Cummings, E.E., 222

"Daisies" (Terry), 184–85

Dandurand, Karen, 172n.33

Darger, Henry, 265

Darwin, Charles, 68, 80, 90–91

Davis, Rebecca Harding, 148, 248

"Day Is Done, The" (Longfellow), 211, 212–13

Democratic Party, 141

Derrida, Jacques, 264

Descent of Man, The (Darwin), 90

Dickinson, Austin (brother), 26, 32, 35, 43, 241

 affair with Mabel Loomis Todd, 252, 257

 building campaign for First Church, 96

correspondence with sister
Emily, 5, 6, 18, 28–29, 41–42,
139, 141, 142, 147–48
education, 9, 242
engagement to Sue Gilbert, 40,
242
Evergreens home, 22, *244*, 245
on father, 52, 81
as father's partner, 22
and Frazar Stearns's death, 159
involvement with church, 71, 77
marriage to Sue Gilbert, 245
as outfitter of Amherst soldiers,
105
portraits, *239*, 242
procuring of Civil War substitute, 156, 158, 248
on Sue Gilbert, 38
Dickinson, Edward (father), 73, 74,
86, 93, 115
Amherst Record "Pen Portrait,"
26–27
as candidate for lieutenant governor, 155, 156, 171n.30, 245
courtship of Emily Norcross,
31–32, 59n.38
death, 52–53, 251
education, 9
finances, 220, 237
friendship with Otis Phillips
Lord, 49
as official of Amherst Academy
and Amherst College, 27,
104, 237
as participant in Amherst local
affairs, 27, 28, 104, 142
portraits, *236*, *250*
public service record, 167n.7
relationship with daughter Emily,
28–30
on slavery, 170n.23
in U.S. Congress, 28, 105, 133–34,
241, 242

as Whig candidate, 138–39
as young father, 20–21, 22
Dickinson Electronic Archives,
60n.39, 222–23, 234n.61,
265–66
Dickinson, Emily Elizabeth (poet)
and African Americans, 151–52,
162
agoraphobia, 26, 58n.21
Amherst home, 20–21, *244*
Amy Lowell on, 25–26
aural foundation of poems,
206–7, 227
Bianchi transcriptions, 258–61
birth, 32
childhood, 32–33
circumference symbol, 88
comic valentines, 36–37, 144–45,
241
compared with Longfellow,
212–13
conflicts about ambitions, 19
in context of other women
poets, 175–200
and conversion, 75–78, 82, 86–87,
98n.13
death, 53, 252, 268
death of father, 52–53
dog Carlo, 30, 55
editions of poetry, 204–5, 255–69
excessive deference as strategy, 41
eye ailment, 5, 15, 23–24, 57n.15,
248
family background, 20–22
family finances, 220
fascicles, 9, 45, 78, 106, 124, 184,
203, 204, 245, 264–65, 271n.26
on father's politics, 140
and feminism, 176–77, 225
and ideology of separate spheres,
105–07, 145–46
illustrated chronology, 235–53
and immortality, 91–92, 95–96

Dickinson, Emily Elizabeth
  (continued)
  LETTERS
    and belief/disbelief, 93
    of Dickinson's maturity, 18–19
    difficulty of identifying
      through, 17–18
    elliptical nature of, 38
    facilitation of biographical in-
      quiry, 18
    from Charles Wadsworth to
      Dickinson, 48
    of maturity, 18–19
    as means of circulating poems,
      148
    network of correspondents,
      146–47
    to Abiah Root, 33–34, 73, 78
    to Austin Dickinson (brother),
      5, 6, 18, 28–29, 30, 41–42, 133,
      139, 141, 142, 147–48
    to Charles Wadsworth, 47,
      249
    to Edward Everett Hale, 78–79
    to Elizabeth Holland, 22, 72,
      133, 135, 136–37, 146, 147, 148,
      161, 237
    to George Gould, 85, 144–45
    to Jane Humphrey, 78, 87, 143
    to Joseph Lyman, 30
    to Joseph Sweetser (uncle), 23
    to Josiah and Elizabeth Hol-
      land, 72, 74, 89
    to Mary Bowles, 44
    to "Master," 46–47, 49, 242, 245
    to Maria Whitney, 251
    to Norcross cousins, 107, 111,
      147, 148, 155, 159, 162, 165
    to Otis Phillips Lord, 50–51, 69,
      146, 265
    to Samuel Bowles, 44, 146, 148,
      157, 159
    to Susan Gilbert Dickinson,
      39, 60n.43, 71, 77, 140, 147,
      148, 204, 241
    to Thomas Wentworth Hig-
      ginson, 13–15, 18, 20, 31, 32,
      37, 53, 54–55, 79, 115, 146, 148,
      150, 152, 158, 163, 164, 188,
      250, 256
    to Washington Gladden, 70,
      91–92
    to women friends, 148
    war references in, 107
    world of, 144–50
  love affair with Otis Phillips
    Lord, 49–52
  manuscripts, 218, 222–25, 228n.5,
    264–65, 266
  modesty, 104
  at Mount Holyoke, 33–35, 142, 240
  and music, 207
  mysterious terror, 14
  poems linking poet with song-
    bird, 207, 229–30n.13
  poetry (specific). *See subhead*
    Works
  poetry of maturity, 19
  and politics, 133–74
  portraits, 239, 240
  as private poet, 104
  readings aloud, 218–19, 220
  relationship with father, 26–30
  relationship with Susan Gilbert
    Dickinson, 39–40, 42, 43,
    61–62n.51, 259
  religion, 67–102, 115–16, 143–44,
    152–54
  reluctance to publish in lifetime,
    16, 106, 130n.23, 149–50, 256
  sets, 46, 245, 271n.26
  social isolation, 6, 23, 24–26, 28,
    44, 163
  speculation on identity of "Mas-
    ter," 46–47, 61nn.50–51
  and Supposed Person(s), 15

"terror—since September," 14–15, 57n.15, 150

transforming experience of artistic empowerment, 78

trip to Washington, D.C., 133–35, 242

in twenty-first century, 201–34

views on death, 37, 53–54, 79, 84

and Wadsworth, 47–48

and war poetry, 103–31, 150–51, 153–54, 156–61, 172n.33

WORKS

"A Bird, came down the Walk," 230n.13

"A Burdock - clawed my Gown," 137–38

"A Prison gets to be a friend," 25

"A science - so the Savans say," 84

"A solemn thing - it was - I said," 198n.15

"Apparently with no surprise," 154

"After great pain, a formal feeling comes," 45

"'Arcturus' is his other name," 91

"At half past Three, a Single Bird," 230n.13

"At least - to pray - is left - is left," 108

"Awake ye muses nine, sing me a strain divine," 241

"Because I could not stop for Death," 259

"Behind Me - dips Eternity," 190–91

"Better - than Music!" 75

"Civilization - spurns - the Leopard!" 151

"Color - Caste – Denomination," 108, 152

"Dare you see a Soul at the 'White Heat'?" 165

"Doom is the House without the Door," 24

"Each Life converges to some Centre," 54

"Exultation is the going," 24–25

"'Faith' is a fine invention," 153

"Further in Summer than the Birds," 185, 207

"Good to hide, and hear 'em hunt!" 17, 225–27

"He fought like those Who've nought to lose," 112

"He gave away his Life," 120

"He touched me, so I live to know," 86–87

"How much the present moment means," 96, 102n.39

"I dwell in Possibility," 4, 16, 54

"I cannot dance opon my Toes," 206

"I felt a Cleaving in my Mind," 155, 190, 191, 193

"I felt a Funeral, in my Brain," 45, 155

"I had some things that I called mine," 104, 267, 273n.37

"I had the Glory - that will do," 55

"I heard a Fly buzz - when I died," 153

"I should not dare to be so sad," 55

"I taste a liquor never brewed," 172n.33, 188, 246

"I think I was enchanted," 206

"I tie my Hat - I crease my Shawl," 179

Dickinson, Emily Elizabeth, WORKS
    (*continued*)
    "I was a Phebe - nothing
        more," 183–84, 197
    "I would not paint - a picture,"
        206–7
    "If those I loved were lost,"
        272n.36
    "If you were coming in the
        Fall," 51
    "I'm ceded - I've stopped being
        Their's," 123
    "I'm Nobody! Who are You?"
        4, 9, 151
    "It always felt to me - a
        wrong," 92
    "It feels a shame to be Alive,"
        119–20, 160
    "It was not Death, for I stood
        up," 44–45, 189, 193
    "Mine - by the Right of the
        White Election!" 87, 152
    "My country need not change
        her gown," 162
    "My Life had stood - a Loaded
        Gun," 111
    "My Portion is Defeat - today,"
        112, 160
    "My Triumph lasted till the
        Drums," 113, 268
    "My Wars are laid away in
        Books," 163
    "Myself was formed - a Car-
        penter," 164–65
    "New feet within my garden
        go," 189
    "Of all the Sounds despatched
        abroad," 191, 201, 206,
        212–13, 247
    "Of God we ask one favor,
        that we may be forgiven,"
        25
    "On a Columnar Self," 153

    "One need not be a Chamber -
        to be Haunted," 185
    "One Sister have I in our
        house," 259
    "Ourselves were wed one
        summer - dear," 43
    "Publication - is the Auction,"
        50, 149
    "Robbed by Death but that
        was easy," 123
    "Sang from the Heart, Sire," 194
    "'Sic transit gloria mundi,'"
        168n.14
    "Some keep the Sabbath going
        to Church," 71, 185
    "Some - Work for Immor-
        tality," 165
    "Soto! Explore thyself!"
        154
    "Split the Lark - and you'll find
        the Music," 193–96, 207
    "Step lightly on this narrow
        Spot," 55–56, 124
    "Success is counted sweetest,"
        111, 112
    "Tell all the truth but tell it
        slant," 180
    "That after Horror - that 'twas
        us," 112
    "The Brain, within it's
        Groove," 155
    "The first Day's Night had
        come," 155
    "The Heart is the Capital of
        the Mind," 108
    "The Lamp burns sure –
        within," 151, 170n.24
    "The Malay - took the Pearl,"
        152, 245
    "The Martyr Poets - did not
        tell," 125
    "The Products of my Farm are
        these," 165

"The Soul has Bandaged moments," 123

"The Soul selects her own Society," 151

"The Spider holds a Silver Ball," 191

"The Way I read a Letter's - this," 17–18

"The Winters are so short," 92

"Their Hight in Heaven comforts not," 19, 154

"There came a day at - Summer's full," 260

"There's a certain Slant of light," 19, 55

"This is my letter to the World," 148–49, 265

"Those - dying then," 67, 68, 70, 79, 94–95, 153

"'Tis so appalling - it exhilarates," 45, 158

"Title divine - is mine!" 157

"To fight aloud, is very brave," 150–51

"To learn the Transport by the Pain," 25

"'Twas like a Maelstrom, with a notch," 44

"Victory comes late," 120–21

"Water, is taught by thirst," 25

"What is - 'Paradise'," 16–17, 89

"What mystery pervades a well!" 88

"When I was small, a Woman died," 112

"Wild nights - Wild nights!" 187

Dickinson, Emily Norcross (mother), 21, 22–23, 30–32, 75, *236*, 240, 242, 251, 252

Dickinson, Francis H., 110, 112

Dickinson, Gilbert (nephew), 24, 252, *252*

Dickinson, Lavinia Norcross (sister), 9, 21–22, 29, 32, 46, 53, 133, 161, 169n.17, 237, *239*, 241, 242, *253*, 256, 257

Dickinson, Lucretia Gunn (grandmother), 20

Dickinson, Samuel Fowler (grandfather), 20, 135, 138, 141, 237

Dickinson, Susan Gilbert (sister-in-law), 22, 26, 38–40, 42, 43, 52, 60n.40, 61n.50, 62n.52, 71, 77, 140, 147, 148, 182, 204, 219, 241, 242, *242*, 245, 252, 256–59, 266

Dickinson, William Austin. *See* Dickinson, Austin (brother)

Dobson, Joanne, 178, 180, 225

Douglas, Ann, 101n.30

Douglass, Frederick, 99n.16

Dwight, Edward, 71

Dwight, Timothy, 81

Eberwein, Jane Donahue, 267–68

economics, 165

Education of Henry Adams, The (Adams), 153

Edwards, Jonathan, 81, 84, 86, 99n.15, 100n.22, 114

electricity, 233n.50

Elementary Geology (Hitchcock), 83

Eliot, George, 80, 92, 148, 245, 249, 251

Emancipation Proclamation, 158, 249

Emerson, Ralph Waldo, 4, 6, 24, 37, 87–88, 103, 138, 153, 162, 176, 206, 209, 241, 245, 258

Emily Dickinson: Face to Face (Bianchi), 144

Emily Dickinson: Woman Poet (Bennett), 182

Emily Dickinson and Her Contemporaries (Petrino), 180

Emily Dickinson and Her Culture (St. Armand), 177

Emily Dickinson's Home (Bingham), 261

Emily Dickinson's Open Folios: Scenes of Reading, Surfaces of Writing (Werner), 265

Erkkila, Betsy, 181–82, 225

evangelicalism, 87, 88

Everett, Edward, 155

Evergreens (Amherst, Mass.), 22, 244, 245

evil, 111–12

evolution, 90–91

Faderman, Lillian, 39, 60n.43

Farley, Abbie, 52

Farr, Judith, 47, 61n.47

fascicles, 9, 45, 78, 106, 124, 184, 203, 204, 245, 264–65, 271n.26

Female Poets of America, The (Griswold), 179

Finney, Charles Grandison, 75, 86, 153

Fiske, Daniel Taggard, 32–33

Ford, Thomas, 129n.8

Frank, Joseph, 216

Franklin, R.W., 9, 67, 183, 184, 185, 204, 205, 223, 224, 263–64, 266–68, 272n.36

Fuller, Margaret, 143, 239, 241

Further Poems of Emily Dickinson, Withheld from Publication by Her Sister Lavinia (Bianchi), 259, 260, 261, 270n.12

Garfield, James A., 161–62, 251

Garrison, William Lloyd, 99n.16

Gettysburg Address, 123, 160

Gilbert, Harriet Arms, 38

Gilbert, Martha, 38

Gilbert, Susan Huntington. *See* Dickinson, Susan Gilbert

Gilbert, Thomas, 38

Gilbert, Thomas Dwight, 60n.40

Gladden, Washington, 70, 91, 96

Gould, George, 36, 85, 144

Graves, John, 42

Great Awakening, 81, 82

Griswold, Rufus, 179, 193

Guiteau, Charles, 161

Guthrie, James, 267–68

Habegger, Alfred, 23, 47, 58n.24, 60n.40, 61n.51, 63n.59, 99n.17, 101n.28

Habermas, Jürgen, 146

Hale, Edward Everett, 37, 78

Hart, Ellen Louise, 61n.51, 204, 205, 219, 265, 266

Harvard Divinity School, 82

Harvard University Press, 255, 262, 268

Hawthorne, Nathaniel, 105, 237, 239, 241, 249

Higginson, Thomas Wentworth, 6, 9, 10, 92, 105, 148, 173n.40, 184, 224, 249

correspondence with Dickinson, 13–15, 18, 20, 31, 37, 53, 55, 79, 115, 146, 148, 150, 152, 158, 163, 164, 188, 250, 256

Dickinson's response to essay in *Atlantic Monthly*, 13, 164, 247

marriage to Mary Thacher, 252

portrait, 247

and publication of Dickinson's works, 63n.60, 149, 253, 257–60, 262

visits to Dickinson, 249

Higher Criticism, 69

Hirschhorn, Norbert, 57n.15

history, 84

History of the Work of Redemption, A (Edwards), 84

Hitchcock, Edward, 83–84, 90

Hitchcock, Edward, Jr., 38
Holiness Movement, 92
Holland, Elizabeth, 22, 72, 74, 79, 89,
  92, 135, 136, 147, 148, 161, 249
Holland, Josiah, 72, 74, 79, 89, 92,
  105, 146, 148, 174n.40
Homestead (Amherst, Mass.), 20,
  21, 242, 244
Hopkins, Gerard Manley, 126
housework, 143
Howe, Julia Ward, 113, 179–80
Howe, Susan, 47, 61n.49, 216, 218,
  221, 222, 223–24, 225, 265, 266
Humphrey, Heman, 81, 84
Humphrey, Jane, 37, 73, 78, 87, 143
Humphries, Rolfe, 270n.12
Huntington, Frederic Dan, 93
Hutchinson, Anne, 88
hymns, 89, 101n.30, 207

immortality, 78–79, 91
Ingersoll, Robert, 80

Jackson, Helen Hunt, 33, 53, 84,
  146, 148, 182, 236, 251, 252,
  256
James, Henry, 249, 253, 255
Jay, Martin, 229n.11
Jefferson, Thomas, 122, 137
Jenkins, Jonathan, 72, 249
Jesus Christ, 114
Johnson, Thomas H., 8, 67, 98n.13,
  107, 171n.28, 183, 185, 204,
  205, 224, 262–64, 266–67,
  272n.36
Juhasz, Suzanne, 178

Kane, Paul, 231n.20
Kansas-Nebraska bill, 28, 134, 242
Kazin, Alfred, 169n.19
Keller, Karl, 177
Kerber, Linda, 128n.2
Know-Nothing Party, 134, 155

Leaves of Grass (Whitman), 221, 243,
  245
Letters. *See* Dickinson, Emily,
  Letters
Letters of Emily Dickinson (Johnson),
  262
Lewis, Wyndham, 215
Leyda, Jay, 207, 263
liberty, 122–23
libraries, 233n.47
Life and Letters of Emily Dickinson
  (Bianchi), 259
Lincoln, Abraham, 115, 122–23, 151,
  157, 160–61, 172n.37, 236, 239,
  245, 249
Lind, Jenny, 81
Literary History of the United States
  (Spiller et al.), 176
Literary Women (Moers), 178
Longfellow, Henry Wadsworth,
  202, 205, 209–13, 226,
  231n.20, 258
Longsworth, Polly, 57n.15, 58n.21,
  58n.24
Lord, Otis Phillips, 49–52, 69, 138,
  146, 163, 172n.37, 251, 252,
  265
Lowell, Amy, 25–26, 261
Lowell, James Russell, 188
Lowell, Maria White, 188–94
Lubbers, Klaus, 258
Lundin, Roger, 68
Lyell, Charles, 68, 83
Lyman, Joseph, 30
Lyon, Mary, 34, 35, 73, 76, 106

McDermott, John F., 58n.21
McGann, Jerome, 203, 217–18, 260,
  264–65, 266
McIntosh, James, 68
McLuhan, Marshall, 215
McPherson, James, 130n.20
manifest destiny, 142

Manuscript Books of Emily Dickinson, The (Franklin), 9, 264

Marx, Leo, 142

Massachusetts, 81, 155

Masteller, Jean Carwile, 259

"Master" letters, 46–47, 49, 185, 242, 245. *See also* Dickinson, Emily Elizabeth, Letters

Melville, Herman, 69, 118, 140, 273n.38

Memorial, The (Osgood), 179

Messmer, Marietta, 233n.52

metaphor, 84

Mexican War, 141–42

Miller, Cristanne, 130n.22

Minister's Wooing, The (Stowe), 100n.23

Mitchell, Domhnall, 219–20, 223, 228n.5, 232n.44, 266

Mitchell, W.J.T., 216, 229n.11

Moers, Ellen, 178

"Monotropa" (Terry), 187–88

Monson Academy, 21

Moody, Dwight L., 95

Mossberg, Barbara Antonina Clarke, 179

Mount Holyoke, 33–35, 73, 76, 106, 142, 240

Mount Vernon, 135, 136, 242, 243

My Life a Loaded Gun (Bennett), 178

Naked and Fiery Forms (Juhasz), 178

Nänny, Max, 216, 232n.37

National Council of the Congregationalist churches, 82

natural selection, 90

Natural Theology (Paley), 83

nature, 83, 87, 110, 153

New, Elisa, 229n.11

New Light Christians, 82, 92

Newton, Benjamin Franklin, 37, 78–79, 87, 241, 242

Nietzsche, Friedrich, 116, 126

Niles, Thomas, 146, 148, 256

Nims, Seth, 141

Noble, Marianne, 62n.53

Norcross, Betsy Fay (grandmother), 57n.10

Norcross, Emily (cousin), 34, 76

Norcross, Frances (cousin), 24, 92, 107, 111, 147, 148, 155, 159, 162, 165

Norcross, Joel (grandfather), 21, 237

Norcross, Lavinia (aunt), 21, 24, 57n.10, 237, 239

Norcross, Louisa (cousin), 24, 92, 107, 111, 147, 148, 155, 159, 162, 165, 219

Oberhaus, Dorothy Huff, 98n.13

Old Light Christians, 82, 92

Olson, Charles, 218

Only Kangaroo among the Beauty, The (Keller), 177

"Opium Fantasy, An" (Maria White Lowell), 189–90, 191–21

Original Sin, 100n.23

Origin of Species, The (Darwin), 90

Osgood, Frances, 179, 180

Ostriker, Alicia, 180

Paglia, Camille, 181, 182, 193–94

Paley, William, 83

Park, Edwards Amasa, 101n.28

Parker, Theodore, 87

Perloff, Marjorie, 228n.5, 230n.17

Petrino, Elizabeth, 180, 181

Phelps, Elizabeth Stuart, 89, 177

Phillips, Wendell, 138

Pinsky, Robert, 232n.43

Piombino, Nick, 202

Plath, Sylvia, 196

Poe, Edgar Allan, 91, 208, 237, 241

Poems of Emily Dickinson (Franklin), 266

Poems of Emily Dickinson, Including Variant Readings Critically Compared with All Known Manuscripts (Johnson), 255, 262
poetry, 201–34
    Bernstein on, 217, 224
    free verse, 230n.17
    Imagist, 216
    memorization of, 220–21
    metrical variation, 209–10
    of nineteenth-century American women, 175–200
    nineteenth-century as aural, 207–8
    nineteenth-century perception of, 202
    typographical elements, 222
    visual elements, 203, 208
    See also specific poets
Poetry of American Women from 1632 to 1945, The (Watts), 175
Poet's Parents, A (Pollak), 59n.38
Polk, James Knox, 142
Pollak, Vivian R., 61n.51, 171n.25, 178, 180
Pound, Ezra, 215, 216
prayer, 74
Principles of Geology (Lyell), 83
Protestantism, 72, 82, 93
Puritanism, 68, 79, 81, 82, 84–85, 143

Quakers, 88

racism, 151–52, 170–71n.25
railroads, 142
"Rain in Summer" (Longfellow), 210, 226
"Raven, The" (Poe), 208
reading aloud, 218–19, 220, 233n.47
religion, 67–102, 115–16, 143–44, 152–54

Religion of Geology, The (Hitchcock), 83
Republican Party, 134, 138, 155–56
revivalism, 92, 100n.25
Reynolds, David, 177–78, 186
Rich, Adrienne, 10, 41, 63n.60
Roberts Brothers, 9, 146, 253, 256
Robinson, John, 85
Roman Catholicism. *See* Catholicism
Root, Abiah, 23, 73, 77, 78, 139
Rosenbaum, S.P., 55
Rossetti, Christina, 176–77
Ryan, Mary P., 169n.19

St. Armand, Barton Levi, 58n.24, 177, 186
Schramm, Geoffrey, 268
science, 83, 90
Second Great Awakening, 68, 75, 79, 81, 89
"Semele" (Terry), 187
Sergeant, Elizabeth Shepley, 258–59
Sewall, Richard B., 47, 257
Shakespeare, William, 5, 26, 219, 221
Shaw, Lemuel, 104–5, 237, 267, 273nn.37–38
Sherwood, William R., 98n.13
Sicherman, Barbara, 218, 220, 233n.47
"Sick Room, The" (Maria White Lowell), 189–90, 191–21
Sigourney, Lydia, 177, 180, 205
sin, 78, 86, 100n.23
Single Hound, The: Poems of a Lifetime (Bianchi), 258
slavery, 133–34, 142, 170n.23, 241
Small, Judy Jo, 207
Smith, Elizabeth Oakes, 180
Smith, Martha Nell, 61nn.50–51, 204, 205, 219, 265, 266

Smith-Rosenberg, Carroll, 39,
    60n.43
"SNO" (Cummings), 222
spatial form, 216
Spiller, Robert E., 176
Springfield Republican, 8, 105, 147,
    168n.14
Stearns, Frazar, 90, 107, 110, 111, 119,
    159, 248
Stoughton, William, 80, 99n.15
Stowe, Harriet Beecher, 89, 100n.23,
    140,148, 151
Strong, Martha Dwight, 99n.17
*Structural Transformation of the Pub-
    lic Sphere, The* (Habermas),
    146
suffering, 111, 114, 160
Sumner, Charles, 134, 161, 173n.38
Suskin, Alicia, 180
Sweetser, Joseph A., 23
Swett, Anna Norcross (cousin),
    219
Syrian Protestant College, 73

Taylor, Edward, 96, 99n.15, 100n.24,
    262
Taylor, Nathaniel, 86, 100n.24
Taylor, Zachary, 142
Terry, Rose. *See* Cooke, Rose
    Terry
theodicy, 111, 114
theology, 85, 90
Thomas, Owen, 267–68
Thoreau, Henry David, 87, 121, 239,
    241
Todd, Mabel Loomis, 9, 22, 26, 52,
    148, 149, 169n.17, 224, 228n.6,
    252, 252, 253, 257–62, 264,
    267
Transcendentalism, 87–88, 153
Trilling, Lionel, 166n.4
Turner, James, 80, 100n.25
Tyler, William Seymour, 157

Uncle Tom's Cabin (Stowe), 151
Unitarianism, 82, 88, 92, 153
Untermeyer, Louis, 260

Van Vranken, Sophia Arms, 38
Vaill, Sarah (step grandmother),
    57n.10
*Visiting Emily: Poems Inspired by
    the Life and Work of Emily
    Dickinson* (Coghill and
    Tammaro), 4

Wadsworth, Charles, 47–49, 53,
    61n.51, 62n.52, 242, 243, 245,
    247, 249, 263
Walker, Cheryl, 178, 180, 182–83
Wallace, Lew, 96, 102n.38
Ward, Theodora, 8
Warner, Susan, 89
"Warning, The" (Longfellow), 211
Washington, George, 135, 136–37,
    165
Watts, Emily Stipes, 175–76, 180
Watts, Isaac, 71
Webster, Daniel, 133, 139
Webster, Noah, 68
Werner, Marta, 218, 260, 265
When a Writer Is a Daughter (Moss-
    berg), 179
Whicher, George Frisbie, 262
Whig Party, 27–28, 134, 136, 137, 139,
    140, 142, 155
Whitefield, George, 81
white race, 151–52
Whitman, Walt, 10, 118, 130n.23,
    173n.40, 176, 202, 221, 227,
    268
Wicked Sisters, The (Erkkila), 181
Wigglesworth, Michael, 100n.23
Wilberforce, Samuel, 80
Wolff, Cynthia Griffin, 20, 47, 68,
    98n.13, 179
Wölfli, Adolf, 265

Woman in the Nineteenth Century (Fuller), 143, 239

women, 55, 88–89, 103, 105–6, 143, 233n.47

"Wood Worship" (Terry), 185–86

"Work of Art in the Age of Mechanical Reproduction, The" (Benjamin), 214

"Wreck of the Hesperus, The" (Longfellow), 209

Yale University, 81

Years and Hours of Emily Dickinson (Leyda), 263